THE IRG SOLUTION

THE IRG SOLUTION

Hierarchical Incompetence and How to Overcome It

DAVID ANDREWS

Souvenir Press

First published 1984 by Souvenir Press Ltd,
43 Great Russell Street, London WC1B 3PA
and simultaneously in Canada

ISBN 0 285 62662 0

Photoset and printed in Great Britain by
Photobooks (Bristol) Ltd
Barton Manor, St. Philips, Bristol

For
Katherine Rose

CONTENTS

ACKNOWLEDGEMENTS

I would like to thank the following people, who helped me significantly with this book, through general discussion of some of the points, or the provision of specialist knowledge, or the correction of errors – or a mixture of all three types of help.

Dr Mike Hussey for numerous discussions on the nature of communication and its failure within organisations; Bob Everett for his excellent illustrations and many helpful comments; Bob Bushaway and John Fletcher for their help on informal aspects of social history; Dr Harry Collins for help on the concept of tacit knowledge; Dr Richard Carter for his meticulous attention to detail and his inside knowledge on the social services; Dr Steve Cousins for long-term encouragement and assistance on the biological areas; Dr Mike Baker for help with computerisation of IRGs; Dr Bob Lowe for many helpful comments; Robin McCombe and Godfrey Boyle for general discussions.

I have also received useful help from Pat Mugglestone, Steve Andrews, Dr Mark Barrett, Dr Ian Clements, Anne-Lize Gotsche, Faith Hall, Martin Large, Peter Worsley, David Olivier, Sue Jeffries, Dr B.W. Meade, John Evans, Jas Gill, Dr Tom Berrie, Dr Sarah Stewart-Brown, Dr David Abercrombie, Dr McGuire, Francis Sealey, Robert Giddings, Dr Marjorie Tew, Hugo Grimes, Nick Cole and Richard MacBride.

I also need to thank above all Jan Hooker, for, ironic as it may seem in a book about communication, it was she who translated my original thoughts into recognisable form before the material went to the publisher.

I am grateful for permission to quote from the following published material: *Selections from Political Writings* by Antonio Gramsci (Lawrence & Wishart Ltd.); *The Mediaeval Foundations of England* by G.O. Sayles (Methuen & Co.); *The Nuer* by E. Evans-Pritchard, *African Political Systems* edited by M. Fortes and E. Evans-Pritchard, and *Godes Peace and the Queenes* by N.J. O'Connor (all Oxford University Press); *A History of Shopping* by Dorothy Davis (Routledge & Kegan Paul Ltd.); 'Vernacular Values' by Ivan Illich, *Resurgence* No. 72, February 1979 (by permission of the Editor); *Language Change: Progress or Decay?* by Jean Aitchison (Fontana Paperbacks); 'Understanding Language' by

Deirdre Wilson and Neil Smith, *New Society*, 24 July 1980 (New Society Syndication); *Backwardness and Educational Failure* by R. Gulliford (© 1969 NFER–Nelson Publishing Company Limited); *Language and Learning* by James Britton, Pelican Books 1972, © 1970 James Britton (reprinted by permission of Penguin Books Ltd.); *Thought and Language* by L.S. Vygotsky, translated by Eugenia Hartman and Gertrude Vakar, translation © 1962 (The MIT Press); *The Plug-in Drug* by Marie Winn, © 1977 Marie Winn Miller (reprinted by permission of Viking Penguin Inc.); *Crosstalk*, National Centre for Industrial Language Training (by permission of the Director); 'Organisational Aspects of Information Flow in Technology' by T.J. Allen, *Aslib Proceedings* 20 (11) 1968; 'An Indian Village Agricultural Ecosystem: Case Study of Ungra Village' by Amulya Kumar N. Reddy, *Biomass* 1 (1981) (© Applied Science Publishers Ltd.); *Integrating the Individual and the Organisation* by Chris Argyris, © Chris Argyris 1964, and *Increasing Leadership Effectiveness* by Chris Argyris, © Chris Argyris 1976 (both John Wiley & Sons, Inc.); *Beyond the Stable State. Public and Private Learning in a Changing Society* by Donald A. Schon (Temple Smith); 'Verbal Violence' by John Fletcher, from *More Words* (BBC Radio 1977); 'Developing Creativity' by Bryan Silcock, *International Herald Tribune*, 6th January 1983 (by permission of New York Times Syndication Sales); 'Freedom to Build - Dweller Control of the Building Process', *Architects' Journal*, September 1982; *Parent Effectiveness Training* by Thomas Gordon, New American Library (© 1970, 1975 Thomas Gordon, Peter H. Wyden, Inc.); *France in the 1980s* by John Ardagh, Pelican Books 1982 (reprinted by permission of Penguin Books Ltd.); *The Victorians at Home* by Susan Lasdun (Weidenfeld and Nicolson); 'Some thoughts on the nature and causes of industrial incompetence' by Norman F. Dixon, *Personnel Management*, December 1982 (reproduced from *Personnel Management*, by permission); *Thought and Reality: Selected Writings of Benjamin Lee Whorf* edited by John B. Carroll, © this edition 1976 by John B. Carroll (The MIT Press); *The Rape of the Earth* by G.V. Jacks and R.O. Whyte (Faber and Faber); *A Golden Thread* by Ken Butti and John Perlin (Marion Boyars); 'Computer Conferencing and Post-Industrial Regional Policy' by Tom B. Ward and Julian Newman, *Working Research Paper Series V, 8*, School of Business Management, Ulster Polytechnic (by permission of the authors).

The following quotations from newspaper articles are reproduced by kind permission of the proprietors concerned:

The Guardian: letter from K. Bandham, 18 January 1978; article by Donald Gould, 22 January 1980; 'How the village of Xinbu learned to love the biogas unit' by John Madeley, 5 August 1982; article by Harold Jackson, 2 January 1982; article by John Ezard, 11 May 1978; letter from Eric Liggett, 20 March 1980; letter from Feona Hamilton, 17 April 1980; report by Rory Johnston, 26 March 1982.

The Sunday Times: article by Hugo Young, 24 October 1982; 'Legacy of Hate' by Neil Lynden in *Sunday Times Magazine*, 5 September 1982.

The Observer: interview with Sir John Hackett by Maureen Cleeve, 4 July 1982; article, 2 January 1983.

While every effort has been made to obtain permission for the material quoted, it has been impossible to trace all the copyright owners, and in some cases repeated written requests have elicited no response. I therefore apologise to those who may read this book and find themselves quoted without permission having been granted.

David Andrews
Bath 1984

INTRODUCTION

Quite a few years ago, when I was about fourteen, I saw one of those David Attenborough programmes about people in far-off places. This particular programme was about 'cargo cults', and showed pictures of shrines dotted about the islands of the southern New Hebrides where Attenborough was filming. The shrines were odd in that they didn't contain the traditional carvings and idols one might expect, but instead, were filled with items familiar to Europeans, such as razors, fountain-pens, and soft-drink cans. These objects were worshipped by the people.

Attenborough questioned them about the background of these strange religious practices, and their leader explained that, one day, the 'ancestors' would bring 'cargo' – all kinds of common Western consumer items like watches, televisions, washing machines, and so forth – in huge aeroplane loads. The ancestors made this cargo, he said, but the evil white men wanted it for themselves, and so confused the ancestors' great white birds, causing them to land on their airfields. By observing certain rituals, and by setting up shrines, however, the people believed that one day the great white birds would land in their own territory and bring a plenitude of cargo. They had conveniently prepared special airstrips, complete with bamboo control towers and radio masts, for the purpose.

Years later, I read more on the subject of cargo cults, in particular in Peter Worsley's study, *The Trumpet Shall Sound*.[1] In the area known as Melanesia, to the north and east of Australia, numerous similar cults have flourished, dating right back to the days when the white men first began to move in and colonise. These cults often took bizarre forms. There are many cases of entire provinces being afflicted by mass hysteria. Cult activities have been recorded from the 1890s up to the present day, and have in numerous cases led to rioting and rebellion in opposition to the colonial government. Sometimes the cults called for the destruction, in preparation for the coming millennium, of all food and money, leading to disruption of local economies and causing great problems for colonial administrators. They have had bizarre names; the Vailala Madness, the Naked Cult, the Taro Cult, Marching Rule, the Mansren Myth, and so on.

Why did they arise? One of the essential problems, from the local people's point of view, was discovering the source of the cargo and the white men. Where did it come from, who made it, and why did the white men have so much of it? Who were the white men?

When the white men were asked where and how to obtain cargo, they told the people to work hard, join one of the many mission stations, and believe in Jesus Christ. In the early days the people tried this, abandoning their old religions, working hard on the plantations, and going faithfully to the mission churches. They soon found, however, that the white men had been lying, for they were still without cargo. And the white men appeared not to work hard; they seemed simply to send out pieces of paper and receive cargo in return. It was also obvious that they were lying about Jesus. Clearly the missionaries did not practise what they preached; they did not put themselves on an equal footing with the people as the scriptures advised, but set themselves above them, living apart from them, making them feed them, and in many cases not even bothering to learn their language. The missionaries also turned a blind eye to the appalling treatment of the workers on the local plantations, many of which they owned. Furthermore there seemed to be no agreement amongst the Christians as to the correct way of worshipping Jesus. In at least one case, an island actually had a fence erected down the middle, with Catholic missions controlling one side, and Protestants the other. And not all the white men believed even in Christianity. One native leader was shown a book describing modern evolutionary theory by a white man, and was completely baffled. He is reported to have blurted out 'But we were right all along, then! We always believed we were descended from apes, but the missionaries said otherwise.'

At the same time as giving manifestly implausible and contradictory explanations of the source of the cargo and himself, the white man was destroying the existing culture simply by being there and interfering with the local way of life. A new power had entered everyday life, one which the people found difficult to explain in any familiar terms. They had experienced other foreigners in the past, but these had eventually left the islands. These new white men, however, did not go away.

Essentially then, these cults were attempts by the local people to explain the situation in which they found themselves. Human beings do not simply see reality in the same way that a camera sees it. All disc cameras, say, form the same image on the film, if they are pointed at the same scene, and the same settings and lighting conditions are used. But what appears on the plate depends on the type of film in the camera. If you took a picture of the Vietnam jungle with two identical cameras, one containing an ordinary colour film, the other an infra-red one, the ordinary film would simply show trees. The infra-red film on the other hand, because it is sensitive to temperature, would show a completely different scene. So if some of the 'trees' were really camouflage netting, these might show up as a completely different colour from the real trees, revealing the enemy's position.

This is analogous to the varied perceptions of human beings. A burglar visiting a country house will notice and recall the alarms, the points of access, portable items of value, the strengths of the various locks, and so on. The ordinary visitor may notice only the aristocratic lifestyle of the occupants. The burglar's internal representational system is different from others'. In this sense, the world he lives in is actually different from the ordinary visitor's.

Similarly, people with emotional difficulties may inhabit different social worlds from others. A paranoid person will persistently misinterpret any form of interaction as some form of threat or rejection, whereas a more confident one could interpret almost any interaction as some form of compliment.

It is clear that how we see reality is also structured by the way we have learned to see it. It would appear that something exists in our brains which stands in the same relation to reality as do maps to a country. So we react to the map and not to the country, or reality, directly. If the map is wrong, or shows only certain features and misses others, then the map-user may run into difficulties.

People become so accustomed to their individual maps that when faced with data that cannot be fitted into it, real discomfort is felt. In one experiment, researchers showed their subjects a series of playing cards at high speed, and asked them to call out what was on the cards. Some of them were trick cards: there was a black four of hearts, or a red six of spades, for example. At high speed most of the subjects correctly called the numbers and the suit of the cards for the normal ones, but for the trick ones adjusted the suit to what it *should* have been. So a black four of hearts might be identified as the four of either spades or clubs. But as the researchers gradually gave the subjects more time to look at the cards, most of them became hesitant, and aware of something being wrong. With longer exposures they became increasingly confused, until quite suddenly most of them realised what the trick was, and thereafter correctly identified the cards.

Some of the subjects, however, were never able to recognise the problem, even at exposure rates of forty times the average. Those who failed often experienced acute distress as they struggled to fit the anomalous data into their internal maps. Just like the people who invented the cargo cults, the subjects were suffering from extreme anxiety and confusion as they struggled to fit something new into their maps of reality.

We can envisage a spectrum, or perhaps a hierarchy, of these internal representations of reality. At one end there is what we might call cosmology, notions of the world that people think they live in as a whole. Before the circumnavigation of the world most people in Western Europe imagined that they were on a flat earth. People who thought the earth was round or circled the sun clashed with the Catholic Church, and were often burnt for heresy. Nowadays we do not live in a flat world, or indeed one where people get burnt very often. Our cosmology has changed. At the other end of the scale there are internal maps for dealing with everyday detail. We can recognise and locate on our internal language map the greeting 'How do you do?' A schizophrenic, with a distorted internal representational system might mis-categorise the question and answer 'How do I do what?'

The problem I want to examine in this book is the way in which people have the ability to extend their internal maps, and the problems caused them by getting stranded with the wrong cosmology.

In 1882 it was found necessary to put up notices in New York hotel bedrooms advising people not to try to light the new electric lights there with matches. This may seem amusing to us today, yet it is only because in our heads we live in a different world from those hotel residents. Our cosmologies recognise and respond to the concept of electricity and so we know how to deal with it. Often, however, the wrong map can be activated, and we can carry on misinterpreting data in the light of a wrong cosmology for a long time, sometimes indefinitely.

Cosmologies also determine the options people think they have. Lateral thinking, as propounded by Edward de Bono, is all about getting people to think beyond the cosmological boundaries they have unwittingly set for themselves. For example, if little Johnny is annoying Granny and won't go into his playpen, what would you do? Most of us, unwittingly restricted in our thinking, would not consider putting Granny into the playpen instead. In many cases, as I hope to show, unintentional but sometimes deliberately self-imposed limitations lead to peculiar and inappropriate technological and social decisions being taken, through failure to recognise the true situation and the real range of options.

Clearly, cosmologies are important in that they control how we see the world, and how we react to it. In short, they may determine what we do, as much as 'real' world events. Cosmologies explain why the Chinese eat dog and the French horse meat, and why both these practices revolt the English. Only some parts of a cosmology can be consciously enumerated. If asked by curious aliens to describe the world in which we live, we might say, 'Our planet is called Earth and it goes round the Sun', but would we say 'We do not believe in putting grandmothers in playpens'?

Cosmologies are learnt. We are usually brought up by parents and educated in schools; we have friends; we work in institutions; we read books and newspapers and watch television. All these influence, mould and modify the way in which we see the world. An aim of this book is to look at how some of these mould our cosmology, for better or for worse. We may think the Melanesians a bit strange when they claim that their ancestors make the razors, cameras, and ball-point pens in their shrines, but to a visiting alien some of our Western beliefs might seem equally odd. Perhaps at this very minute we are on intergalactic television, with an intergalactic David Attenborough explaining why it is that '. . . every few thousand years these interesting Earth people go through a ritual called "civilisation", involving the creation of many fine buildings, great art, literature, music, and so on, along with a few military adventures. These civilisations,' he might continue, 'seem to last a few thousand years and then, for reasons we are not quite sure of, they peter out. They often seem to come to an end due to the destruction of natural resources, for many "civilisations" have certainly left behind ravaged treeless areas with massive soil erosion. Whatever the reasons for ending, we are a little worried about the most recent one. It is bigger than the others, and the inhabitants seem to be carrying out the destruction of their environment in a far more efficient way than ever before. They've even invented what they call nuclear weapons, which could wipe them out for good.'

I'm also going to look in this book at some more mundane (but I hope equally interesting) problems from this point of view, and will try to shed some light on why people working within organisations behave in 'irrational' ways when viewed 'rationally' from outside.

Numerous pieces of research have shown that most engineers make virtually no use of mathematics above 'O' level standard in their professional lives, yet maths is taking up greater and greater proportions of their study time.[2] Why?

Surveys have shown that 20 per cent of all scientific research has been done before by someone else.[3] Why should this be so?

Of all hospital admissions, 10 per cent are the result of drug side-effects, and studies have shown that groups of heart patients who are put on a course of drugs actually do worse (ie. more often die) than those patients who are left alone.[4]

During the Second World War, with its shortages of fresh fruit and vegetables, the RAF devised for their crews cooking methods which preserved the maximum amount of vitamins in the food. Today, the NHS is still ignoring these techniques, and serves food in hospitals which is deficient in vitamins because of inappropriate cooking methods. In some cases it actually *leads to* vitamin deficiency in hospital patients. Why?

Some of the survival swimming awards for which school children currently compete at the rate of up to 4,000 a day, could *lead to* death by drowning rather than preventing it, a ROSPA report warned recently.[5]

Official studies have shown that, apart from in certain inner city areas, the crime rate in this country is not increasing dramatically. Other studies have indicated that crime prevention methods such as simple alarms, stronger locks, locks on windows, and so on, are ineffective in deterring burglars. At the same time, the Home Office is promoting the use of such crime prevention methods, in a campaign that must inevitably increase public unease about crime by emphasising its 'common' occurrence, and thereby create a climate which must actually encourage crime. By far the greatest deterrent factor is location, detached houses being seventeen times as likely to be broken into as terraced ones, but this fact is not widely publicised.

A senior American academic and advisor to the US government has claimed that the more money is spent on health, the more the indicators of health decline, and its cost rises. In 1976, during a doctors' strike in Bogota, it was estimated that the death rate dropped by 35 per cent. The same thing happened in Israel in 1973, when the doctors went on strike, but in this instance the death rate dropped by 50 per cent.[6]

There are industries in this country that are, on the one hand, using up precious resources, yet at the same time are throwing away waste products which could be used instead of their raw materials. One such example is the Central Electricity Generating Board, which each year allows to pass into the atmosphere, via cooling towers, enough heat for the entire building stock in the country.[7]

I hope in this book to make some of the above oddities of individual and organisational behaviour a little more understandable. I have mentioned some of the factors responsible for moulding people's cosmology which, I hope to show, is in many cases responsible for the bizarre behaviour outlined above. These contradictions cannot simply be put down to crude desire for profit or personal gain, for in many cases the actors would gain more by behaving less 'irrationally'. Nor can they be put down simply to incompetence or stupidity.

I have already mentioned some of the influences forming our cosmologies – parents, education, friends, media, and so on. I will examine how cosmology is affected by different types of media and different types of organisation and then look at how, in turn, actions are affected. One of the key distinctions I shall make is between *central* and *lateral* media. The distinction can be made clearer by reference back, once again, to the cargo cult example.

Firstly, what are lateral media? Before the coming of the colonialists, the Melanesians lived in small villages whose relationships with neighbouring villages were frequently hostile. It is certainly fair to say that, in general, the villagers did not mix with one another, except for specific reasons such as trade and intermarriage: the focus of an individual's life was his own village. Ritualised warfare between villages was common. The Maring of Papua, New Guinea, who we shall look at in more detail in Chapter 2, spent most of their time growing yams, raising pigs, and, every twelve to thirteen years, having a war with their neighbours. When the colonialists came, it was therefore fairly easy for them to subdue these divided villages. Each cargo cult sprang from a particular person having what we would call a religious experience. This vision or revelation explained where the white men and their cargo came from, how they could be destroyed and their cargo acquired,and how lost power could be regained. These revelations often took the form of instructions for the adoption of certain codes of behaviour, such as no adultery, no lying, performing certain rituals, eating only certain foods, or the operation of communal gardens instead of individual ones. The emphasis was often on brotherly love and the abandonment of old tribal customs and rituals. The prophet would reveal that, if the people followed these rules strictly, then *in a few weeks*, at the appointed hour, the sky would darken and the ancestors would arrive, usually in a single large ship or boat. Then the people would rule over the whites, or the whites would simply disappear. Peace and prosperity would come, but only to believers.

The cargo cult idea is in fact similar to the way our Western political parties promise us a return to former glories, or a period of bliss and material well-being, but only if we will believe in moneterism, nationalisation, hanging, discipline, or whatever it is they propound.

Initially, the doctrines of the founder prophet of the cargo cult would be spread by assistants and aides. But once a cult had started, numerous other local prophets would receive similar revelations from their ancestors. This would be taken up and repeated by still more, rather like a Chinese Whisper, the doctrines gradually being modified and distorted to suit particular local conditions. There was often ill-feeling and suspicion between different sects, but, at the same time, a strong sense of being part of the same movement. Thus we may envisage a network of communication between the people of these regions, with anyone capable of passing on the message doing so, albeit a slightly modified one. Or they might initiate a new message, perhaps inspired by earlier ones.

It has been shown that these cults, and the interaction between them became a powerful influence over the years in unifying the people in the face of colonial oppression. Ultimately it helped the development of indigenous political parties. It also led to a growth in a feeling of nationalism. We may think of such poly-centred, self-assembling networks as *lateral media*. Examples closer to home are Old-Boy networks and grapevines.

Central media are different. It has been shown how the cults changed gradually over the years. As each failed to deliver, conventional political parties, better able to oppose white rule and to demand a better deal for the people, evolved out of the cults. Political movements eventually led to important concessions being granted by the colonial authorities, so the people had actually acquired 'cargo'. The cults themselves gradually changed their programmes and promises, adopting more conventional political methods and demands. But some cult-adherers increasingly turned their backs on the 'real' world of politics, oppression, and lack of cargo, and instead focused more on internal spiritual matters, such as defining precisely the cult's organisation, its exact doctrines, rituals, modes of behaviour and so on.

Cults similar to the cargo cults are not unique to Melanesia. They have been recorded all over the world in all cultures and throughout history, typically when one group has been oppressed by another, as were the early Christians under Roman occupation.

In fact, it has been shown by, for example, the Gnostic Gospels and the Dead Sea Scrolls, how early Christianity was just such a polycentred lateral media, as the cargo cults, with as many versions of the basic Christian beliefs, as there were rival sects. Rival versions of the Garden of Eden story, for example, do not give women the role that has justified their abuse down the ages. All the early Christians believed that when the Messiah came, then would be ushered in the millennium. The Romans would be vanquished, and those who conformed to the correct rituals would enjoy earthly bliss. Gradually what was to become the Roman Catholic Church increased in power and was able to force its particular version of Christianity on everyone else and, along the way, formed a convenient alliance with the rulers of the remains of the Roman Empire. What had been a polycentred lateral medium, where everyone could have a share in talking about, and defining the Christian message, and could commune directly with God, was transformed into a centralised hierarchic structure, where only one man, the Pope, could talk directly to God and he could impose his views on everyone else.

Thus central media can give the same message to everyone simultaneously in monologue, and lateral media deliver numerous different messages in dialogue.

Central media in our own society include the civil service, large hierarchical organisations, and most forms of mass communication such as newspapers and television.

With the distinction in mind, between lateral and central media, I hope to examine reasons why some of the phenomena already described, and others not yet touched upon, seem to occur, quite readily in our own allegedly rational culture.

1 SKIMMERTON RIDES, MAY DAY AND THE TRADITIONAL SENSE OF COMMUNITY

A visitor to the Somerset village of Pilton on a certain day in 1905 would have witnessed a peculiar sight. In one of the cottage gardens the villagers had gathered to re-enact a recent local event, each person playing a role in the drama. Afterwards a mock court was held and the defendant was found guilty. The peculiarity lay in the fact that the 'defendant' was represented by an effigy of one of the villagers who had committed an offence. The effigy was burnt later that evening, and the following day the malefactor left the village, never to be seen again.

What happened to precipitate this strange event? It had various names, being known as a 'Skimmerton Riding', 'Rough Music', or 'Riding the Stang'. The event leading up to this particular 'ride' had been the seduction of a 15-year-old serving girl by a lay-preacher in the village. Because he was fond of moralising, the villagers looked very unkindly on the seduction of the young girl, and the fact that she was a servant in the preacher's house was a further cause for outrage. The Skimmerton Ride was their response.

This type of activity was once very common throughout English villages, dating back to Elizabethan times. There is, in fact, a frieze in Montacute Abbey from that period, depicting such a ride. The effigy to be burnt was frequently of a man and woman on horseback, with the woman riding behind the man. This was because in those times much 'illicit' sexual activity supposedly took place on horseback; the image of a man and woman on horseback together was thus considered very scandalous and was widely used to represent offensive behaviour.

This kind of village justice has almost died out, and certainly no institutionalised form survives, although there have been several twentieth-century examples. In 1972, for example, there was a Skimmerton Ride in a Suffolk village, following the death of a girl at the hands of violent parents. The ride for Maria Caldwell took place in the village where she died. Sometimes rides assumed greater importance. In Wells there are records of a stage being constructed, and the words of a play, burlesquing the activities of certain local malefactors, were distributed to the audience.

These rides are an example of self-government, or informal control. In pre-industrial England the sense of village community and popular morality was much stronger than it is today. Numerous forms of 'control' had emerged that held people together and let it be publicly known if one of them was not conforming to community requirements. The novelist Thomas Hardy, familiar with the customs of his native Dorset, describes a ride in *The Mayor of Casterbridge*. It was not a completely blind or inflexible form of justice; only if an adultery, for example, was considered exceptional would it bring the sanction of the village. A man whose wife was a notorious nag or 'scold' might avoid such treatment.

Nowadays, when few of us live in closely-knit villages, this kind of community policing is very rare. In the rather anonymous urban landscape where most of us live, with its attendant decline of a sense of community, anyone committing an offence is liable either to be ignored by the passer-by, or else 'they' will be called in to deal with it. Throughout the history of the English village, however, the regular occurrence of unofficial forms of control was very effective in holding the village together as an entity.

This ability of small groups or communities of people to govern themselves, in terms of organising acceptable behaviour within the community, seems to be a widespread and natural phenomenon. As a feature of society it has declined with the development of modern man, but it reappears in any situation where people come together in small groups away from official control.

Examples abound. In the wagon train crossing early America, the people elected a leader, the wagon master, and agreed to be bound by the laws that he made for them. For anyone severely infringing these the ultimate sanction was banishment from the wagon train, meaning almost certain death. Minor infringements were punished proportionally. In rural areas in Britain it was common practice until the mid-nineteenth century for the harvesters to elect a 'Lord of the Harvest', and his pastoral equivalent was 'Captain of the Shearers'. Workers in eighteenth-century Marl pits would also elect a 'Lord', and during the same period printing chapels usually had a 'Father', who was the oldest printer in the shop.[1]

The point about all these groups is that their members shared a common cosmology or view of the world, which more or less defined each group. They saw the world and experienced its problems in the same way, and this shared experience enabled them to agree on how best to live in order to ensure the survival of the community and its members. In this context Antonio Gramsci's concept of 'common sense' is useful. He refers to a 'spontaneous philosophy',[2] which '. . . is contained in: 1) Language itself, which is a totality of determined notions and concepts and not just of words grammatically devoid of content. 2) "Common sense" and "good sense". 3) Popular religion and, therefore, also in the entire system of beliefs, superstitions, opinions, ways of seeing things and of acting, which are collectively bundled together under the name of "folklore".'

Gramsci distinguishes 'common sense' from taught knowledge, or state education. He uses it in a much wider sense than the English meaning of the phrase, to refer to the cultural experience of the greater part of society, as distinct from that of the ruling or governing class. 'Common sense', to Gramsci, is a non-institutionalised, informal view of life and the world. I shall return to this important concept in Chapter 5, on the allied theme of 'tacit' knowledge.

Writing of the Anglo-Saxons, and their clash with the invading Romans, G.O. Sayles makes clear the difference between the custom-aided social control of a tribal society, and the legal control of the state:[3] 'Fundamentally we are observing the outcome of the clash between a Latin civilisation and a German civilisation with their differing conceptions and traditions. The Romans taught the world to look upon law as the legislative act of a supreme and sovereign authority in the state: the Germans regarded law as the ancient and unchangeable custom of the people, equally binding upon all members of the community, whether king or not. The Roman Empire saw the evolution of principles which paved the way for absolute monarchy: the German peoples looked upon kingship, however divine the origin and hereditary in its nature, as essentially an office created to be of service to themselves, particularly in war, and they emphasised the close personal relationship between themselves and the king who was their tribal chieftain, their leader in battle and their protector in peace.'

These self-control, or 'homeostatic', mechanisms emerge from *homo sapiens'* tribal history and culture. Man is essentially a social animal, and it has been our ability to form these self-governing groups, and to co-operate within them, that has accounted for our success. It was a misinterpretation of the theory of evolution, the oft-quoted 'survival of the fittest', that gave us the idea of our survival being due to our violence as a species. We may well be violent as a group, but an examination of human history shows that *homo sapiens* has been extremely adept at forming fair and democratic self-governing systems, or at least systems which minimise damage in the settlement of conflict, in the same way that apes and carnivores generally do not fight to the death. Ritual display of, for example, buttocks usually halts an aggressive victor. It was certainly not the case that each tribe was ruled by a despotic tyrant who was the biggest, strongest and most violent, as the popular conception of 'survival of the fittest' might lead one to expect. Man has survived because he can co-operate. Furthermore, few tribes until the last 6,000 years or so seem to have been 'imperial', that is to say aggressive expansionists. The proper interpretation of the theory of evolution in terms of 'survival of the fittest' means survival of the most suitably adapted to his surroundings, and man's success has been based on his ability to adapt his small group to the varied conditions in which it found itself. It was this 'fitness' for his environment that enabled man to flourish without significantly unbalancing that environment. Only in recent times, the last 6,000 years or so, compared to the three million years' duration of his evolution, has he dominated, and begun to destroy nature, that is to say, become 'unfit'.

The popular mythical view of early tribes holds that the chief was both self-appointed and ruthless, ruling purely for his own aggrandisement. In this version, primitive savagery prevailed until the coming of the white man to introduce law, order and justice. This was certainly the image which post-Imperial school history lessons used to instil. In fact, anthropological evidence shows that this is largely an inaccurate view. Numerous tribes and societies did not have an identifiable chief or ruler at all.[4] E. Evans-Pritchard, in his book on the Nuer of the Southern Sudan, provides an example of such a society:[5] 'The lack of government organs among the Nuer, the absence of legal institutions, developed leadership, and, generally, of organised political life is remarkable. Their state is an acephalous kinship state and it is only by a study of the kinship system that it can be well understood how order is maintained and social relations over wide areas are established and kept up. . . The Nuer is a product of hard and egalitarian upbringing, is deeply democratic, and is easily roused to violence. His turbulent spirit finds any restraint irksome and no man recognises a superior. Wealth makes no difference. A man with many cattle is envied, but not treated differently from a man with few cattle. Birth makes no difference. A man may not be a member of the dominant clan of his tribe, he may even be of Dinka descent, but were another to allude to the fact he would run a grave risk of being clubbed.'

In numerous tribal situations the chief, if one existed, was elected. He was chosen as the one most likely to bring harmony, stability and good laws. He was often, in fact, very weak. He was the servant of the tribe and its quintessence. His job was basically to interpret the wishes of the tribe's members, and it was judged whether or not he was a good chief by the stability and order he brought by his good laws and settlement of disputes.

Max Gluckman writes of the Zulu:[6] 'From his subject's point of view, one may say that the main duty they owed the king was military service, including labour service. The king was also entitled to certain royal game, though he had to reward the hunters. In addition, it was customary to give him gifts of grain, beer, cattle and, some say, girls. As he also received most of the cattle and women captured in war and fines for certain offences, he was easily the richest man in the nation. In return for this, he was expected to feed and help his people generously. He had to care for his regiments and give them their shields; in famine he was expected to help his people and also at all times those in difficulties.'

There were all sorts of mechanisms within the tribe to make sure that the chief did not become too powerful. The ultimate sanction was for his tribesmen to leave and join another tribe. And he was powerless without their support. In this sense Anglo-Saxon kings were tribally elected chiefs, and there are numerous examples of Anglo-Saxon kings being deserted on the eve of battle. If the king led them into a battle they did not think worth fighting, or if they did not consider the king worth fighting for, they would desert him. This happened, for instance, to Richard III. The chief could always, if necessary, be deposed. And if the tribe became too large, it could split up.

Another mechanism for controlling the chief or king was his accessibility. His public and private life were not separated. The tribesmen could discuss the law and the activities of the tribe around the campfire in the evening. Everyone had access to the chief. A modern example of this survives in the Saudi Arabian monarchy. Among the Bedouin it is a capital offence to prevent a tribesman coming to see his king, and it is also a capital offence to search him; this is how King Feisal came to be killed by an ordinary tribesman.

The role of the chief was essentially to keep harmony within the tribe, not to preserve his own power. The motive was not so much an allegiance to abstract concepts such as justice, fairness or public service, but the fact that every man had the same idea of the origin and purpose of the tribe and every member shared the same concept of harmony and reconciliation. When an offence was committed, the relations of the malefactor were frequently fined. This obviously encouraged families to keep a potential trouble-maker in line. Banishment, rather than capital punishment was often the ultimate sanction. Once a person had been banished from one tribe it would be difficult for him to join another, and this would ultimately often lead to his death, since it would be very hard for him to survive outside society.

There were many and varied mechanisms for keeping the peace and reaching harmony within tribal societies. The Eskimos, for example, had drumming contests as a means of controlling and dissipating conflict.

John Fletcher describes how many tribes had highly ritualised forms of violence which limited real damage: 'Until very recently verbal violence often took the place of physical violence. Primitive people always appear so barbaric to us because they look so fearsome – they are literally dressed to kill – and because their epic poems and histories are filled with gruesome and bloodthirsty "Old Testament" descriptions of battlefields and victories over neighbouring tribes. When anthropologists have attempted to discover precisely what took place, however, on these hallowed battlegrounds, a very different picture emerges. Hours would be spent before battle while witchdoctors ritually and exhaustively damned the other side, to the wild football-supporter cheers of their own. Eventually, the two highly emotional and vocal armies would wobble in the general direction of each other. At extreme weapon range, two or three brave souls from each side would then dart forward and hurl their spears, resulting in one or two generally minor injuries to the other side. Honour thus vindicated and heroism proved, both sides would get down to the real purpose of battle, namely, rushing back home and composing blood-curdling epic poems extolling their bravery and heroism – an ancient version of war memoirs.'[7]

So, if we look more closely at tribal societies, we find that they were more sophisticated well-balanced mechanisms than we may have thought. It is evident that there was a series of mutually demanding relationships between the tribesmen and their chief. In examining these relationships Victor Turner uses the concept of 'liminality',[8] which, he says, 'implies that the high could not be high unless the low existed, and he who is high must experience what it is like to be low.' Thus in many tribal societies with chiefs there are rituals involving role reversal. Maundy Thursday is a survival from such a ritual.

Similar rituals from the late Middle Ages include the 'Lords of Misrule'. These, normally the lowliest servants, were elected to be Lord of the Manor at Christmas. Over Christmas everyone was obliged to treat them as the lord. Boy bishops were also common. In this case, the lowliest choirboy was made bishop for St Nicholas' Day.

These types of role reversal were common in tribal societies, and were mechanisms for making clear the mutual dependence of tribesmen and chief. Such relationships existed between adjacent parts of the tribe, and between one tribe and another. It was not possible for one part of the Nuer, for example, to grow in strength at the expense of

another. The interlocking relationships, alliances and duties derived
from the kinship and age-set systems prevented this. Such mechanisms
ensure stability and minimise or contain an outbreak of violence.

There have, of course, been numerous occasions when one tribe, or
part of it, has eliminated another, due perhaps to population growth,
climatic change or new weapon technology. Nevertheless, numerous
examples exist of tribal societies characterised by interdependent
(albeit hostile) relationships. It was through mutual 'control' of these
'feedback loops' that *homo sapiens* populated the earth in an apparently
stable manner for millions of years prior to the emergence of
civilisations. And the gentle Tasaday people of Mindanao, for instance,[9]
live in much the same way as their Stone Age ancestors. It is only in the
last 6,000 years that civilisations have emerged to disrupt such
stability, and it is far more recently that tribal relationships have been
obscured in industrial countries. Such loss of stability is shown by the
relatively short-lived existence of most civilisations preceding our own,
set against the sweep of man's history, and by the great ecological
damage that has been inflicted on our surroundings.

The value, and hence the survival of some of the elements of tribal
society until recent times can be demonstrated by a look at the history
of England. After the Norman Conquest tribalism gave way to
feudalism; the chiefs, living closely with their people, were replaced by
barons, who were remote from their serfs and protected by armed men.
It was still very much a mutual relationship, however. In return for the
serfs' labour, the baron gave them protection, looked after them when
times were hard, and settled disputes where necessary.

Following the Black Death in the fourteenth century, and the
resulting labour shortage which marked the end of the feudal system,
serfdom began to die out, making it easier for peasants to leave a
particular lord. A different fundamental relationship prevailed: that of
lord of the manor and peasant. There was no middle class as yet, except
in the towns, to blur the distinction between the common people and
aristocrats. The growing merchant class of Elizabethan times, which
gained land and power following the Dissolution and the Reformation,
had little effect on relationships in villages.

Until Victorian times the great majority of English people
continued to live in scattered villages, hamlets and small towns. A
closer look at the structure of the village during this period reveals that
it developed a whole series of rituals, holidays, festivals and feasts
through which it governed itself. These events and activities not only
gave the villagers the opportunity to enjoy themselves, but also
ensured, by their performance, that their government was being

properly undertaken. The process of government was thus inseparable from the processes of enjoyment and of work. This is in contrast with modern society, in which work and leisure are rigidly separated, and the activities of religion, government, social services, psychiatry, policing, education, and so on, are all carried out by specialists set apart from the average person.

Contemporary seventeenth-century chronicles, quoted by N.J. O'Connor, describe a theatrical demonstration in a Lincolnshire village.[10] A large group of villagers was organised by Talboys Dimock into a procession, with drums, flags and reeds tied together like spears. Everybody marched in procession, and there was much visiting of alehouses along the way. 'On the last Sunday in August, Talboys Dimock did frame and make a stage play to be played in for sport and merriment at the setting up of a maypole in South Kime, because the same day should make an end of the summer lord game in South Kime for that year.'

The maypole would go up on May Day, and come down on the last Sunday in August, when it was meant to have lost its power. On this occasion it was also an excuse for putting up a stage and acting out a satirical play in which all the powerful and unpopular people in the area were satirised, in particular the Earl of Lincoln.

N.J. O'Connor describes the event.[10] 'All the hundreds (a unit or organisation of a number of villages) came, venison was served at lunchtime, followed by the play, and then by dancing round the Maypole. After that came a brief satirical interlude. Talboys opened this interlude in a speech imitating the Earl of Lincoln. In it the Earl of Lincoln was hauled off by the devil, and then a song or dirge was sung lamenting the passing of the Earl of Lincoln, wishing him well in hell, and then naming all the whores in London, Lincoln and Boston. The fool then came in and gave his last will and testament, leaving his wooden sword to the Earl of Lincoln, and the coxcomb to all who would not join against the Earl of Lincoln.'

So we see that popular demonstrations were a chance for public protest, as well as a chance for public celebration, the two going together.

The strong sense of community within villages was manifested in the fact that almost all marriages were contracted within a village or with an adjoining one. There was a strong sense of mutual help and neighbourliness, frequently combined with strong hostility to other more distant communities. This was shown in inter-village cricket or football matches. Groups of villagers would rescue one of their own from an alien authority, another town's or another lord's, a whole posse going over and rescuing him. Factional fights would also often break out between different groups of mummers and wassailers. Church orchestras often met each other on their rounds, and fights would ensue.

There were community entertainments which played an integrative role: the May games, climbing the greasy pole, chasing the greasy pig, all dances and sports, were not only good fun, but also brought people together. The Puritans in Stuart and Elizabethan times drove these games from the church, where many had previously been played, to the ale-house. In the late eighteenth century Methodism also attacked popular sports. But bull-baiting was still common in the early nineteenth century, as was folk football.

Remnants of the mediaeval 'largesse' pattern also survived. This was the means whereby the squire gave back to the peasants some of what they contributed to him during the year. Great festivals took place at Christmas, Easter, Whitsun, and also on Guy Fawkes Day. At these there was liberal feasting and drinking at the squire's expense. It was not only a celebration, but also an integral part of the economic system. On Plough Monday, in January, for instance, all the 'plough lads' would go round to the large houses in the village and be given food and drink. If none was forthcoming, they ploughed up the front gardens of the uncharitable householders.

Another example of the mechanism of village self-government is through church orchestras. The minstrel gallery is still a familiar sight in a number of old churches. Prior to the introduction of the church organ, played by the schoolmistress or the squire's daughter, these orchestras were the sole source of music during church services. It is not commonly known that these institutions were suppressed by Victorian tractarian ministers in the nineteenth-century drive for piety and respect for authority. This suppression caused much ill-feeling amongst villagers, and there were many riots. In Little Walsingham the organ, with half the church, was blown up during a Guy Fawkes night celebration.

How did these orchestras function as informal control mechanisms? They were mainly composed of artisans from the villages - the blacksmith, the shoemaker, and so on. These individuals, who worked hard practising and composing, produced, by all accounts, beautiful music. Their position in the church gave them far greater control of the church service than an organist would have nowadays, and they could use this for their own ends. If, for example, someone in the village had offended one of the orchestra - be it the squire or one of the villagers - they could select an apt psalm for the occasion. It might be a psalm which mentioned 'nests of vipers' if an over avaricious squire was the object of attention, or 'adultery' if he were an adulterer. Psalms were believed at the time to have magical properties, and at the appropriate moment the whole choir and all the people in the church would turn and face the malefactor, and sing the psalm *at* him. This was bound to have a powerful effect on the guilty party.

The original function of a market town was to serve as a centre for the weekly exchange of produce. As Dorothy Davis says:[11] 'Most towns up to Elizabethan times were smaller than a modern village, and each of them was built around its weekly market where local produce was brought for sale, and the townsfolk sold their work to the people from the countryside, and provided them with refreshment for the day. Trade was virtually confined to that one day, even in a town of a thousand or so people. The trade of markets was almost wholly concerned with exchanging the products of the nearby countryside and the goods made by local craftsmen. The producers and consumers of these things met face to face, and consequently the genuine retail trader, the man who bought only to sell again, had very little place. Nowadays shopping hours are restricted in the interests of the retailer, and not because of the scarcity of goods. It is one measure of the difference in their way of life that mediaeval people restricted the market hours in the buyer's interest, so that every buyer should have an equal chance to buy a fair share of whatever was going, and also to enable the authorities to keep an eye on all transactions and make sure that no one made a corner in some commodity and engrossed it – that is, forced the price up.'

Governments, that is parliamentary governments, and the landed class they represented, tended to be paternalistic in the Tudor and later periods. The Tudors thought it their duty to protect the common people's right to bread at a fair price, and laws which restricted middlemen from cornering the market were rigidly enforced. In succeeding centuries, however, as the rich merchants and landowners became more powerful, and the king derived more and more of his income from the emerging middle classes, these laws were gradually watered down. The middlemen, from Elizabethan times onwards, attempted to gain control of the market in certain products, in particular, the grain market. This frequently led to a great popular outcry, which was expressed in riots. Over the years these developed into a ritualised and accepted form known as 'bread and blood riots'. If the people believed, for example, that corn was being sold at above its fair price, they would assemble in the market place. Frequently they would have two spears with two loaves of bread impaled on them at the front of the crowd. The people would then march through the town, break open the granaries and sell the grain at what was believed to be a fair price. The money was then handed over to the merchants. This practice developed into a well-understood and perfectly normal routine. When troops were sent to deal with these riots, the aristocratic officers would, as often as not, side with the people, because they thought their action reasonable. So the riots were immediate, rough-and-ready community justice – instant correction of a perceived wrong.

There was also a great tradition of public justice, as opposed to the rather impersonal justice of today. Justice had to be seen to be done. We have been led to think that the crowd went along to jeer and enjoy themselves at public executions. In fact, unless a particularly foul murderer, or a very clearly anti-social individual was to be hung, the crowd went along to display affection and concern for the victim, and to give him as a good an execution as possible. They would, for instance, all sing hymns together beforehand. The same was often true when it was thought that someone had been unjustly placed in the pillory.

Displays of public humiliation and public support are, as we have seen, both present in non-institutional rituals. In this case a state ritual was turned back on the authorities themselves. This kind of direct expression of public displeasure was considered perfectly normal and occurred from time to time all over the country. The last 'bread and blood' riots took place in 1867 and affected all parts of the country.

Up until 1890, it was for local authorities to decide whether or not to intervene in a riot. In the 1890s, following a colliery riot in which three people were shot dead, a new Act was introduced which gave the authorities no leeway. If a riot was in progress, then they were bound to intervene to put it down. Following the introduction of the modern police force in the 1830s–40s, rioting was already much more easily suppressed. Indeed, Lord John Russell, who was Prime Minister in the 1840s, complained when he was an old man, that there weren't anything like as many riots in the 1850s–60s as there used to be in the past. He claimed that in the old days the ruling classes always knew if they had done something wrong because their coaches were jostled by the mob in the street. The general tightening-up of authority, and the repression of the informal mechanisms followed not only the intro-duction of the police force but also the development of railways, meaning that troops could be moved rapidly from place to place. It became much more difficult for the ruling classes to gauge whether or not what they were doing met with the approval of the masses.

Ordinary people in the nineteenth century, even though they may have been obedient Christians, shared a coherent cosmology which was part-Christian, part-pagan. It provided an integrated world view, in which the stars influenced human society, influencing the plants that grew, the animals that bred, and so on. And the universe they inhabited included spirits, forces, immanences and powers, through which they had to steer a perilous course.

The purpose of this brief look at the social life of England in the centuries preceding the Industrial Revolution is to demonstrate, through the somewhat unusual perspective of the festive side of ordinary people's lives, that features of tribal society were retained in village life. Each village was a small, and to some extent independent, unit. The lord of the manor was its head, but mutual responsibilities bound him to the villagers, who saw themselves as part of a cohesive unit, and as a potent force in the day-to-day running of that unit. Life may have been hard, but it had these compensations.

These features of tribal society were more or less extinguished during the nineteenth century. Their suppression with the aid of troops and police caused bitter resentment among the common people, who looked forward to their various annual festivals and ceremonies as a means of expressing themselves, as well as seeing them as occasions for enjoyment.

Gradually, however, such popular festivals were successfully suppressed. Troops were used in Lewes for four to five weeks in 1847, and in Guildford for several months, in 1861 and 1863. The festivals caused widespread fear among the new 'respectable' middle classes, who looked to the authorities to get rid of them.

As the Industrial Revolution began to bite, more and more of the features of custom-aided social control went into the melting pot. Middle-men emerged between the lord and the villagers, those with more land and better education. They formed oligarchies within the parishes, and took over most of the mechanisms by which they were governed, and they brought in their wake a social revolution.

So as the eighteenth and nineteenth centuries progressed, the nature of villages changed. Prior to Enclosure, each villager tended to have his own small-holding and was to an extent self-sufficient. He had to give either labour, money or produce to the lord. In return the lord had certain obligations to him, such as largesse, protection, the provision of alms-houses, and so on.

From the mid-eighteenth century, private legislation brought about the enclosure of much of the common land by farmers and the landed aristocracy, and instead of subsistence agriculture, farming for profit was introduced. The majority of people from then on lost their common right to land and had to work for wages and live in tied cottages. The amount of land allowed to a labourer for an allotment was the subject of endless debates in parliament. He needed enough land to feed himself, and keep himself healthy enough to work, but on the other hand there was a risk he would become independent by producing enough to sell for himself.

In Victorian times the intrusion of a more capitalist system in terms of both economics and social relations completely dissolved the old village ties and customs. The festivals which had symbolised the mutual dependence of farmer and labourer were suppressed, sometimes with the aid of the police. After the sanitisation of the church service the church no longer served as a focus of social activity. The Church of England tightened its grip on education and the new middle classes consolidated their hold on parliament and the law courts.

Thereafter the establishment of the first modern bureaucracy led to the construction of the first modern state – a development I shall later return to in more detail. For the time being, let us consider what I have been describing with the aid of a speeded-up film of the history of *homo sapiens*. For nearly three hours of this film there are millions of small independent groups dotted around the earth's surface, all living separately and autonomously, and in a stable relationship with the 'carrying capacity' of their environment. Then suddenly, in the last 36 seconds, the pattern changes with the appearance of the first civilisations. A succession of very large groupings arises, each centrally controlled by rich élites. Most of these expand by imperialist activities and the subjugation of the dispersed tribes surrounding them, or through victories over other, weaker, central systems. The destruction of the environment at the centre necessitates the importation of materials from surrounding areas. By the end of the film, all of these systems have expired, or become severely weakened, due to a combination of resource-destruction, pollution, and political and social problems.

2 *NATURAL LATERAL CONTROL SYSTEMS*

The purpose of presenting the historical snapshots in the previous chapter was not to draw conclusions about whether the past was a better or worse time than the present. It was to highlight the fact that organisational systems were different in the past. What was different about them being that the day-to-day activities of most people were largely controlled by the lateral media contained within communities, by people living close together. People today, by contrast, have a much weaker sense of community, giving their allegiance instead to smaller nuclear families or to more nebulous concepts such as profession, class, the law, country, and so on. They are controlled by laws and regulations produced by politicians and bureaucrats in remote places such as London or Brussels to a greater extent.

This centralisation of control obviously has its advantages. Our higher standard of living derives in part from our ability to centrally control large numbers of people in a co-ordinated way. The advantages are obvious: some of the hidden disadvantages of centralisation are what I am more concerned with here. I believe it possible to demonstrate that the organisational system in which we live is in fact out of control, and that current attempts to improve the situation are merely worsening it. The point is not that we must do away with centralised systems, but that there are different types of centralised systems that we could use, and by considering decentralised ones, perhaps we can gain important insights into how to improve them. In order to do this we must look at some control models.

Suppose you were a police commander, and wanted to search a large area of open land. You would need to use several hundred policemen. We have all seen this kind of activity on television – a line of policemen gradually moving forward, combing the undergrowth. There are, in principle, two different ways of organising this sort of activity. In one, the sensible way, the police commander says to his men: 'Spread out between these two points and gradually move forward combing the ground, remaining equidistant from one another.' By judging their own position in relation to others', they spread themselves out, a regular distance apart, gradually covering all the ground. We can call this 'dispersed control'. What keeps all the policemen equidistant from one another is a process of continuous interaction between them and their relative positions.

At the other extreme in the same situation we could postulate a megalomaniac police commander who insists on his right to total control of his subordinates; the policemen would then behave as automata, only responding to specific orders. In this case the commander would continually have to order each policeman to his new position: 'Move forwards, Jones; a bit to your left, Smith; back a bit; right' and so on. To keep several hundred policemen moving he would have to give instructions to them simultaneously, so he would also need several hundred assistants at headquarters, operating radio links.

Obviously the latter method is a ludicrous way of proceeding, and could probably not be done in practice. But it illustrates an important law in cybernetics, the scientific study of organisations, the 'Law of Requisite Variety', or Ashby's Law, after its discoverer.[1] For our purposes, Ashby's Law states that for a control system to be effective, then its complexity must match the complexity of the system that it is trying to control, or that the control system must be able to adopt the same number of states as the system being controlled.

In the police search party, the number of states is the number of policemen, and all the possible positions they could take up. For the hypothetical central control case, the 'control system', the room containing the controlling officers, must have enough officers and radio links to cope with the number of searching policemen, and the mind of the police chief must be able to recognise the position of each policeman and any deviation from the desired path, and also be able quickly and clearly to communicate his desires to the controllers. Whatever the combination of individual positions the searchers adopt, the control system must have sufficient capacity to recognise those states, and appropriate instructions must be issued. In cybernetics' jargon, the number of states of a system is called its 'variety', so Ashby's Law is really stating that the variety of a control system must equal the variety of the system being controlled, hence the Law of Requisite Variety. This has important consequences for society, for there are frequent mismatches in variety between systems and their controls.

There are two possible ways round the problem: either the variety of the control system must be increased or reduced, or the variety of the system being controlled must be increased or reduced. One way of bringing down the crime rate, for example, would be to attach an incorruptible policeman to everyone in the population, thus increasing the variety of the control system. This sometimes applies to small rural communities, where everyone may be an unofficial policeman to everyone else, and the crime rate may consequently be proportionally lower than in large cities. An alternative control method would be to institute a curfew which, by limiting the number of states that a potentially criminal population could take up, would reduce the variety of the 'crime generating system' to limits which could be handled by a relatively small police force. This strategy is similar to that followed by insurance companies, which, by making individuals fill in standard forms, reduces their variety to within the limits that the company can handle.

If we apply cybernetic thinking to human society, we can see that the early traditional societies were stable, and must, therefore, have satisfied Ashby's Law. The control system within tribes was other tribesmen; between tribes it was other tribes, and the environment; it was in fact what we have called dispersed control. It could be seen working in, say, the mutual dependence of the tribesmen and the chief. Remnants of such dispersed control systems until quite recently still survived, as described in Chapter 1, as Skimmerton Rides, church orchestras, and so on. The collapse of previous civilisations can be seen in terms of their failing to satisfy Ashby's Law.

Another important result of cybernetic theory is that, to be effective, a control system must contain an accurate model of what it is controlling.[2] In a modern bakery, for example, the various ingredients must go through certain processes, storing, mixing, proving, baking, cutting, and so on. In the plant there is a control room with what is called a mimic diagram on the wall. This is a stylised map of the flow of materials in the plant, a bit like an underground railway map. Sensors at the various processes send information back to this diagram, and various lights are illuminated to show what is happening; the operators can then check that each process is functioning properly. Cybernetic theory says that the mimic diagram must be an accurate copy of the bakery processes, otherwise these will not be properly controlled. Applied to previous civilisations, cybernetics indicate that they were unable to accurately model the situation they were in, or to take appropriate action based on that model to ensure long-term survival. I shall return to this idea in more detail in a later chapter. For the moment, let us look at some other examples of dispersed control systems.

The first 'system' I want to examine has the somewhat undistinguished common name of 'slime mould'. It is an organism responsible for the damp woody smell you get in a wood when it has been raining, and is, in fact, an amoeba, a single-cell animal which is found in water, or any damp place, such as the surface of leaves. The slime mould is a 'social' amoeba, and is particularly interesting, since it can at different times be a single cell or a single organism composed of millions of such amoebae. Several million of them, moving about independently, feeding on a leaf, look as shown in Fig 1.

Gradually there comes a point when the food runs out for the amoeba. When this happens, they somehow recognise their situation and an extraordinary thing happens. Although at the beginning there were millions of amoebae spread out on the leaf, when the food begins to run out, each starts to move towards a central point; together they take on the appearance (shown in the figure) of a river, or several rivers, all converging towards the centre. This is an astonishing thing to watch speeded up on video. It may take several hours, but over a period of time they will all stream together towards a central point. They then form themselves into a slug-like shape and move off as an organised entity. This traverses the surface of the leaf, changes into a spore body and distributes spores, which change back into amoebae. The process then starts all over again.

The question is, how do several million amoebae move in this organised way towards a central point? And secondly, once they are there, how do they form themselves into an entity that is actually capable of moving off? The tendency of the human observer is to feel that the operation must be co-ordinated by some central signal-giving agency – or at least that a master-plan must exist – but this is not the case. What happens is that each amoeba begins to send out pulses of a complex chemical called cyclic AMP. Each is sensitive to high concentrations of this substance, and each is programmed to move into the gradient, that is, towards the greatest concentration of cyclic AMP. The process is rather like being blindfolded and being ordered to move into the wind by the use of a wet finger stuck in the air. As the amoebae begin to accumulate in the centre of the leaf they reinforce the tendency of this spot to initiate the maximum concentration of these pulses. The more amoebae that accumulate in the centre, the more signals there are to attract others to join them. The accumulation of amoebae in the centre of the leaf is a dispersed phenomenon, and is purely an outcome of chemical dialogue between cells. Another way of saying this is that the organisation of the slime-mould into the slug state is an emergent feature of the communication between amoebae. The use of these pulses as a chemical language has another effect, in that only those amoebae that can recognise the pulses are capable of joining in. Any amoebae that can't – any foreign ones or any that are damaged – get left out. The process is similar to policemen organising their formation for a groundsearch. In place of pulses, they are told to respond to the observed position of their colleagues by keeping an

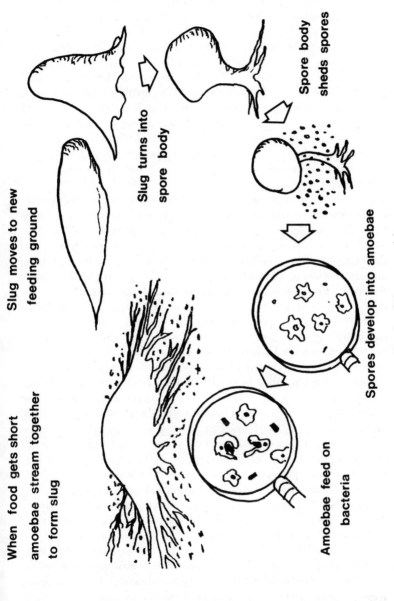

Slug moves to new
feeding ground

Slug turns into
spore body

Spore body
sheds spores

When food gets short
amoebae stream together
to form slug

Spores develop into amoebae

Amoebae feed on
bacteria

Fig 1   Slime mould

arm's length away. How the slime-mould actually manages to move off as an organised entity still defeats observers, but that, too, appears to be organised in similar fashion to the dispersed communication which brought the amoebae together in the first place.

Exactly the same sort of dispersed control occurs in an ecosystem such as a forest or an ocean before man interferes with it. Why don't the wolves eat up all the moose and then die of starvation? Why don't the lions kill all the wildebeest? Why don't sharks eat up all the fish? In natural ecosystems various homeostatic mechanisms have evolved whereby individual species keep within certain limits. These complex controls have evolved alongside the evolution of the different species. Their overall tendency is to keep the biological production of a given natural habitat at a maximum, and composed of a wide diversity of species, so that biological catastrophes do not wipe out all life.

How do these controls operate? Take the case of the wildebeest, many thousands of which roam, say, Tanzania's Serengeti, preyed on by lions and other predators. The predators kill wildebeest in insufficient numbers to have much impact on their growth rate, and the homeostatic mechanism that keeps the population from growing and destroying its habitat is apparently that the young wildebeest simply get lost, and starve to death. In large herds, this happens very easily.[3] In this way the population size is self-limiting, the predators merely helping the process along. By contrast, many plants are controlled by their predators. The prickly pear cactus, which was introduced from the United States into Australia at the close of the last century, nearly overran Australia, making 60 million acres of land useless for sheep farming by the 1920s. Finding that dynamite, flame-throwers and bulldozers made no impression on it (lack of requisite variety), the Australians tried importing moths whose caterpillars feed on the cactus from the United States. Within a very short time the caterpillars had almost eradicated the prickly pear (increased variety of control system). Almost, but not quite; a small number survive, and support a small population of the moth. So both the moth and the prickly pear population are now controlled by one another.[3]

Similar mechanisms control other animal populations. The feedback between species and their predators, between species and their environment, and the species themselves, create stable ecosystems. Numbers of each species are kept within certain limits, at the same time ensuring that every niche is colonised by a wide variety of species.

In the past, before the advent of settled civilisations, human societies appear to have developed control mechanisms similar to those that can be observed in nature. Contrary to popular belief, this mechanism was not warfare. Among the Yanomamo in South America, reckoned to be one of the most warlike tribes, the average number of deaths in adults attributable to war is 15 per cent.[4] Since most traditional societies are polygamous, any shortage due to male war dead has little effect on population growth, since the widowed females simply join the ménage of the dead's brothers or uncles. Even in the Soviet Union, where in the Second World War one in ten of the male population was killed, the population was almost back to where it would have been had the war not occurred, after only one generation.

How then do traditional societies regulate themselves? Martin Harris' plausible explanation[4] is that such societies have subtle and sophisticated controls intrinsic to their way of life. The Maring, for example, are a remote group of New Guinea tribesmen. They have a twelve year cycle of peace, which is followed by warfare with neighbouring clans. The cycle is apparently driven by love of pigs. During the year preceding the battles, the rival Maring slaughter their pigs, and feed themselves and their allies. This has the effect of propitiating the ancestral spirits, who will aid them in the coming battles. The battles themselves are highly ritualised. One side often flees as soon as someone is killed or injured, as this is a sure sign that not enough pigs were killed to satisfy the ancestral spirits. Even in the most bloody battles recorded, only some twenty out of a possible three hundred were killed. After a defeat the losers abandon their village and gardens hacked from the jungle, but the victors do not take them over for fear of annoying their ancestors, so their gardens are allowed to return to their natural states. The defeated side, meanwhile, joins its allies, and hacks out a new area, to start the process again, growing food and raising pigs ready for the next war, in twelve years' time. Harris points out that this is precisely the time taken for the agricultural system to reach the point of breakdown, from soil exhaustion and pressures on the women from the care of children, the pigs and the gardens. When pigs from rival groups invade and eat other groups' produce, the outbreak of war becomes inevitable.

The mechanism that controls the population is not the warfare, but the placing of a premium on men, who do the fighting. The society has a tendency to nurture male children more successfully than female ones, resulting in a ratio of 1.5:1. According to Harris, this factor has a far greater effect on population than losses in battle. Together with protecting cultivation, this population control does not arise from a set of rules, or any such formal system, but is generated by the cosmology of the people, their belief that their ancestors like pigs, and must be propitiated, and the inevitable fact that as the cycle reaches its climax, friction will break out between rival groups. Societies without such controls presumably either died out or suffered rapid population growth, and there was an attendant necessity to import large quantities of food and raw materials in order to survive.

The control systems I have described, enabling ecosystems and traditional human societies to maintain their stability without sudden surges and crashes of population are dispersed control systems. They do not have a central control, and only when they have suffered disturbance do these become necessary.

I have mentioned feedback between the various elements of an ecosystem. Feedback was a term originally taken from a branch of control systems engineering. It is a term that has now crept into general usage: people, for example, speak of a local council getting feedback from the community about their plans for a new hypermarket and neurotic couples wail about not getting enough feedback from one another.

To illustrate what feedback really is, consider the humble electric toaster, or bread-toasting system. Many people will have experienced burning toast in the more primitive types of toaster. The reason is twofold: different breads require different periods of heating, and when the toaster has warmed up it cooks more quickly than when it was first turned on. Toasters usually have a simple timer in them which has to be adjusted to suit the particular bread being used. This, once set, is oblivious to whether that piece of bread is white, brown, stale or fresh, and toasting on such an implement is consequently a very hit and miss affair. In theory we could design a toaster which incorporates feedback, having an electronic eye which detects when toast is beginning to burn: the machine would then automatically eject it.

Two different feedback situations can be represented, as in Fig 2. In the second case, the timer gets information fed back to it from the toast and adjusts itself according to its condition. The feedback from the electronic eye to the timer creates what is known as a closed feedback loop between the timer, the toast and the sensor.

Any ecosystem incorporates feedback, or closed-loop control systems such as the electronic toaster. In a healthy, stable organic system, these feedback loops are ultimately negative, negative not being used as a pejorative term. It simply means that the control signals always function to restore the state of the system to some fixed value or range of values, reversing any trend or tendency to change the system's state. All stable, healthy living systems are collections of 'things' interacting through predominantly negative feedback loops.

Multiply-interlocking feedback loops give an ecosystem, or a human

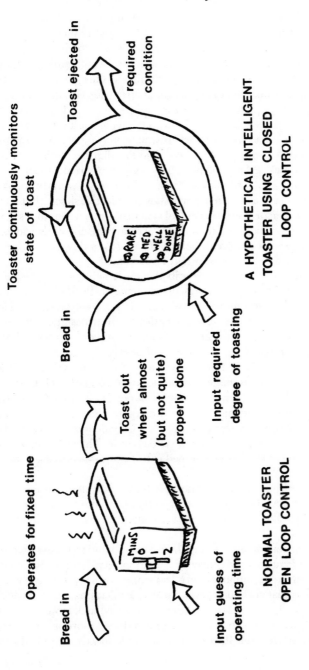

Bread in

Operates for fixed time

Toast out when almost (but not quite) properly done

Input guess of operating time

NORMAL TOASTER OPEN LOOP CONTROL

Toaster continuously monitors state of toast

Toast ejected in required condition

Bread in

Input required degree of toasting

A HYPOTHETICAL INTELLIGENT TOASTER USING CLOSED LOOP CONTROL

Fig 2   The toaster

body, natural stability. But, there are limits to everything. If the wildebeest in the Serengeti, for example, were reduced below eleven thousand, the approximate number required by their main predator, lions, each year, it is probable that the lions would entirely eliminate the wildebeest, and so themselves. Similarly, the system for regulating the body's plasma (see Fig 3) can stand up to wide variations in external conditions – climate, activity, diet, and so on – and still maintain a constant body temperature. However, giving the individual a nasty shock, such as bad news or a severe injury, may overcome the capacity of the body's control system. We then say that the individual is in a state of shock. Many of the body regulators break down and the condition is fatal without treatment. I hope to show in this book that the human race as a system is in a state of collective shock, that is to say, that the intricate complex control systems, which for millions of years kept a balance between us and the carrying capacity of the earth, and between groups of human beings, have broken down and also show how these control systems might be recreated.

The traditional systems described in the last chapter were essentially homeostatic, examples of closed-loop control. Pre-industrial villages and small communities were also stable systems. Modern societies, however, have lost the characteristics of the tribes and villages that made them homeostatic, and have shifted to open-loop control. Worse than that, in many cases, elements of positive feedback have crept in. Positive feedback is frequently undesirable, despite sounding so benign. In common usage we hear, for example, polytechnic lecturers or politicians say, 'I'm getting a lot of positive feedback'. In strictly technical terms this means something quite different from what they are presumably intending to say. The equivalent of positive feedback in vernacular terms is, in fact, a vicious circle. The inflationary spiral, for example, is frequently claimed to be a positive feedback system (see Fig 4).

Toast-burning is another positive feedback system. As toast begins to burn it gets darker, and, as is well known, darker surfaces absorb more heat. The darker the toast becomes, the more rapidly it burns.

The purpose of introducing these concepts and terms at some length is to enable me to apply them to human society. For positive feedback loops operate in human society and cause problems that are not only severe, but that are bound to worsen at an accelerating rate. It is one of the aims of this book to identify these positive feedback loops, and to look at how we might be able to reintroduce appropriate forms of homeostatic control. If we do not, we will follow the fate of all systems

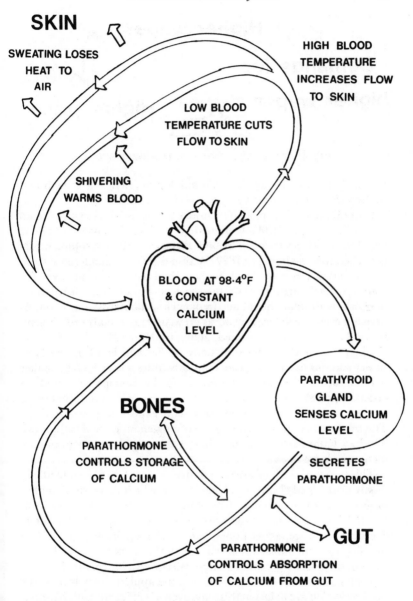

Fig 3   Blood temperature and calcium content are some of the many properties of blood which are controlled by the negative feedback loops shown in this diagram

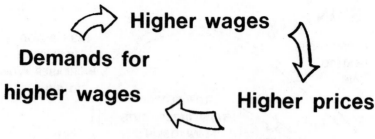

Fig 4   An alleged positive feedback system

in which positive feedback predominates: accelerating growth and sudden catastrophe – we will burn our ecological toast.

As a preliminary step, let us consider how some of these ideas could be applied to a practical and immediate problem facing us: supplying consumers with electricity in Britain. Electricity was first commercially produced in Godalming in 1897. Within five years, hundreds of small power stations run by local councils had sprung up all over the country. Each area had its own power station and distribution network, with different voltage frequencies, standards, and so on. As demand grew, these local networks grew, and, as a final development, they all became interconnected, giving us the now familiar National Grid. It was quickly realised, notably by Ferranti in 1910, that large power stations had certain economic advantages over several smaller ones, so successive governments encouraged a monopoly in supply in order to prevent competition between many small producers using smaller, and what were thought to be more expensive, power stations. The result is that all Britain's electricity is generated in less than two hundred large power stations. Half of that supply comes from only forty very large ones.

This policy, though advantageous up to a point, has brought about highly-centralised electricity production in which there are a number of severe disadvantages and diseconomies far outweighing the advantages. Power stations of the current size and type waste a lot of energy, even large modern ones being extremely inefficient. A large British power station is at best only about thirty-six per cent efficient. That is, sixty-four per cent of its input energy is wasted in the chimneys or cooling towers of the station. The same applies to nuclear power stations, which are in fact in this sense even less efficient than coal-fired power stations. The loss of energy does not end there. A further nine per cent of what we get from the best stations then gets lost in transmission from the power station to the consumer, mainly due to inefficiencies in the transformers. Taking all these factors into account, including the consideration that not all power stations are new and efficient, overall, the efficiency of the Central Electricity Generating Board in converting coal in the power station to power in the plug in your home is only about twenty-nine per cent. In other words, the CEGB wastes more than two-thirds of the heat energy of the fuel that is delivered to it in heating up the countryside.

Each year the CEGB wastes more energy in its cooling towers, chimneys and river cooling water systems than the heat requirement of all the buildings in the country put together. Furthermore, the heating of buildings is the biggest single user of energy in this country – that is to say about forty per cent of all energy used in Britain is for heating buildings or producing domestic hot water in them. So if the hot water from all the power stations were piped to our homes and buildings, instead of being wasted in cooling towers, rivers, and chimneys, we would use hardly any fuel in our buildings' boilers.

We can't, of course, pipe all that heat to all our buildings. The policy of building fewer and fewer but larger and larger power stations has meant that they have had to be sited far from urban settlements. It would, therefore, be very expensive to pipe the waste heat, or reject heat, as it is euphemistically known, to all the buildings requiring it. Nevertheless, studies have shown that bringing heat from many of these power stations is economically feasible and would save a lot of energy, despite the fact that such Combined Heat and Power stations (CHP stations) are slightly less efficient in terms of electricity production. Overall, of course, they have a much higher energy efficiency.

Whether or not the CEGB is right to cling to its faith in the large electricity-only station is a matter of continuing controversy. In a number of other European countries – Germany, Denmark, and Holland, for example – many power stations are smaller and have been located close to the cities, so that the waste heat can be used for local heating. For every unit of electricity production lost due to the lower efficiency in the power station, ten units of useful heat can be used. In Britain there are several hundred small power stations where waste heat is used for heating, for example on Slough Industrial Estate, but these are mainly in private hands.

Such small CHP stations can be eighty per cent efficient, compared with the CEGB's thirty-six per cent. Their average size is about 10–50 megawatts, compared with the CEGB's 2,000 megawatt stations. The problem for the CEGB with its present operational method is that a large number of small power stations, although more efficient, would be very hard to control. At the moment, its two hundred power stations can quite easily be centrally controlled by issuing a plan of expected demand a few days ahead, and supplementing this by phone calls on the day. The CEGB has a sort of league table, called the merit order, with the cheapest power stations at the top and the most expensive at the bottom. As demand rises, it switches on more and more power stations, starting with the cheapest first, and gradually going down the list to the more expensive. With a very large number of power stations this system would be difficult to operate, due to Ashby's Law.

For similar reasons, the CEGB has always argued that large amounts of electricity derived from renewable energy sources cannot easily be incorporated into the grid. This inflexibility is serious, in view of the potential shortage of fossil fuel. Renewable energy sources such as wind, wave, hydro, and probably in the long term solar, are now in principle as cheap as nuclear power, but within the present system cannot easily be used, because these sources are uncontrollable and therefore unreliable, without additional expenditure on electricity storage schemes and supplementary fuels.

Another disadvantage of CEGB policy is that very large power stations take about ten years to plan, design and build, so forecasts of demand have to be made at least that time in advance. It is very difficult to accurately forecast for years ahead, and so the tendency is either to have too few power stations, as in 1955–6, or too many, as we have now. Both tendencies cost the consumer money.

As if all this were not enough, a major failing in the system is that there is no rapid feedback between the availability of supply and the demand for it. With the exception of certain large industrial consumers, the CEGB's twenty-one million customers can place whatever demand they like on the CEGB. People can turn on as many lights, fires and machines as they choose, and the CEGB must, by law, have sufficient power stations running to meet that demand. The system must also be able to cope with any sudden surges in demand, such as at the end of a TV programme, when millions of people switch on their electric kettles at the same time. It does this by keeping plant operating, but not producing full output, in readiness for turning up at short notice. This 'spinning reserve' and 'hot standby' - plant which can produce power at short notice - costs money to build and operate, and is a charge passed on to the customer.

A related problem is that most customers pay the same amount for their unit of electricity irrespective of how much that particular unit cost to produce. There is only very crude feedback between the consumer and the varying cost of a unit at different times. This is an example of the

Law of Requisite Variety, existing tariffs only crudely coping with the variety of consumers. A unit purchased from the CEGB during the summer, when its cheapest and most efficient plant is running, costs the same as a unit in winter, when its oldest and most expensive plant is operating. So the users of power in winter – those with electric central heating, for example – are being subsidised by the all-year-round users. 'Economy Seven' and certain industrial tariffs do create some feedback, but it is so gross that it has no short-term effect on the CEGB supply and demand mismatches.

What we see when we look at this cumbersome, unwieldy and unresponsive system is that it would now be possible to introduce elements of homeostatic control which would ultimately resolve many difficulties. Based on the relative cheapness of modern microprocessors, their use is under active discussion and development by certain sections of the electricity industry. Field trials of parts of the system are proceeding.

The concept is simple. All previously existing electricity tariffs would be abolished, and, instead, two 'spot prices' would be substituted: a 'spot selling price', the price at which the CEGB could sell electricity, and a 'spot buying price', the price for which the board could buy electricity from private producers. These prices are broadcast by the CEGB or Area Boards to all consumers, say, every five minutes. The signals are received by a 'smart meter' which is installed on the consumer's premises. This displays the current spot prices to the consumer, so he can actually see that it would be cheaper to vacuum-clean or use an electric drill in the afternoon, say, rather than at any of the peaks of electricity demand.

The result would be that peak consumption would not reach such heights as it does now. This, in turn, would mean less use of the older and less efficient power stations, and, consequently, lower fuel and electricity costs. While the consumer would save money, he would not use less electricity: he would simply use it at different times of day, in the same way that people try to use the telephone in the afternoon rather than in the morning.

That is one effect of the system. But the smart meter is capable of more than that. It can be programmed by the consumer to switch certain appliances on or off by signalling over the house wiring to 'intelligent' plugs, which are nowadays very cheap. This would mean that the householder could, for example, programme the smart meter to turn off the freezer and immersion heater whenever the spot price exceeded, say, 10p a unit and turn them on in cheaper periods. Such implements can quite happily be switched off for several hours at a time, without any problems. How would this benefit the consumer? As soon as the CEGB were to receive a sudden surge in demand, such as the huge one at the end of the Royal Wedding in 1981, it would simply raise the spot selling price until enough freezers and fridges were turned off by the smart meter. This would enable an exact balance to be maintained between demand for power and supply, without necessitating such a large standby margin. It would mean far less likelihood of power failure, and lower electricity bills. The mechanism would be quite sensitive, in that consumers would all have slightly different settings on their smart meters, and hence different criteria for turning off different appliances. So, by gradually raising the spot price, the CEGB would gradually reduce demand. These appliances would only be cut off for short periods, since the peaks would not last long.

The application of this system would also enable all sorts of people to install and operate small power stations based on windmills, photo-voltaic cells, and highly-efficient car engine sized micro-CHP modules such as the Fiat Totem (see Fig 5). These small power stations could be controlled in exactly the same way as electrical appliances, using the spot buying price and a smart meter. The fluctuating output of renewable energy sources and private producers could then be absorbed into the power network by manipulating the spot selling price. Under the present system this is impossible; if it is a very windy and sunny day with all the photo-voltaic cells and windmills giving their full output, any change in the weather might cause a sudden drop of power. To cope with this at present, many large and expensive standby power stations would need to be provided. Under homeostatic control, as soon as the output from the renewable sources dropped, the spot price would be raised, thereby shedding load instantly, until the crisis was over. The spot buying price would be also raised, encouraging small private stations to begin increasing their output. In this way a perfect match between consumers and producers could be obtained, always exactly balancing supply with demand.

Many other advantages would follow. Very small power stations can be installed in months rather than years, so the time-lag problem of the CEGB would be solved. If an all-nuclear future were to be chosen, homeostatic control could still greatly assist. Nuclear power stations have to be built in large sizes, and the sudden failure of one of their large generating sets is a serious matter compared with a similar failure in a small power station. This has led to the creation of huge pump-storage schemes, such as Dinorwic, whose main function is to cope with a sudden failure, or other surges in load. Homeostatic control is a much cheaper way of doing this. It has, in fact, been estimated that the

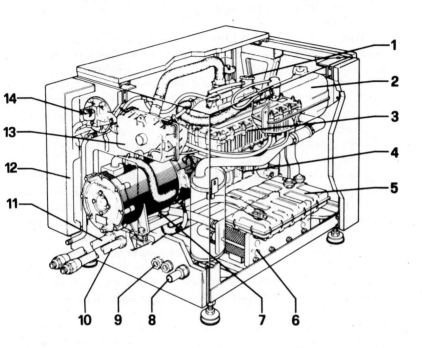

1 - 27 ENGINE	8 - GAS EXHAUST
WATER RESERVOIR	9 - ELECTRICAL CONNECTION
GAS/WATER HEAT-EXCHANGER	10 - HOT WATER OUTLET
OIL/WATER HEAT-EXCHANGER	11 - COLD WATER INLET
OIL RESERVOIR	12 - THERMAL AND ACOUSTIC INSULATION
WATER/WATER HEAT-EXCHANGER	13 - AIR INLET
ELECTRIC GENERATOR	14 - GAS FEED

Fig 5   The installed capital cost of the Totem micro CHP module (in £s per kilowatt) is less than a large CEGB power station, the electricity it produces is cheaper (in pence per kilowatt hour) and overall it is more than twice as efficient (88%)

introduction of homeostatic control now would lead to annual savings of £1,000 million,[5] in proportion to the CEGB's annual turnover of £3,500 million.

What we are proposing in control terms is that we exchange an open-loop system, with no rapid, effective feedback between the moment-by-moment cost of power and the demand for it, for a closed-loop system. The full application of these potential homeostatic control mechanisms to the buying and selling of electricity would amount to a fundamental shift of control from a central to a dispersed source, dispersed in fact among the entire population of producers and users. The result would be a cheaper and more efficient power supply system, and one that is in the long run more sustainable.

Many of the problems of the CEGB can now be seen to stem from its attempts as a central control system to satisfy the Law of Requisite Variety. In order to be a good control system it must model the situation it is in, and plan appropriately for electricity demand, for a few seconds as well as thirty years ahead. But performance to date indicates that this model has not always been very accurate. The building of power stations, in particular, has demonstrated conspicuous failure. In the late 1960s there were too few power stations, resulting in the disconnection of consumers during peak periods. At present, there are too many power stations, representing premature investment which is passed on to the consumer as a cost. Since it is impossible to project future demand with any certainty, and new power stations have to be started ten years before they are needed, it is not surprising that both shortages and over-abundance in the provision of power stations have arisen.

With homeostatic control, and the ending of the CEGB's monopoly on power supply investment and supply, the decisions as to when to invest, and in what, can be shifted to all consumers. Based on their individual situation – roof angle, house position, local climate, wind speeds, cost of fuels, demand for waste heat, and so on – each consumer with adequate funds could decide whether or not he should invest in power supply. He could use his own models of the future. Does he think certain technologies will become cheaper? Will the recession end? And so on. In other words, there would no longer be any central model of the situation, or the future; it would have been dispersed among all the participants, who would be linked by the fluctuating price of power. As a shortage of power developed, with more load-shedding at peak periods, more people would respond by investing. Since they would be installing small plant, local CHP plant, windmills, photo-voltaic cells, and so on, which would take only about two years to install, any mismatch between supply and demand would be greatly reduced.

In this chapter I have elaborated the concept of dispersed homeostatic control. In our culture, whenever something needs to be organised or controlled, the tendency is to try and set up some form of centralised system. I hope to show in subsequent chapters that in many cases this simply does not work, because such solutions frequently lack requisite variety. What is needed instead is the implementation of more forms of dispersed control, for these are much more likely to possess that variety. Electricity generation is a concrete example of one application of this approach. In the perspective offered so far I would suggest that the phenomenon known as civilisation emerges when the type of dispersed control mechanisms I have described break down, leading to uncontrolled growth at the expense of the environment. Many previous civilisations have declined because of their destruction of their environment and exhaustion of locally available materials, necessitating the importation of large quantities of raw materials, and ensuing tensions with rival powers. Our society would seem to be well down this path. But the only solutions on offer seem to be packaged in more central control. My argument is that we must try to create conditions in which homeostatic dispersed control can reassert itself in a form resembling the network of interactions occurring in the slime mould and in Maring society.

3 LANGUAGE AND COMMUNICATION

The crucial factor in the dispersed control of complicated natural systems such as the slime mould is the communication between the system elements. It is the multiple and mutual signalling links between these that close the feedback loops and maintain the stability of the system. In my example of the electricity supply industry, my proposed alterations would introduce an analogous complexity of signalling using electronic devices. For most of the interactions in human society, however, language is the medium used. Here we have hit on a serious problem. For it is my contention that many of the notions held today about the nature of communication and language are inappropriate. As a result, the design of organisational systems, media systems, educational and child-rearing and professional systems frequently militate against successful and effective communication.

In order to consider this idea, we need to look at what language really is, and how communication takes place. The popular view of this subject appears to be the sort that is derived from language lessons at school, and from exposure to books and television. It suggests that we use words which have fixed and specific meanings, and that communication is the sending out of streams of these words, which can then be understood by others. So in order to be able to transmit ideas, all that is necessary is to know enough words, or to have a good dictionary, and to know the grammatical rules for using the language. We can call this a 'monologue' concept of language. Such attitudes are frequently encountered by language teachers. Students of English as a Foreign Language, in particular, are sometimes bemused by Western methods and clamour for more 'rules'. A friend of mine who teaches EFL was recently asked by a high-ranking Saudi government official for extra private lessons in which he could learn the rules. He had the idea that it was knowledge of the rules, rather than everyday use of the language, that would make him fluent.

People have, of course, managed to use language successfully throughout history without the aid of rules or a classical education. The first grammar of modern times did not appear until 1492, in Spain. Not everyone was impressed, none less than Queen Isabella de la Catholica, who commented: 'It is impressive that finally someone has done for our Castilian tongue what so far has only been done for the sacred tongues of antiquity. But I am aghast at the uselessness of this undertaking, which has taken Nebrija so many years, because grammar is a tool to teach language, and I do not see why a spoken language should be taught.' She continues with a gloriously royal linguistic theory: 'Because in our Kingdoms every single subject is made by nature in such a way that growing up he obtains a perfect dominion over his tongue and it does not behove the King to interfere in this domain.'[1]

The notion that there is a correct form of a language, and that it requires to be taught, is a relatively modern one. In fifteenth-century Spain there was no such thing as 'correct' Spanish; there were simply different regions and different classes. Since the culture of Spain at that time did not recognise any particular standard or correct form of Spanish, this caused few problems: people using different dialects were accustomed to adjusting their speech to communicate with one another. In England there was a similar situation, with widely differing local dialects. The written language also had many forms even among the literate, and there were widespread variations in spelling and grammar, which were accepted as perfectly normal and natural. How, then, did the conviction arise that there is such a thing as a fixed, correct language, with words having fixed, correct meanings? For this is the attitude which still underpins most contemporary lay thought about language.

Until the end of the fourteenth century, such central government as there was in Europe interfered very little in the details of people's lives, compared with the plethora of laws and regulations to which most of us are now subject. But in the fifteenth century central government started to take a greater hand in people's lives. The increasing wealth and mobility of the ruling classes prepared the way for the breakdown of the feudal system, with its emphasis on the lord and serf relationship and mutual aid. In Britain, this process reached its climax in the eighteenth and nineteenth centuries, when the Enclosures, and the mechanisation of agriculture, forced people off the land. They congregated instead in large numbers in towns. The Industrial Revolution mopped up many dispossessed agricultural workers, but their arrival in the towns gave rise to an enormous problem of poverty. The poor had previously been looked after by the lord of the manor, or the parish, or by family and neighbours, informal links rather like those of the old tribal systems, but these broke down in the growing cities. To attempt, belatedly, to cope with this drastic state of affairs, the Reform Act of 1832, followed by the Poor Law Amendment Act of 1834 (referred to by Cobbett as the Poor Man's Robbery Bill), introduced, among other measures, a new Poor Law and the associated Poor Law Commission. This step was a revolution, in that it set up the first modern bureaucracy, which was to be the prototype of the Civil Service as we know it today. Similar bureaucracies had of course developed in previous civilisations.

From 1832 onwards, central government departments increasingly controlled the actions of the people. This meant that a standardised form of English had to develop, so that there could be effective communication between London and the provinces. There could be no argument about what London meant, and London had to be able to understand its incoming mail. At the same time elementary schooling for all was introduced, thus enabling a standardised language to be taught.

This standardisation of language led to the loss of much of Gramsci's 'common sense', the 'spontaneous philosophy' which 'is contained in language itself, which is a totality of determined concepts, and not just made of words grammatically devoid of content.'[2] The same point is made by Thomas Hardy in *Tess of the d'Urbervilles*, (first published in 1895) when describing the divide between Tess and her mother: 'Between the mother, with her fast-perishing lumber of superstitions, folk-lore, dialect, and orally transmitted ballads, and the daughter, with her trained National teachings and Standard knowledge under an infinitely Revised Code, there was a gap of two hundred years as ordinarily understood. When they were together the Jacobean and the Victorian ages were juxtaposed.'[3]

Attempts to codify standard English preceded Victorian England, of course. In the mid-eighteenth century Johnson produced his dictionary, which noted primarily current middle class usages. Bishop Louth, however, who in 1762 wrote *A Short Introduction to English Grammar* was unrestrained by such pragmatism. This publication had an extraordinarily far-reaching influence, perhaps because of Louth's status as Bishop of London. As Jean Aitchison writes, 'Many modern rules about usage can be traced to him. Where Johnson used current usage, Louth simply elevated his own idiosyncratic views on good grammar to the status of absolute law. For example, contrary to general usage he urged that the prepositions at the end of sentences should be avoided: "The Preposition is often separated from the Relative which it governs, and joined to the Verb at the end of the Sentence, as 'Horace is an author, whom I am much delighted with . . .' This is an Idiom which our language is strongly inclined to; it prevails in common conversation and suits very well with the familiar style of writing; but the placing of the Preposition before the Relative is more graceful, as well as more perspicacious; and agrees much better with the solemn and elevated style." As a result the notion that it is somehow wrong to end a sentence with a preposition is nowadays widely held.'[4]

The problem with the idea that language is, and should be, standardised, is that although in practice no standard language has ever existed in a large civilisation, those who believe that it does also believe that they alone speak it. These people then emit messages which are comprehensible to themselves, but incomprehensible to outsiders.

The public school background, from which most of our leaders come, has only served to exacerbate the difficulty. Following the Reform Bill of 1832, the role of certain élite schools changed to preparing the sons of the new middle classes for public service, to run, for example, new bodies such as the Poor Law Commission. The classical basis of the education offered, however, did not greatly change. For obscure reasons it was, and still is, thought that training in Greek and Latin enables a man to run a modern civil service. The result is that even today almost all civil servants, and particularly those in senior positions, tend to think and write in Latin- and Greek-based thought modes. The following is an extract from a letter in an engineering journal: 'During my period as a temporary civil servant, I dealt with a large number of top civil servants and administrative trainees and usually asked after their academic backgrounds. I was dismayed at first to find that most did, indeed, have degrees in classics, languages and history, with a strong Oxbridge bias. . . Indeed, I have seen a classicist who took meeting notes in Greek arguing more convincingly and numerately than a mathematician who was occasionally as woolly-minded as the worst sociologist.'[5] At one time the paperwork spawned by such classically-educated administrators reached such a peak of incomprehensibility for the unfortunate recipients that Sir Ernest Gowers was commissioned to write *The Complete Plain Words*; a case of trying to close the linguistic door after the horse had bolted.

The trouble is that believers in the monologue concept and the 'universality' of language think, quite erroneously, that there is no need to check whether their message is understood. In fact, satisfactory communication can only occur under one or both of two conditions: between two people who share *exactly* the same language, monologue communication is sometimes possible, in practice this means people from the same community or background. In the case of local dialects, for example, this means the same village; in the case of civil servants, the public school or Oxbridge system. Even in this situation monologue can still be ambiguous, however, and lack of understanding can have disastrous results. In the famous murder case of Chris Craig and Derek Bentley, accused of murdering a policeman in Croydon, much hinged on what the defendant meant when he shouted to his armed accomplice, confronted by the policeman, 'Let him have it, Chris!' Did he mean 'Give him the gun' or 'Shoot him'? The defendant hung, some say, wrongly.

Under the second condition, between two people who are not certain whether they have a common language, there must be feedback or dialogue. A speaks to B, and B responds with 'Am I right in thinking that you are saying. . .?' This feedback is often subconscious on the part of the listener. In Ireland, for example, a pattern of conversation is often heard in which the important word of each utterance is repeated:

'So I went to the pub.'
'Pub!'
'And I met Murphy there.'
'Murphy!'
'And we had a Guinness.'
'Guinness!'

And so on. This simple fact about language and effective communication is not widely embodied in our modern usage, and has, over the years, been responsible for endless trouble. Lack of feedback has also accounted for arguments over historical texts by long-dead authors. Differing interpretations of what the Bible says have, over the centuries, caused not only confusion, but bloodshed. The Protestant Church, for example, holds that the Roman Catholic Church bases its entire doctrine on such linguistic confusion. The Roman Catholic Church's claim to a monopoly of knowledge of Jesus and God, and mediation between them and us, is believed by many to be founded on a misreading of Jesus' words. What did Jesus actually mean when he said to St Peter 'Thou art Peter, and upon this rock I will build my church'? Did He mean to set up a strict hierarchy under the Pope, as the Roman Catholic Church believes, or to establish a loose collection of individual meetings in members' homes, as, for example the House Church Movement believes? The disagreement is hardly surprising in view of the fact that only three hundred and twenty-five years after the death of Jesus bishops began physically fighting one another over their interpretations. The Roman Catholic Church has since claimed that all other forms of religious service but its own are invalid, and, in consequence, countless people have been put to death. Equally, one hundred years after the death of Karl Marx, there is at least one great division of opinion between the Soviet Union and China about the philosophy expressed in his writings, with each side calling the other 'revisionist'.

The monologue concept of language involves a fixed array of words, with fixed associated meanings. What is needed is a different concept of language – closer to what actually happens when people learn to use languages. I will call this the dialogue concept of language.

It seems that what actually happens is that the human brain has a system for recognising situations, and then correlating the situations with the words that are being used by others at the time. After several encounters with the situation and the new word, the person may try the new word out – feedback from the people he is trying the new word out on guides him to the word's acceptable usage, and tells him if he has got it wrong or only nearly right. At the same time, the person's misuse of the word, if it is appealing, or attractive in some way, will in turn affect the usage of the word by others. For example, our son, aged $2\frac{1}{2}$, after much exposure to people taking photographs, squinting through a viewfinder saying 'smile', uses the word 'smile' to mean looking through an optical device. If he wants to look through my binoculars, he says, 'Want to smile your noculars.'

But these correlations can also be a joint process. Two or more people, sharing the same experience of reality, can create new language by setting up, unconsciously, tacit agreements about how they will label certain external phenomena. This is not a conscious, formal process.

A good example of how meaning arises from shared experience is when two people try to move a large piece of furniture. If they are inexperienced, it is extremely difficult for them to explain to each other what to do. Their hands are tied by holding the object, so they can't use gesture, and they have no useful mutual vocabulary. After some experience of moving furniture up and down stairs and round narrow doorways, however, various tricks become part of the mover's repertoire: backing into rooms, lifting things over banisters, going downstairs, and so on. When this experience is shared, various phrases, such as 'Let me change hands', 'Twist your end', which would be meaningless out of context, acquire new meaning. This is all done at an unconscious, tacit level.

In French the word for radio is TSF, which stands for telegraph without wire. It might be thought that when the French use the word, the image of the tap-tap-tap of the old morse-code telegraph appears. But of course it doesn't. It did originally, but the young nowadays identify TSF as a thing with knobs and dials that produces music, in the same way that we don't think of a 'wireless' as being a 'wireless telegraph'. 'Blueprints' for survival, for new towns, for rescue operations, for dramatic action by governments, are relentlessly produced, although architects, engineers and planners know that what were originally blueprints became obsolete years ago. The point is that the meaning of a word to an individual is how it *appears* to be being used by others. This must inevitably mean that in time the meanings of words will change. For example, a word currently *changing* its meaning in English is 'refute'. Politicians are continually heard 'refuting' allegations. Originally the word meant to 'produce incontrovertible evidence to disprove an allegation' not merely to 'deny'.

Wherever attempts are made to halt the change of language, by shifting to the monologue concept, it is apparent that in fact miscommunication is the main effect. The legal profession is a good example. The attempt accurately to define what is meant in Acts of Parliament and case law by the use of legal terminology leads to the proliferation of incomprehensible jargon and confusion.

The same process of gradual change applies to the grammar of a language. It is learnt in context, so it also changes. A number of studies have also shown how people vary their grammatical styles according to the situation. A schoolboy, for example, when talking to his headmaster, will produce 'correct' language. When with his friends he will use much 'looser' grammar, with rules of its own. Context and usage can, in fact, impart bizarre new meaning to apparently familiar words and phrases. To a couple who have lived together for years, during which time the man has always taken the dog for a walk at nine o'clock, the phrase, 'It's nine o'clock, dear', means, precisely, 'Time to take the dog for a walk; I'll put the cocoa on'. The association with normal habit makes the utterance meaningful to the participants, if opaque to outsiders.

All social interchanges are suffused with these special shared meanings. A drug-dealer can phone his confederate and ask, 'Is the stuff ready for collection?', meaning something like, 'Have you got the heroin and is it safe for me to come and get it now?' The point is that people don't usually agree explicitly on meanings. They possess the normal mechanism for generating tacit new understandings.

Such mutual construction of private language is a basic social activity. It arises naturally from dialogue. A rugby team, or research group, gradually builds up a set of words and phrases which are invested with new intrinsic meanings. These then act as special coded signals signifying membership of that group, a group cosmology developing.

Such private languages of necessity emerge from the desire to properly communicate. If you want to convey an idea to a stranger, you may emit a stream of words without making any concession to your listener, unconsciously adopting the monologue concept of language, and so surrendering any guarantee that you have been understood. If, on the other hand, you unconsciously subscribe to the dialogue concept, you will know that you first have to check that your listener is hearing you, and you must then learn his cosmology. In other words, if effective communication is to take place, you must find out fairly quickly about the world he lives in, and present your message in terms of concepts both you and he understand. You have to discover shared experiences. It is this process of searching for common ground, this ability to carry on successful dialogue, which underlies much of personal and social relationships. Those who are known as bores, or as particularly irritating, are people who ignore the cosmology of others and do not modify their own world views. They are unable to give or receive feedback in the course of communication, so that conversation takes place under open-loop control and is thus largely ineffective.

According to the Bible, this is how Jesus created such a big contemporary following. His parables were full of symbols and relationships which He knew His listeners would understand. His terms were mainly agricultural, and His metaphors based on agriculture, or village life. It was inevitable that the Pharisees, Greeks and Romans, with completely different cosmologies, would not find the message so appealing. The Sermon on the Mount, for example, was effective because it was obvious from His use of language that Jesus had spent time among His people, living a simple agricultural life on the shores of Lake Galilee. Good communicators like this show by their language that they have bothered to learn beforehand something of the cosmology of the group being addressed, and to synchronise with it.

The idea that I have outlined above flies in the face of much conventional wisdom, expressed in a regular flow of letters and articles complaining about the state of the language, as if it were a car, or a house, that actually existed in an unchanging form. In the same way that considerable philosophical thought has been given to determining theoretically how people know what sentences mean, much linguistic research has been dedicated to working out how people know what to say. Noam Chomsky has postulated a sort of universal grammar which is capable of generating the apparently infinite number of sentences that a person can produce. As Deirdre Wilson and Neil Smith have commented:[6] 'Chomsky's constant concern during the last 20 years has been the relation between language and mind. For him, since it is individual human beings who know and speak languages, the essential questions about language are questions about human psychology: What constitutes knowledge of a language? How is it acquired? How is it put to use in speaking and understanding? His answers to these questions have also remained largely unchanged. It is the rule-governed nature of language which provides the essential connection between language and mind.

'The claim that language is rule-governed is one of the most frequently disputed of all Chomsky's claims – and one of the most misunderstood. So far as we know, it provides the only possible explanation of how people can produce and understand utterances they have never heard before. Suppose each person has a set of rules which describe a set of grammatical sentences and give each a pronunciation and a meaning. Someone who knows this set of rules – this grammar – will then be able in principle to produce and understand any of the sentences it describes, whether or not he has heard that sentence before. It is, of course, possible to produce and understand ungrammatical utterances, too; but the claim is that unless these can be related to some grammatical sentence or sentences which do have a meaning assigned by rule, there will be no means at all of predicting how they will be understood.'

This search for a universal grammar is in some ways a search for a central control system for all possible sentences. It may be possible to show by reasoning related to Ashby's Law that, in principle, this type of grammar cannot exist. Certainly, so far no linguist has ever managed to construct a grammar capable of generating more than a small fraction of the meaningful utterances produced by one person. And yet a child of five can produce an apparently limitless variety of sentences. The reason is that the control of grammar, in exactly the same way as word usage, comes from the context in which each type of utterance is originally learnt. At scientific conferences people speak differently from the way they talk in the bar afterwards, or at parties, or to babies or lovers. People have as many different grammars, styles and vocabularies as they have memories of situations. Control of a person's grammar is dispersed among all the talkers he has been exposed to; and the factor that controls what you say is your memory of all the other similar situations that you have experienced. This is not, of course, a conscious memory, but rather the sort used in learning to ride a bike or play tennis. So I think it is unlikely *in principle* that a finite set of Chomsky-type language rules will be discovered.

I have elaborated the contrast between these two conflicting concepts of language because in my view numerous problems can thereby be illuminated. In general, there appear to be four main areas of difficulty.

1 *Specialist groups develop private languages and world views, and don't speak to other specialist groups.*

Such groups develop private languages for obvious reasons: they need to be able to discuss reality through the prism of their own particular speciality. This enables sociologists, for example, to come up with jargon like the following extract from a social service report: 'This elderly geriatric female has multiple joint problems which limit her perambulation. Absence of verbal intercourse aggravates her detachment from reality and reinforces isolationism. She is unable to relate to events at this point in time. Psycho-geriatric considerations in the context of conceptual distortion and paranoia is also a parameter in the total dimensions of her problem.' (Translation: 'This (83-year-) old lady has arthritis, cannot get about and is lonely, confused and frightened.')[7] Though this is an extreme example, all specialist groups are guilty to some extent.

The problem, however, arises from the fact that sociologists or lawyers or architects don't talk to 'ordinary' people very often, each much preferring to socialise with his own professional group. Put a sociologist and an architect together, however, and the situation changes. Their different worlds collide and retreat, unless one of the participants is willing to be bored or dominated. Positive feedback is therefore very easily set up whereby sociologists and architects have little informal contact and begin to see the whole world in terms of their professional specialisation, with the result that they only see part of it. The outcome of this may be buildings designed by architects without much thought being given to the people who will actually live in them.

It may be inevitable that separate specialists develop different and to some extent mutually incomprehensible ways of looking at the world. But it would seem that the educational and communications systems which presently prevail make the situation worse than it need be. The problem is that in many cases the real incompatibilities between differing world views only become apparent when it is too late for anything to be done, when the building has been finished and the heating and ventilating engineer finds he cannot fit his pipes and ducts, or the people who move in are unhappy because the children playing in the gardens cannot be seen from the fifteenth floor. These incompatibilities cannot be foreseen and dealt with merely by better formal education as they are simply too numerous and varied to be so captured. The key to the problem of separate specialist groups would seem to lie in some method of promoting informal contact and discussion between them, which would lead to wider mutual understanding.

2   *People thrown together in an organisation tend to form sub-groups within it, each with its own cosmology, language and aims. The aims of the sub-groups may run counter to the organisation's, and their existence may inhibit communication within it.*

A group of individuals thrown together for a period rapidly develops its own group feeling. This is expressed by the private language, slang and mythology which is used to reinforce their togetherness. Regimental group feeling is what General Sir John Hackett has described as being of fundamental importance to military effectiveness:[8] 'You don't join the army, of course, you join a *regiment*. A man on the battlefield does not go into action for Queen and Country, nor for a cause. He goes in with his mates. The Americans have got it all wrong. They run the army like a big industrial enterprise; they have tried to replace leadership with management.'

Frequently, however, groups within organisations inhibit the correct functioning of that organisation. A friend of mine worked as a consultant to a water authority. One department of the authority dealt with the water treatment works and associated pumping stations, and another solely with the pipes along which the water was pumped. When this consultant was shown round the works, he noticed a surge-arrester, a device to prevent damage to the main when the pump is suddenly turned off. When he asked the operator, 'What's that?', he was told 'Oh that – that's never worked.' When he moved on and met the people in charge of the pipes, he found that they had persistent trouble with one of the pipelines. 'Oh, that pipeline – we've always had trouble with that pipeline ever since it was commissioned,' they said. To the outsider it was obvious that the pipeline failure was due to the non-working surge-arrester. It proved impossible, however, to get the two groups of engineers to accept this. In the end it took the consultant a year to arrange a meeting between the parties even to discuss the possibility.

This illustrates the extent to which non-communication between groups, and antipathy to the cosmology of other groups, can go, even though they are in the same organisation with, nominally, the same aims. Each group had absorbed either the non-operation of the surge-arrester or the pipeline failure, into its cosmology, and did not want to disturb it. The rival group was seen as being made up of trouble-makers, best avoided.

Attitudes like this can cause enormous problems for large organis-ations. Successful multinationals recognise this and cope with it by hiring management consultants. These vary in their approach, but often come up with a reorganisation which shifts people around and breaks up the rival groups. This approach also treats the associated problem of anomalous situations being absorbed into the cosmology of those familiar with them, and accepted as normal. Similar problems in this area range from that of the Queen who had to ring her alarm bell for half an hour without the police responding when an intruder came into her bedroom, to that of personnel in nuclear reactors who ignore warning signals. In both cases the cause is a succession of false alarms that have led to the apparatus being disregarded when the need arose. In the cosmology of those who work with alarm systems, the possibility of a real crisis is subconsciously eliminated. Frequent rotation of personnel can help reduce this problem.

Seen from this view, it is ludicrous to attempt to reform criminals by sending them to prison. There could hardly be a better place in which to inculcate group feeling against the perceived common enemy, society. Many prisoners come from emotionally impoverished back-grounds, where they are unlikely to learn to communicate effectively or, in consequence, to feel part of a wider society. In prison for the first time in their lives they go through an experience with people who really understand how they feel. Not surprisingly, criminals have a well-developed argot, or professional language, based on their common experience of being caught, jailed, and labelled as outsiders. And few policemen or crime reporters would disagree that most large 'firms', or criminal gangs, are born in jail. A recent *Sunday Times* article on the IRA describes the phenomenon: 'A hardline, left-wing generation has emerged from the child street-fighters and the young men detained in the Maze Prison without trial in the Seventies. The Maze was described then as a university of terrorism; the description is now being justified by events.'[9]

3 *Private cosmologies are extremely durable and resist change.*

In the same way that human beings form groups which then ensure their own stability and continued existence, there are strong forces working to maintain inter-relationships within them. These forces arise, as we have shown, from the group cosmology which is chiefly 'stored' in the language of group members as Gramsci suggested in his concept of 'Common Sense'.

Groups tend to be reluctant to accept new ideas which might change their structure and function, even though these could be to the benefit of the group or to society as a whole. Tacit rules develop which actually inhibit the use of new or threatening terms. An example of how this dynamic can impede progress was shown when the CEGB cosmology in the shape of its philosophy of large electricity-only power stations was under threat. When the government, in the form of the Marshall Committee, looked into the whole issue of Combined Heat and Power, the Committee was repeatedly asked by the non-CEGB members to include, in their deliberations, the small, cheap, highly efficient, low acid-rain, 'combined cycle' type of Combined Heat and Power station. This request was repeatedly turned down by the CEGB. One of the chief CEGB representatives reportedly could not bring himself even to say the words 'combined cycle', as if saying the name would invest it with an uncomfortable reality. Obviously conscious linguistic censorship in the light of crude self-interest is not a sufficient explanation of the operation of taboos on words like this. Part of the business of running a large organisation means imposing a framework on the problems being addressed, and in order to function within such a framework, and to get on, members have to accept what is imposed by their superiors. Any deviation from this tends to be regarded by superiors as heresy or insubordination, so those who rise tend to have the dominant means of describing problems deeply ingrained within them. This is what lies behind the inability of the CEGB man to say 'combined cycle'. I will be looking more closely at this, and other aspects of hierarchic organisations, in a later chapter.

4   *Outsiders experience the language of professionals as jargon, but professionals can't help using it*

Professionals cannot help inventing new languages for themselves. Doctors and lawyers, for example, need to chop up their own realities (by speaking about them) in different ways. It is necessary, and part of the job. The trouble is that once they have developed a private language they are unable to stop using it outside their group. They begin to see the world solely in terms of their profession, and become so used to their linguistic shortcuts that they cannot avoid them, even when talking to outsiders. They are often quite unaware of what they are doing. In a book review decrying the use of professional jargon Philip Toynbee wrote 'I suspect that there is a natural process by which the demotic is constantly invading, and constantly re-creating, the mandarin.'[10] As an Oxbridge literary man, Toynbee was apparently blithely unaware that words such as 'demotic' and 'Mandarin' are obscure to people from backgrounds different from his own, who would tend to feel alienated by such literary jargon.

It is my contention that in any society, and ours in particular, as there is a shift towards central media, central religion, and hierarchical central control, then there will also be a shift to the monologue concept of language. This will inevitably bring about mis-communication, non-communication, confusion, the obscuration of important issues, a massive increase in the amount of monologue communication (ie paper) and a gradual collapse of society under the weight of the monologue processing systems, ie bureaucracy, and their attendant non-solutions.

4 TELEVISION AND ITS LONG-TERM EFFECTS

For socially successful and well-adjusted people, language and communication is a system of relevant responses. Children in a playground, and adults chatting in a pub, are not just talking to themselves, but are responding to one another. One person speaks or uses a gesture which creates ideas, thoughts and sensations, which cause the listener to reply. His response may be insulting, friendly, witty or perhaps just a grunt to indicate that the talker can continue, and that he is being understood, but what he says must follow from what the speaker says.

The skills and sub-skills required for taking part in conversations are formidable. They are for the most part subconscious, progressively accumulated during childhood. The critical period for acquiring language is under debate; at the very latest it is puberty: 'After puberty, the ability for self-organisation and adjustment to the physiological demands of verbal behaviour quickly declines.'[1] This does not mean, however, that learning to speak can commence equally easily at any age during the period up to puberty. If there is a departure from the normal progression in which the basics of speech are established before the age of three, then the retardation of development can only be put right by considerable remedial work or specialist treatment. This sort of therapy has, in a few much-quoted cases of abandoned or isolated children, proved quite effective. A girl called Isabelle, who had been imprisoned with her deaf-mute mother until she was six, as well as twins who were neglected and isolated until they were seven, all showed great acceleration in development once they were put under specialist care. But these children at least had continuous contact with either their mother or their twin during their early deprived years. The case of Anna, who had virtually no one with whom she could interact during her infancy, is different. In 1938, a social worker discovered the little girl tied to a chair in an attic room on her grandfather's farm in Pennsylvania. Anna had been confined there by her mother during most of her short life because her grandfather resented her illegitimacy and did not want to be reminded of her existence. Although nearly six years old when found, she did not talk, smile, cry or respond in any other way to the people around her. When she was moved to a foster home, she eventually became less apathetic, but remained socially and mentally retarded, and never learned to speak more than a few sentences.[2]

There appears to be a time in childhood when the ability to speak can most easily be activated, and if this opportunity is lost, only intensive remedial language work can make up the lost ground, the late learner probably never catching up.

The remarkable fertility of the language-learning aptitude in children is shown in the rare instances of twins or siblings being brought up almost exclusively in each other's company developing their own private language or ideoglossia. These sound fast and fluent to the outsider, and appear to be potentially unlimited in the number of statements that can be made; and are genuine new languages. This phenomenon is confined to childhood.

In order for this aptitude for language development to be activated, however, the child must be provided with the raw material. If circumstances fail to provide this, the deprivation brought about by failure to learn to speak is far greater than the mere inability to manipulate words. For language is a sort of key which opens doors to all kinds of development. The child's growth is closely dependent on it, and any backwardness in language-learning will be associated with educational and other problems. 'Language is the economical and efficient means of preserving the results of learning and thinking, applying them in new situations and modifying them with experience. Words play an important part in thinking itself, facilitating the reasoning processes with which the child examines and orders his experience. Children whose language is retarded (deaf children, children from verbally impoverished homes) are also likely to be to some degree retarded in intelligence.'[3]

The eminent Russian psychologist Luria studied the language that children use when talking to themselves, and showed how the development of motor skills followed its development. 'He showed that both "narrative speech", a recounting the past, and "planning speech", anticipating action, arise from the running commentary once a child's language transcends the bounds of the immediate present. And in particular that the act of formulating a plan in words has the effect of increasing a child's ability to resist the distractions of other cues in the environment and carry the plan to its conclusion. The verbalising has in fact a regulatory function.'[4] His work was supported by experiments which showed, for example, that with three-year-olds, performances in button pressing were clearly improved when they used their own speech to accompany action, that is, improvement in speech development brought about significant behavioural advances.

The importance of play, not just with toys, but with ideas, has also been fully described by psychologists. 'Play with sounds and with ideas – rhyming, punning, making outrageous statements or teasing jokes or other kinds of nonsense – these occupy a considerable place in many children's talk of all kinds. The function of this play, as with all play, is that it strengthens the child's understanding of reality and what is normal . . . a means of reinforcing what he has learnt about actuality.'[4]

Make-believe play is another kind which increasingly preoccupies the two to five-year-old. In it he can make anything happen that he wants to happen, and he brings the whole of his experience into it. Piaget explained its purpose: 'Imaginative play reproduces what he has lived through, but by means of symbolic representation. As he reproduces it in play, he may work upon it, assimilating reality to his desires in order to come to terms with it or compensate for it or reduce its threat.'[4] In other words, play helps the child to adjust happily to the world around him, and appears to be a necessary part of absorbing all the new information presented to him. 'The child from two to five is at his busiest as an explorer – if we are to judge merely by the rate of increase of his discoveries about the world: it is at this stage that make-believe games are at their peak. To use a rough analogy, it is as though the immense data-collecting task necessitated an equivalent in intensive data-processing sessions.'[4]

The most serious effect on an individual of an impoverished language-learning background is probably the effect it has on the development of personality and communication. Vygotsky, another Russian psychologist, observed how during the period between three and seven years old, social speech developed, while the running commentary, or monologue, slowly withered away. His explanation was that the child's monologue became internalised, becoming 'inner speech' which it was no longer necessary to speak aloud. He described the subsequent relationship between speech and thought in the following terms: 'Inner speech is not the interior aspect of external speech – it is a function in itself. It still remains speech, ie., thought connected with words. But while in external speech thought is embodied in words, in inner speech words die as they bring forth thought. Inner speech is to a large extent thinking in pure meaning. It is a dynamic, shifting, unstable thing, fluttering between words and thought, the two more or less firmly delineated components of verbal thought.'[5] Without internalised speech the flowering of the personality would seem impossible.

Another experiment underlines the twin points I am making – the paramount importance of speech as a basis for later development, and the importance of providing the right pre-school environment in which it can flourish:[4]

A survey made not long ago by an American psychologist called Samuel Kirk reported some interesting research into the language ability of disadvantaged children. Twenty-four children of one-and-a-half to two years old, living in an orphanage, were divided into two groups, matched for 'measured intelligence' – as far as it could be measured at that age: what is clear is that both groups showed *low* ability. Each of the twelve in one group was sent to be looked after by an adolescent girl living in a mental home: the other group was left at the orphanage. After two years the group that had been living with the girl showed extraordinary increases in measured intelligence (well over twenty points), while those in the orphanage showed a *decrease* of similar proportions. What is more astounding still is that after *twenty-one years*, the experimenter was able to trace the children and discovered that the average of the final school achievement of the group looked after in infancy by the girl was twelfth grade (work normal for seventeen to eighteen-year-olds) whereas the average for the other group was fourth grade (work normal for nine to ten-year-olds). Samuel Kirk reports also that a recent check on the abilities of children under school age in the poorer Negro districts of New York revealed a small number of children of distinctly higher ability than the rest. When these were followed up it was found that there was in each case a grandmother living with the family.

This is not a plea for importing grandmothers . . . it is important as evidence that suggests that talk in infancy with an older person may make all the difference: and not necessarily the intelligent talk of educated parents. Evidence from the same survey proved that timing is crucial: the advantage of providing a talking environment is greatest around two years of age and falls off sharply after five.

It seems, then, from this evidence that if a child does not learn to speak (or communicate in some other way by, for example, sign language), he will not learn to think with any degree of sophistication. Obviously the term 'thinking' covers all sorts of possible mental activities. But I am using it to refer to what a human being can do in contrast with, say, a chimpanzee. These animals are capable of many mental activities that are similar to those carried out by humans: they can receive stimuli, communicate with their fellows in a limited way, seek food, and perform other more sophisticated tasks. But there is little evidence that they can think about the world in the same logical way that we can, assisted by the medium of unarticulated words. If someone does not learn to think we can surmise that he will never fully develop into a person with a personality, because that is based on an individual's thoughts and ideas. Similarly we can make graduations of this statement and say that if a child's speaking ability is to some extent retarded, the development of his personality will to a commensurate extent be retarded. His thoughts, ideas, adjustments to reality and to his fellow human beings will, in fact, be unnecessarily limited. And my contention is that for the past twenty years societies have been increasingly preventing their children from learning to speak with all that this entails.

There is no dearth of evidence for decreased verbal ability in Western societies. On an anecdotal level Ivan Illich wrote in 1979:[6] 'I was invited to New York by a former pupil of mine, now married, living in a very miserable slum in the East Bronx, voluntarily with his family, as a social worker. He wanted me there because he wanted me to co-sign a petition for pre-kindergarten language instruction for the under-privileged children who live in that area . . . We went there from apartment to apartment. To Jamaican, to Puerto Rican, to Southern White to Southern Black homes, where I saw those children, who even at ten could not speak a word, although the television was blaring, sometimes two televisions in the same welfare apartment.' Not very scientific or quantitative, perhaps, but telling.

In the United States, also, College Board exams are taken by American high school children. A range of abilities is measured, including verbal aptitude and reading skills. From 1964 to 1975 scores of verbal aptitude steadily declined and still had not levelled off by 1975.[7] In France, the French military authorities keep meticulous records of the performance of past conscripts on written verbal aptitude tests, which are kept as nearly as possible to a constant standard. A recent report by the military authorities expressed alarm at the severe decline in performance on these tests, complaining of an inability to follow verbal or written instructions.[8] In Britain many further education colleges are now starting to offer courses on speaking and social skills which were originally designed in the 1970s for North American Indians making the transition from one culture to another; the courses have been adapted to suit the needs of illiterate 'a-verbal' young Westerners. The Manpower Services Commission, in organising Youth Opportunities Programmes, has also had to devote con-siderable resources to teaching the basics of reading, writing and social skills. Teachers at the other end of the educational system are also noticing how the speaking abilities of the children entering nursery and primary schools have declined. Their vocabularies have contracted and they are not communicating as they used to do. In Birmingham, for example, a programme has been instituted to encourage mothers to talk to their children, in order to counteract the trend of children entering school with very limited vocabularies.[9]

This trend is attributed to a lack of opportunity for conversation, allied to too much use of the television as a child pacifier. 'The most pervasive toy is television. Gone are the days when mum, and especially dad, read a story to his child before lights out. Now it is a dismissive peck on the cheek before Coronation Street.'[9] When we begin to look for causal relationships for the decline in verbal ability, television-watching becomes a prime suspect. The year 1964, when American College Board exams began to show declining verbal aptitude, is precisely when the first children who had earlier been exposed to large doses of television began to take the tests. In 1950, only four million television sets were sold in the country; by 1955, 67 per cent of all American households had a set. Before 1950 American children presumably spent most of their spare time playing with one another.

The reason suggested by the French military authorities for the decline in verbal and written aptitude that they identified was the extraordinary amount of television watched by French children. As a result of their report on their findings, many schools in France have replaced more liberal aspects of education, such as painting, dancing, drawing and nature study, with language and reading lessons. The problem is regarded as so severe that these changes have been introduced for all years at French schools, not simply for the new year's intake.

Other evidence for the effects of television watching on children is also being accumulated. The amount of time that children spend watching television is beginning to cause especial concern. Pre-schoolers in the United States in 1970 watched on average over four hours a day.[7] Another American report, putting it a different way, says that 'By the time a child reaches fourteen, he has watched the violent assault or destruction of nearly 18,000 human beings. As he graduates from high school, he will have spent nearly 22,000 hours in front of a TV - twice as many as in school.' And perhaps 5,000 of these, nearly half the hours in school, will have been spent watching commercials.[10] In Britain the average for children is twenty hours a week.[11] One survey by a deputy headmaster (which I shall refer to later) reported that most parents exercise no control whatsoever over the number of hours their children watch, or what programmes they see.

Data about the harmful effects of television watching on children's language, to add to the many expressions of personal observation and opinion, are also becoming available. A four-year study of 350 American families has come up with some disturbing news about the effect of television viewing on the reading and speaking skills of children. It finds that by the age of six real differences have appeared between children who watch television for three hours or more a day and those who watch for one hour or less. The heavy viewers are more likely to be retarded in reading and comprehension and limited in their conversational range, using fewer adjectives and adverbs and shorter, simpler sentences. 'The idea that TV affects reading, languages and comprehension is not just conjecture,'[12] Dorothy Singer said, one of the Yale researchers responsible for the study. 'Now we know for certain that this is so. What the study tells us is that watching TV is not enough to give a child a vocabulary. Unless words are used in their own experiences and reinforced with play the words will not be internalised.'

American research has also demonstrated that there is no such thing as good television for children. '*Sesame Street* . . . was created by child psychologists, ad men, teachers and producers to prepare pre-school children for school by pushing basic literacy, numeracy and verbal skills in the programme. One hope was that the programme would help improve the verbal skills of children deprived of the opportunities for conversation that middle-class children are supposed to have.'[13]

The educational benefits of *Sesame Street* were widely publicised in the United States in the early 1970s by the Educational Testing Service. It purported to show that pre-schoolers learned much from the programme, and these benefits were also made widely known in Britain. The ETS research was, however, criticised severely by the Russell Sage Foundation in *Sesame Street Revisited*, published in 1975. This found that the gap between advantaged and disadvantaged children may have in fact become wider, as a consequence of watching *Sesame Street*. And when 'heavy' viewers of the programme received visits from interested researchers, it was found that they were stimulated to watch more attentively by parental involvement. The *key* factor in children's progress was found to be adult encouragement of, and interest in, the experiment, rather than the programmes. And 'light' viewers showed more gains in cognitive skills than 'heavy' ones in the group of 'unencouraged' children in the research.

It would seem that what is so damaging to the development of language in watching television is that it is a completely passive activity, while learning to speak is an interactive process, which can only be learnt through such interaction. In the same way that no amount of watching a cyclist would enable a child to ride a bike, no amount of listening to or watching others speaking by itself enables a child to speak and communicate. The only way to learn to do so is to participate in massive amounts of communicative interaction, for there is more to conversing than meets the ear.

David Lewis has written:[14] 'Recent research in Europe and America has confirmed what sensitive parents may have suspected for years. Long before children can speak they are able to talk to each other with ease by means of a silent and secret language.' The book also makes clear that skill in this language can only be acquired by imitation and interaction with other children, and that learning the appropriate responses in this language is essential to development, since they are the prototypes for later behaviour. But television does not provide that necessary interaction: 'Studies have shown that toddlers sit motionless in front of television sets, their faces drained in totally passive submission. When interrupted from the hard-hitting events of the screen, they are startled – as if awakened from a dream.'[10]

In every culture there are special subliminal signals – angle of head, eye contact or its absence, pitch, pauses, grimaces, gestures, and so on – which carry much of the content of any conversation being carried on. People who do not get enough opportunity to practise these conventions at a susceptible age are to some extent socially handicapped. The features are used to indicate boredom, interest, permission to speak, not to speak, attempts to take over the conversation, and so on. The fact that these apparently unimportant and universal 'para-linguistic' features are both essential to effective communication, and specific to each culture, is demonstrated in a study by the National Centre for Industrial Language Training,[15] concerning problems arising from this area for non-native English speakers. There are fundamental differences, for example, in the conventions for signalling politeness in Indian languages and in English. For example, 'Thank you' or its equivalent are used in Indian languages only in return for special favours. Their use implies some social inequality and a high degree of formality. The same is true of 'Please'. Other formulaic phrases such as 'I would like', 'Could I have' also imply social inequality and tend to be avoided in ordinary speech. Respect, humility and apology in Indian languages are conveyed through special words or through professional or other titles, and not through verb constructions, as in English. This means that many Asian-English speakers use English–English conventions somewhat differently. Some of the difficulties and misunderstandings which can result from these systematic linguistic differences between Asian–English and English–English can be summarised:[15]

What can confuse English people and lead to irritation	*What can confuse Asian people and lead to irritation*
Certain uses of high or low-pitched voice and loudness eg., raising voice in 'No', to contradict.	Tone of voice: high pitch or stress on *particular* words, which can sound emotional and impolite eg., when English speaker wants to explain or emphasise a point.
Lack of stress eg., not clearly marking the difference between *last* week and *this* week.	
Use of 'yes/no' eg., saying 'yes' but not meaning that you agree.	Apparent not listening eg., in longer chunks of discourse the English speaker may switch off or change subject.
Lack of cohesive features in discourse so that the Asian speaker appears boring or confused eg., misleading intonation patterns, unclear pronoun references.	Many forms of inexplicit or indirect statements and questions.
Wrong use of turn-making eg., persistently interrupting in the middle of the English speaker's utterance.	Apologetic or polite and repetitive uses of English.

Without the feedback provided by conversation, then, a child or a new language learner cannot make progress, for he requires continuous feedback to build up his repertoire of responses. The result of such continual deprivation of live interaction and such prolonged and passive exposure to a system for transmitting monologue involved in television watching is that the ability to participate fully in communication is impaired. People affected in this way are experienced by others as boring, irritating, irrelevant, people who don't listen, who talk too much, and so on. Television can deprive a child of his only chance to learn the responses which make him a fully social person.

If we accept the evidence that watching television deprives children of experiences which allow full development of their communicative skills, and of the personality growth that is dependent on those skills, we would expect to be able to predict major adjustment problems with the generations who became adult in the late 1960s and after. And we find that some evidence, again largely anecdotal, does indeed point towards the fact that television has already caused pervasive damage to the first generation to grow up with it. For instance, the anthropologist Edward Norbeck has written:[16] 'Playing children are motivated primarily to enjoy living. This is the major rehearsal value of play and games, for without the ability to enjoy life, the long years of adulthood can be dull and wearisome. There are indeed signs among the generation that grew up watching television that adult life *does* seem dull and wearisome, that something is missing in their enjoyment of life, something, perhaps, that a childhood of normal play might have provided.' 'Many Rebels of the 1960s Depressed as They Near 30' reads a headline in the *New York Times*.[7] The article describes young people who matured during the late 1960s, who are now experiencing 'a generational malaise of haunting frustrations, anxiety and depression', a malaise reflected in the increase of people in their twenties and early thirties receiving psychiatric help, the rise in suicides and alcoholism in this age group, and other manifestations of an inability to 'enjoy life'. 'I've got a good job, I'm successful, and I want to kill myself. Life doesn't mean anything,' says a person quoted in the article. 'It cannot be a coincidence,' the article continues, 'that the people suffering this strange new malaise represent the first television generation. And it cannot be insignificant that they represent the first generation whose normal play activities were curtailed (in some cases virtually eliminated) as a result of involvement with television. "Pity the monkeys who are not permitted to play," writes Harry Harlow in a discussion of his experimental work. What about the children who have spent their childhood *watching* instead of playing?'[7]

Another article, this time in *The Guardian*, gave further details of 'this sickening upsurge in childhood suicides in the Western world'.[17] Five thousand young Americans between 15 and 24 kill themselves every year, but the United States is not alone in having an alarmingly increasing suicide rate in young people. 'Successful and attempted suicides among the young have only reached worrying proportions within recent years. Now, however, suicide is a major cause of early death in the inaptly-labelled "developed nations". An official Japanese report in 1978 revealed that 784 young people below the age of 20 had taken their own lives during the previous 12 months.' The writer of the article put forward the theory that television exposed children prematurely to too many ideas, bringing about a cynical view of life, and feelings of despair.

The previous two articles may seem somewhat subjective, and perhaps suffer from the tendency of newspapers and popular books to exaggerate and sensationalise, but a similar view comes from another source. In his resignation letter from his post as New York's Commissioner for Mental Health Retardation, Dr Herbert Fill wrote, 'I have become increasingly concerned with the fact that although we are spending hundreds of millions on better and more efficient programs, we still have more and more mental disturbances, alcoholism, drug abuse, vandalism, crime. The mental state of our population in general is steadily deteriorating and psychopathology now reaches epidemic proportions. We do not seem to gain on the problem by focusing solely on casualties, by increasing services. I have become convinced that it is our social attitudes and our social institutions that are now actively creating mental disturbances. It is becoming increasingly clear that the way we educate, use technology and exploit media, for instance, engenders mental harm and disruption on a massive scale.' Dr Fill sees television as exploiting man's need for lost imagery, the 'electronic hallucinogens' which it provides bringing to children's 'open and trusting minds, precocious intellect, depersonalisation, aggression, violence, indifference to suffering, cheap and degrading fantasies – all when they only seek humanity and self-assurance.'[18]

It would seem then, that young children who spend a large amount of time watching television at a crucial developmental stage never learn the full extent of their language, and that this retarded language development produces adults whose personalities are likewise retarded. The available evidence suggests that the result is people who communicate less effectively than they used to, experience less satisfaction in their lives and possibly have greater anti-social tendencies. I find it astonishing that the massive intrusion of television into our lives should have occurred with so little comment, question or research. In a later chapter I shall also consider other forms of mass media.

5 TACIT KNOWLEDGE AND LATERAL MEDIA

There are two distinct kinds of knowledge: formal and tacit. Formal knowledge is the kind that most people are aware of, probably as a result of the way we are educated, and is knowledge that is capable of being written down or stated. It exists in the form of, say, 'The distance from London to Brighton is 50 miles'; 'Polaris submarines weigh 40,000 tons'; 'The moon is not made of cheese'; and so on.

Tacit knowledge, by contrast, is much more elusive. Riding a bicycle can again serve as an example. If most bike-riders were asked how they turn right on a bicycle when travelling in a straight line, they would reply, somewhat surprised at the question, that they turn the bars to the right. In fact, in order to turn right on a bicycle, it is necessary first to turn the bars slightly to the left, throwing the bike over to the right, which then enables the bars to be turned in that direction. It simply is not possible, as most people maintain, to 'throw the bike over to the right' without adjusting the bars first; once the bike is balanced and moving in a straight line, it follows from Newton's Laws of Motion that it is impossible to throw it off balance.

Now hardly anyone who rides a bike is aware in 'formal knowledge' terms of how they turn right. That is to say, they would be unable to give the description above of what they do, Similarly, instructing someone who had never ridden a bike before to turn the bars to the left before he turned them to the right, would not help him to ride the bike successfully. And yet riding it is almost as easy as walking. It is learnt by almost anyone who wishes by getting on the bike, practising riding it, and responding to feedback from the situation in which he finds himself until it is mastered. The rider therefore comes into possession of the tacit knowledge that he requires; mere formal instruction would be unintelligible.

Another example comes from the teaching of algebra. As Collins elaborates, algebra cannot be reduced to a set of formal rules.[1] 'All types of knowledge however pure consist in part of tacit rules which may be impossible to formulate in principle. For instance the ability to solve an algebraic equation includes such normally non articulated knowledge as that the symbol 'X' usually means the same whether it is written in ballpoint, chalk or print or spoken irrespective of the day of the week or temperature of the air. But in another sense 'X' stands for anything at all and may only mean the same - exactly (eg. 2.75 grammes, 2.75 inches, etc.) - on coincidental and unimportant occasions. Again, sometimes a capitalised X or an italicised X may have a distinctive meaning. Capital X in the equation $X = 5Y$ is the *same* as X in the equation $5Y = X$, but is not the same as in $X = 5Z$, unless $Y=Z$. On the other hand, 'X' is being used in the same way in all the equations. This list of tacit rules as it is extended becomes more confusing, and comes to resemble a list of all the examples of the uses of X which have ever been made. But such a list cannot serve at all as a guide to the use of X in the future. Learning algebra consists of more than the memorisation of sets of formal rules; it involves also knowing how to do things (eg. use 'X' correctly - use logical inference) which may have been learned long before.'

Algebra is learnt, then, by being shown examples, trying out solutions, asking questions, being corrected, and so on. It is similar to learning to ride a bicycle in that they are both learnt through trying the activity and getting corrective feedback.

Learning to speak a language is, as we saw in the previous chapter, the acquisition of tacit knowledge. Children learn their mother tongue without access to an *Introduction to Syntax*, or a dictionary. They learn by observation and participation, and by storing the feedback they receive from each situation for future use. Indeed, there is evidence that attempts to interfere with this process by teaching formal rules can be counter-productive, as having once arrived at a generalisation children are also extremely resistant to explicit correction from adults.

The process of learning and storing appropriate responses can be observed in a small child doing something he is forbidden to do, such as taking an object off a shelf. He is repeatedly told not to do it. Eventually, he will carry on trying to remove the object but start saying 'no' as he does so: he is beginning to internalise a piece of corrective feedback from the world. 'No' is appearing in his head because he recognises the situation from his internal map; his internalised feedback has appeared. Finally, he will learn to associate 'no' with negative experience, and will stop trying to remove the forbidden object. In the same way phrases like 'Pull yourself together', 'Don't panic!' 'Keep cool' and so on spring into an adult's mind under stress. Almost all aspects of speech and behaviour are acquisitions of tacit knowledge, which is held only in the minds of individuals.

Tacit knowledge is vital for successful 'in the world' operations, be they social ones such as making friends or technical ones such as building power stations or motorways. But tacit knowledge cannot be transmitted in written form. The reason for this lies in its difference from formal knowledge, which tends to be of a general or 'coarse-grained', and static, nature. Tacit knowledge is more dynamic and fine-grained, more concerned with minute, constantly-varying detail. Formal knowledge such as 'All swans are white', is fixed and rather general. Formal knowledge about why the bars on a bike must be turned to the left before it can go to the right are a general derivation from Newton's Laws of Motion. But such knowledge doesn't give any information about the detailed second-by-second adjustments of the bars that are necessary to maintain balance. The internal feedback map of someone who has successfully learned to ride a bike provides him with continuous instantaneous adjustments. The moment he begins to fall to the left, his brain subconsciously recognises the situation and the brain signals his arm muscles to move the bars to the left, thereby correcting the fall. People who are still learning generally tend to react too late and over-compensate, causing the bike to wobble or lurch. As time progresses the internal feedback map is refined, and the rider learns to apply just the right amount of control at the right time. It is impossible to give a series of formal instructions for such action because there are too many, they are too complex, and they would take too long to transmit, understand and act on.

In the same way learning to function successfully using a language cannot be reduced to a set of formal rules, since there would simply be too many rules, and because communicating is essentially a feedback process. The feedback occurs at two levels between the speakers externally and internally. In the latter case the speaker will be trying to get a point over and will be gauging the correspondence between what he is trying to say and what he thinks his listener has grasped. Equally the listener will be trying to 'update' the tentative model he is receiving from the speaker. Similarly the process of developing personality, and a place in society – enculturation or socialisation – which is depen-dent on, or co-emergent with, learning the mother-tongue, is also the process of acquiring tacit knowledge or building this internal map.

Kinship webs explored by anthropologists have revealed how intricate families ties can be, and how firmly these can control behaviour. The Aboriginals of Northern Australia live in extended families in which almost everybody is inter-related, but social maps allow everyone to know how to behave and how they are expected to behave.[2] Western man has a similar, though more complex, map showing how he should behave to his girlfriend, the used car salesman, his boss, a policeman, and so on. It includes all the categories in the person's experience, and enables him to recognise the situation and the feedback it provides, and to respond in his own interests.

The subconscious operation of the internal feedback map is illustrated in many day-to-day situations. We recently had in our house a door that had been sticking for months and which had become part of our cosmology. Eventually I was persuaded to plane the bottom of the door. Before this, every time I opened the door I had anticipated it sticking, and applied a slight extra force and an anticipatory twist of the hips at the appropriate time in order to pull it past the sticking point. Following my planing of the door, I still involuntarily make the extra bodily adjustments, which result in my slamming it against the wall. Although my formal knowledge system had been updated, my tacit knowledge system, my internal feedback map, had not.

The significance of the map for my purposes is that in order to do anything effective or useful in the world, to achieve the required results, whether personal or institutional, it is necessary to have the appropriate map, otherwise inappropriate or counter-productive courses of action will be taken. A 'successful' lawyer, accountant, engineer, teacher, lover, banker, or Dutchman, has acquired an appropriate map. A Dutchman has more words for water-conveying structures than an Englishman, because he is required to chop the world up and label it to suit situations particular to him.

As we saw in the previous chapter, the ability of children to develop and change this map diminishes with time. The children of globe-trotting parents pick up local languages or phrases very rapidly, and drop them for new ones as they move to a new area. There is a rapid drop in this facility after the age of ten, and after puberty a notable decline. The older an immigrant is when he arrives in a new country, the greater the retention of his accent and the tendency to lapse into his mother tongue at any opportunity. The fact that linguistic flexibility and its internal equivalent decline causes problems. Children who have had linguistically impoverished early experience, or have been exposed to abnormal or distorted home-life situations, tend to develop restricted or inaccurate maps. This leads to later misinterpretation of situations and the production of inappropriate responses.

There is claimed to be a successful therapy system, based on the idea of changing the internal map, called 'neuro-linguistic programming'. It is a synthesis of successful therapeutic techniques developed in the United States. The basic premise is that people begin to confuse their internal map with reality. This causes socially inept people relentlessly to repeat the responses indicated by their map, rather than attempt to change it. When a social strategy goes wrong, say in an attempt to gain esteem, the 'normal' reaction is to pursue the previously learned inappropriate response more vigorously - boasting for example - rather than question the map and the response which it provides. The developers of neuro-linguistic programming claim to have developed methods of getting people to change their internal map, or 'representational system' as NLP terms it, enabling them to generate new and more successful strategies for dealing with life.

Here, however, I am interested less in people's personal problems than in the social consequences of distorted maps. I am particularly concerned with the maps of specialists, experts and professionals, since these are people with power in our society, and it is insufficiently realised that their maps are in fact only supplied by systems of formal knowledge with broad outlines. The detailed, useful and applicable parts of their skills come only from personal contact and experience.

An experience of mine as a freshly-graduated civil engineer will perhaps illustrate the point. The consulting civil engineers for whom I first worked, were undertaking a sewer survey in which I took part. This involves noting the position, type and condition of sewers. One of my tasks was to be on the watch for 'infiltration', that is, where groundwater leaks into the sewer or the manhole. This is very dangerous and has to be stopped, because it can undermine the whole sewer network; it is the cause of those holes that suddenly appear in roads. I discovered one manhole which had water pouring into it as if through a fireman's hose. I reported this and enquired, out of interest, what could be done about it. It was impossible to see how cement could be put in to seal a leak against such enormous pressure. 'Simple,' replied an older engineer, smugly. 'We hammer a large pipe with a tap on it into the hole, and then hammer rags in around it, which makes the water come out of the pipe. Having done that, we pack cement around the pipe, fixing it into position. When the cement has hardened, the tap is turned off and we connect a cement pump to it, open the taps and pump cement into the pipe, filling all the voids around the manhole.' What struck me at the time was, firstly, the neatness of the solution, and secondly, the fact that I hadn't been taught anything like it at university. I said, 'How am I supposed to learn this?' 'By asking questions,' I was told.

Most skilled jobs get done because there are people in possession of nuggets of information like this one. There are people around who 'know about sewers' - or about picture-restoring, or draught-exclusion or accountancy, or whatever. The information they carry may or may not exist in some formal system, but it is really unavailable to others unless it first exists in someone's head, blended with his own particular experience. Only then can it spring into service at the right place and time.

I was once present at a meeting of about 20 people discussing a monitoring project for a low-energy dairy supported by the Ministry of Agriculture. The project included a solar water-heater. During the meeting the organisers demonstrated a computer programme which aimed to predict how solar energy would be absorbed by the collector over the year. A great deal of debate then ensued about whether the programme accurately modelled the effects of shading due to an adjacent tree. This was discussed in great detail and at some length until somebody pointed out a simple fact: 80 per cent of collectable energy is gathered between midday and two o'clock, and since the tree only shaded the collector until about 10 o'clock, the effect would be negligible and the amount of energy lost unimportant. This nugget of information stemmed from a correct appreciation of the problem; in other words, the supplier's internal map recognised the situation and located the one fact that was most relevant to the discussion at that point. The relevant information no doubt occurs in various formal sources of knowledge, where it is embedded in graphs and figures and prose. Its application has to be seen and remembered by somebody before it is of any use, and that is what arises from discussions such as this.

It is necessary to have the right internal map, or way of looking at the world, to generate effective action. Successful 'doers' from any field of activity have to acquire the right map of their particular activity. Doing things requires know-how and know-how comes largely from experience. This is what most employers recognise when they ask for 'experience' when taking on new staff. Let us look a little more closely, however, at how such experience is acquired: obviously not from scratch by every individual every time.

Let me first propose a model of how this type of knowledge passes from one person to another. In any area of endeavour, a group of people develop a particular or private cosmology relating to any situation. New extensions to the map are passed around from person to person within the group as and when required, with 'apprentices' picking up the map bit by bit simply by being present. Every time a gap in an 'apprentice's' map is noted, by a question being asked, or ignorance being displayed, the missing piece is added to his map space. Information travels much as gossip or an illness spreads through a community.

The medium which passes information on in this way is variously known, as we have seen, as lateral media, or the old-boy network. Several interesting studies have looked at their role and functioning. In a detailed study entitled *The TEA Set: Tacit Knowledge and Scientific Networks*[1], Collins looked at how a new type of laser was constructed in Canada, and how the art of constructing such lasers subsequently spread over a network of other constructors in Britain. The diffusion network, the path taken by knowledge about the laser from lab to lab, person to person, looked like Fig 6.

A number of interesting points emerged from Collins' study, indicating the importance of such networks of informal contact. In the first place, the original laser was developed in contradiction to existing formal knowledge. 'The construction of the first device involved trial and error pragmatism, in the face of written and verbal assurances that the principle could not possibly work.'[1] Even when the device had been constructed it was not really understood. One of the scientists is reported as saying: 'We are even now discovering things about how to control the performance of these devices which are unknown. I have four theories for how they work which contradict each other.'[1]

The unsystematic nature of the laser development was further demonstrated by a British group who built what was, as far as they could see, an exact copy of a laser successfully operated elsewhere; theirs failed to work. They were at a loss to explain this, and simply gave up. Another correspondent reports being particularly impressed by one design of laser because he had actually seen it working. Normally, he reports, laboratories don't demonstrate their big lasers, ' "because they don't work". They will work perhaps one day in five, unpredictably.' Collins adds, 'In fact to date no one to whom I have spoken has succeeded in building a laser using written sources (including pre-prints and internal reports) as the sole source of information, though several unsuccessful attempts have been made, and there is now considerable literature on the subject.'[1] Indeed, he found that many of the published articles were actually misleading, in that they followed the practice of keeping back useful information. As one scientist put it, 'What you publish in an article is always enough to show that you've done it, but never enough to enable anyone else to do it. If they can do it, then they know as much as you do.'[1]

The major point that emerges from the study is that *the transmission of skills is not effected through the medium of the written word.* Collins describes how transmission does take place: 'All the laboratories studied here (other than the originating laboratory) actually learned to build working models of TEA lasers by contact with a source laboratory, either by personal visits and telephone calls or by transfer

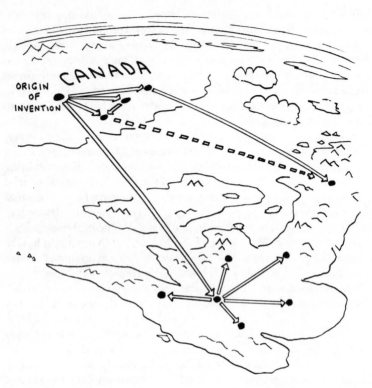

Fig 6 The diffusion of an invention, the transversely excited atmospheric laser from laboratory to laboratory, largely through informal friendship links

of personnel. The number of visits required depended to some extent upon the degree to which appropriate expertise already existed within the learning laboratory, but many capricious elements were also involved. Attempts at building which followed visits to successful laboratories often met with failure, and were backed up with more visits and phone calls.'[1]

The importance of social connections in the setting up of information exchanges also emerges from Collins' study. Fruitful information exchanges were set up as an indirect result of these social contacts. One of the American relations was set up as a result of a member of the seeking laboratory having been best man at the wedding of a member of a different department of the source laboratory. The one relationship, set up by writing a letter to the source laboratory, threatened to be very brittle at first, but was reinforced by placing students at the source laboratory.

Another example of the importance of informal networks in bringing about change is highlighted in a study of the introduction of a new drug by physicians in the United States.[3] When such a drug is launched, physicians are inundated with advertising material promoting it. Some doctors respond and some don't. The study discovered that the decision to use a new drug appeared to diffuse throughout the acquaintanceship network connecting doctors, those most strongly linked to the network prescribing it more quickly than weakly-connected doctors. The authors of the paper theorised that certain innovative doctors prescribed the new drug first and re-ported doing so in their discussions with colleagues. As a result of these the colleagues changed their minds and began to prescribe it too. They in turn discussed it with *their* colleagues, and the decision to prescribe the new drug diffused throughout the network in the same way as a plague or a rumour. The study found that a doctor's degree of inte-gration amongst his colleagues was strongly and positively related to the date of his first use of the new drug. This finding is illustrated in Fig 7.

So decisions get made and things get done not just because of what a book says, or a handout, or a conference paper, but because people are influenced by someone they know. It appears that dialogue through a network of acquaintances is particularly effective in extending and altering an individual's internal representational system of the world. Another American study looked at how engineers working in research laboratories contracted to the US government on the space programme got their ideas for things such as spacecraft power supplies, methods of landing on planets, and so on. The government had many different contracting laboratories working on the same problems, enabling the investigators to compare successful and unsuccessful groups of technical innovators, and then to examine what caused particular groups to be successful. The results support the contention that dialogue networks are vital in the transmission and generation of ideas. It found, like the TEA Set study, that the scientific engineering literature was very little used by the engineers. 'The engineers just do not read. They have little contact with the literature'; and, later: 'When we look at the amount of contact between the average engineer and his technical literature, the situation is somewhat distressing.'[5] The author of the study goes on to suggest that the people who talk to one another within their laboratories produce better technical solutions. He is referring here to the same phenomena already described.

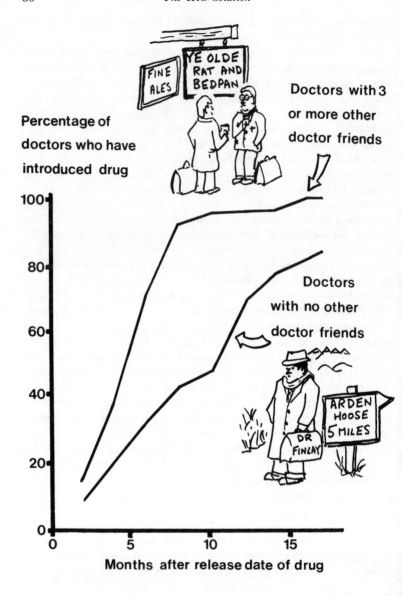

Fig 7   The take-up of the drug Gammanym was very dependent on the friendship links of the doctors prescribing it

The closed appearance of groups, however, is not the full story. It emerges that the successful US laboratories appear to contain people described as 'technological gatekeepers' who have access to many contacts outside the laboratory. 'There appear to be two distinct classes of individuals within this laboratory. The majority have few information contacts beyond the bounds of the organisation. A small minority in contrast have rather extensive outside contacts and furthermore serve as sources of information for their colleagues. There is then evidence of a two-step flow of information in the laboratory studied. Six or seven individuals act as technological gatekeepers for the rest of the laboratory. As further support, it was found that two of these six or seven people were responsible for introducing all four of the "most important technical ideas" that had been introduced into the organisation during the preceding years.'[4]

One of the reasons for the very minor role that literature plays, in comparison to personal networks, in the world of engineering is that of necessity it contains very general information, whereas an individual engineer's needs are very specific. A particular technical journal will specialise in, for example, space research or radio transmission, but an individual working on a specific problem is unlikely to find the information he needs. In addition, such sources provide information which is public knowledge, so it will not help an engineer to produce a better solution than a rival laboratory. Such information needs are not suited to 'central media', books, newspapers, journals, television and radio, which have to cater for the general informational needs of large numbers of people.

In addition, it appears that actually doing things, as we have shown, involves having the right internal map, or tacit knowledge. Many skills can only be transmitted by dialogue, because the cosmology that has to develop is implicit in a set of responses based on feedback. Only then can the engineer, say, recognise categories or situations on his map and call up appropriate responses.

What I am saying applies to every area where skill is applied in working life, from banking to ballet. But now we come to the nub of the problem: if you do not have the right internal map, or informal knowledge, then no amount of computer data bases, books, journals or conference papers will help you solve a problem or make a correct decision. If your internal map cannot identify the problem correctly, then your model will be wrong, and your model determines what *formal* knowledge you will seek. Lacking the right model you will only get part of the right information.

What is called the 'relevance paradox' is at the root of many costly and disastrous mistakes, as well as small-scale irritations. Unless you see the relevance of certain information, you may not seek it.

Take a major contemporary problem: bilharzia in the Third World, a disease caught by bathing in contaminated water. Tiny organisms bore through the skin and enter the human body, where they release eggs which cause enormous damage. The eggs are finally released into the water, where they re-infect snails, which subsequently release more organisms and continue the life cycle. Since the 1950s a document has been available from the United Nations pointing out the risk of bilharzia, and the engineering steps that can be taken to control it. Measures can be taken which can be incorporated in the design of irrigation schemes making the disease easier to control. But in spite of the existence of this information, numerous irrigation schemes around the world have been designed since the 1950s by Western engineers, oblivious to bilharzia and its effects, and the result has been an enormous increase in the number of sufferers. There are now something like 200,000,000 victims world-wide and the number is still increasing. In Egypt alone, one-third of the population has the disease.

In 1980 I was present at a symposium on the disease, a three-day meeting between doctors, engineers and biologists. On the third day an engineer stood up and asked, slightly shaken, as the full impact of the problem was becoming clear, 'Are you telling me that any body of water in Nigeria near habitation is liable to become infected with bilharzia, and that the population will always become infected because they will always bathe in it and use it?' The answer from the assembled experts was, 'Yes, this is the case.' The engineer said, 'I'm horrified. I've been project engineer on a new town development in Nigeria and we've deliberately sited the new town close to an abandoned gravel pit as an amenity and you're telling me that these people are all likely to suffer from bilharzia.' The reply was 'Yes, that is so.'

This engineer had not previously had the concept of bilharzia, and its association with water, included on his internal map. So when he sought the information he thought he needed, he found out about new towns, roads, climate, local materials, and so on. But he had no tacit knowledge to prevent him siting the town near the lake. He had never heard of it and no librarian had guided him to the UN publications. Similarly, engineers on irrigation schemes go out and get information on water flows, levels, materials, and so on. They will not take into account the bilharzia factor because they are unaware of its existence and its relevance to their job. They are victims of the relevance paradox. Central media are clearly inadequate to bridge the gap. Civil engineering journals mostly confine themselves to orthodox civil engineering information, and even though in this case articles had begun to appear, most engineers at the symposium seemed not to have come across them. It is also clear that dialogue between members of different specialist groups had, effectively, not taken place. Doctors, engineers, biologists, economists and politicians in the countries concerned did not form a working community, but separate, closed groups.

Such problems – and there are many, many more examples – arise from a failure of what we can call *lateral communication*. Pieces of vital technical knowledge do not, by their nature, propagate through formal systems; nor is this problem likely to be aided by the proliferation of the new electronic media. People simply cannot and do not look for a certain piece of information unless they know it is there. They cannot look for a solution unless they know there is a problem and they can only recognise the problem if they have the correct internal map.

6 INTERLOCK RESEARCH

We have seen that informal acquaintanceship networks are vital in transmitting the tacit or informal knowledge that enables people to do things efficiently, and which provides them with much of the information they actually need rather than what they think they need. Breakdowns in these networks, due to organisational barriers, often lead to expensive and counter-productive mistakes or to missed opportunities. The important role played by 'technological gate-keepers' – individuals who seem to act as intermediaries between different groups, or different parts of an organisation – is vital. Let us now take a closer look at the role these key figures play, and the networks they belong to, to see if it is possible deliberately to create similar phenomena, or at least to enhance their present use.

Consider the position of a university researcher interested in investigating the potential benefits of integrating the activities of the agriculture, water, waste disposal and energy sectors of the economy. His position is much the same, in fact, as that of anyone requiring information on which to base a decision – whether in government, industry or the social services. Our researcher comes to believe that it would be better, cheaper and less polluting, if some of the processes carried out by the various sectors could be combined. At Croydon, power generation and sewage treatment were for years effectively combined. The two processes took place side by side, with waste water from the sewage works being cleansed whilst being used in the power station water cooling circuit. In this case there were considerable savings in both building and running costs. Another example where integration could be advantageous is cattle or pig-farming. Modern intensive farms produce large quantities of waste which offends local residents and is expensive to dispose of. It is possible, however, to 'digest' the effluent in large tanks, which in turn produce a gas that can be used for heating, or for driving generators (see Fig 8). Mini power stations running on it are cheaper to install than large conventional ones. And if all cattle and pig slurry and surplus straw were digested, they would provide enough gas to produce more electricity than is now used by all British farms, at far lower cost than purchasing it from the National grid.[1] A by-product of the digestion process is an inoffensive nutrient solution, containing nutrients equivalent to the original waste.

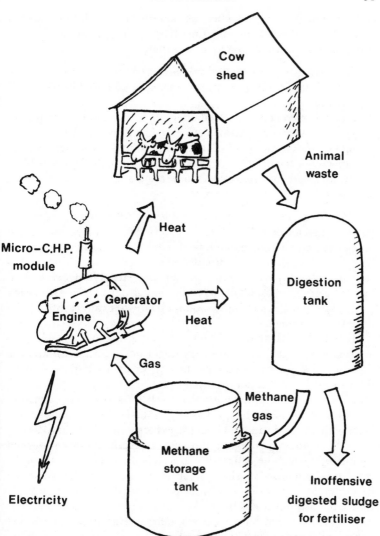

Fig 8   Without the digestion system, intensive animal farming produces offensive wastes that are expensive to dispose of. Digestion plus micro-CHP (see Fig 5, page 49) transforms the situation – the previously offensive waste is changed to inoffensive, easily transported fertilizer. The gas can be used for electricity generation and the heat from the micro-CHP to warm the digester and heat the animal houses. Capital costs are repaid in less than 5 years

To return to our researcher, he is aware of possibilities such as these which are worth investigating. If he carries out normal research procedures he will take the following steps:

1 *Study each sector*, and obtain relevant and correct information on the possibilities for integration, the attendant costs and benefits, and any snags.
2 *Prepare a model* of his proposed integration which would balance resource flows and interaction between activities in the various sectors.
3 *Inform relevant authorities* of useful results, and encourage them to implement them. (This stage would not normally be undertaken by an academic researcher; nevertheless it frequently follows research.)

At each stage he will run into problems. When he approaches a particular sector he will find that it is very difficult for an outsider to reach any depth of understanding about it. Each has its own body of tacit knowledge, which is normally only acquired by a degree in the relevant subject, plus several years of being part of its network. This makes it very hard for an outsider not only to get a real grasp of each sector, but to make sensible decisions about what can realistically be done between them.

He will also find that institutions do not generally like giving out information to outsiders, since they might misunderstand it and use their misconceptions to precipitate attacks on it. It may then be difficult for the institution to defend itself.

As a consequence of these problems, when the researcher comes to his second stage and attempts to set up a model for interaction, he is beset with uncertainties. Not being an expert in each field, how does he know his figures for resource flows are correct? Has he overlooked problems of which he is unaware, and is he therefore a victim of the relevance paradox? In theory, for example, a market could be developed for selling digested waste as fertiliser. But he may not know that pig waste must not be used on land grazed by sheep, since it contains copper, which may poison the sheep. He may propose the use of straw on farms as a fuel, unaware of one of its major uses as a building material. There are many such snags for the researcher, familiar to those in each industry, but difficult for an outsider.

The third stage, trying to get the results implemented by the relevant authorities, in many respects poses the worst problem. It is notoriously difficult for individuals to influence institutions, particularly if they are outsiders. The fixed cosmologies that tend to form in groups and institutions are resistant to new ideas, even from insiders, let alone from outsiders who may be speaking a different language.

We can conceive of a method of research, which I will call 'interlock research', which can help to circumvent these problems, and which I have experimented with at the Open University.[2] I will use the same specific 'hard' technical problem to outline both the concept and the method. I believe this can be applied to any situation where a decision has to be reached, individually or collectively, by such specialists as politicians, economists, academics, engineers, investors or bureaucrats. The 'researcher' should proceed like this:

Step 1:   Drawing up a provisional interlock diagram

The researcher takes a cursory look at the system in question, and draws up a provisional interlock diagram. In our example it might look something like Fig 9.

Here the boxes represent the elements of the system, and the lines the interactions between them, in this case material flows. In a non-technical case, its elements would still be organisations, or sections of them, but the lines would be policy interaction. The interlock diagram in Fig 10 represents the interaction of the DHSS, old people, and hospitals. If the DHSS cuts back on home helps for old people as an economy measure, there is an external effect on the health service of more old people being retained in hospital, and the hospital beds they occupy costing about twenty times as much as the home help.

Step 2:   Finding a gatekeeper for each sub-system

The researcher finds a professional who has worked, or still works in each sub-system. This person could be a decision-maker, who designs power stations or intensive rearing units or is influential in policy-making in the Ministry of Agriculture and Fisheries, briefing Ministers. Such people have accurate tacit knowledge, access to correct data, and know what is feasible; they will also be in a position to act on any new ideas acquired as a result of the exercise. The aim is not to find 'moles' to leak information which could be damaging to the institution, but people with whom trust can be built up. I have carried out this exercise, and my experience shows that it is possible to locate individuals who will help and provide information within most institutions. They are willing because they know the information they give will not be abused or misunderstood, but used responsibly, by someone who is aware of the industry's wider problems, and may also be doing research that will benefit the institution itself. Furthermore, they may learn something in return and will in any case enhance their circle of contacts, which may be professionally advantageous.

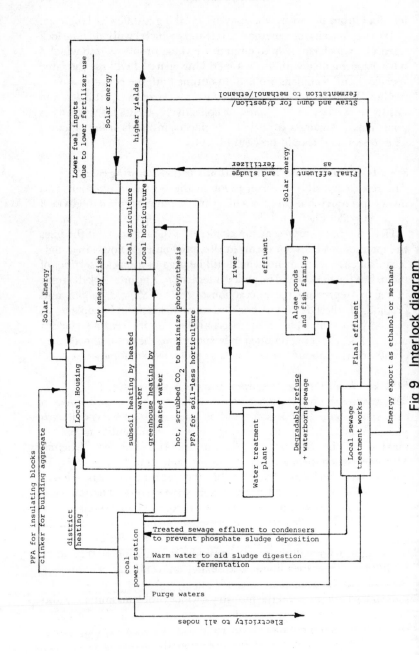

Fig 9 Interlock diagram

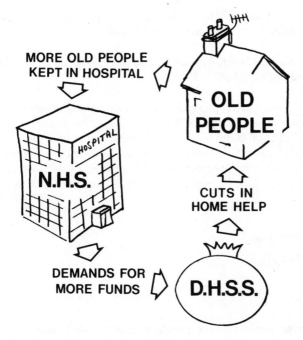

Fig 10   Interaction of the DHSS, old people and hospitals

Step 3:   Stimulating lateral communication between gatekeepers

Having identified a gatekeeper for each sub-system, the researcher must then get them to communicate with one another, wherever an actual or potential resource flow or policy interaction is indicated by the provisional interlock diagram. This is achieved in two ways: firstly, each gatekeeper gives a seminar on the activities of his sub-system, with particular reference to the interactions indicated by the diagram. To these other gatekeepers and interested people are invited. It is recorded on paper or tape and made available to people who join the process later, or who could not originally attend, or who did not appreciate the relevance of it at the time. During these discussions unforeseen possibilities come to light, as well as the snags and dead-ends of proposed advances: that is to say, the relevance paradox is thwarted.

Secondly, as the seminars proceed, the researcher asks all his gatekeepers and other interested parties, to fill in a profile. This records what information, expertise, and experience each individual already has, and what information he is interested in obtaining. Over time the profile can be adjusted to suit the particular needs of the situation. The record sheet set out below has been found to be successful.

Agriculture, Water, Waste and Energy Seminars (AWWE)
Registration slip (MK 111A)

A set of the entire proceedings (lectures and discussion) will be available as transcript or cassette. Together with the indexed proceedings will be an indexed set of these registration slips. This will enable discussion to continue indefinitely outside the seminars, along with the arrangement of meetings and site visits, by network members. A full set of address labels can be supplied to network members.

Name: *Profile No:*

1   *Organisation(s):*

    Address(es):

    Tel. No(s):
    Date:

2   *Seminar related activities* (practical projects, profession, etc.)

3   *Seminar related interests:*

4   *Information available* (articles, reports, contacts, experience):

5   *Information sought* (articles, reports, contacts, experience):

6   *Other Information Routeing Groups that you are in:*

    Please fill in and return, preferably typed, preferably in the format of the samples, by return.

Every member of the evolving network is given a fully indexed set of these record sheets, as they come in. A computer can easily process them, so that each new member has a full set of profiles, and an index for each of the main headings (see opposite).

Seminar Activities

(Extract from index on Page 96)
profile number

25 Pollution Control
 2 Power Generation
 3 Power Station Cooling Water
31 Power Supply
15 Prevent Pollution
22 Recycling of Domestic Solid and Liquid Wastes
22 Sewage Effluents
35 Sewage Effluent
 3 Sewage Sludge Studies
26 Sewage Treatment
28 Solar Energy in Agriculture
 1 Solid Waste Processing and Handling Plant
13 Spectral Energy Distribution of Diffuse Sunlight
 1 Steel Tanks, Corrosion Resistant
 1 Waste Processing and Handling Plant, Solid
34 Water

This process means that the group of fifty or so people can now operate as a network. Channels for communication have been opened up through which the members can communicate laterally with one another. The number of possible interactions between sub-systems is extremely large, and if seminars were the only vehicle for dissemination of information there would be a long and long-winded series of them which would bore many of the members much of the time. But record sheets and the index, together with access to telephone numbers and addresses which they provide, enable numerous private dialogues to occur, without the need for central control. This lateral medium can, by its composition, cope with the complexity of all possible interactions

Step 4: Progressively modifying the interlock diagram
Once the network is in operation, the next step is to redraw the interlock diagram with the help of the gatekeepers. More gatekeepers and more boxes may be required, as well as the scrapping of irrelevant or impracticable boxes. The process is repeated, with each stage becoming more accurate as more information becomes available. Finally, by consensus, a stable interlock diagram is produced. At this stage, it represents feasible and economic possibilities for integration. The seminars and the private interactions will almost certainly have identified these possibilities for the researcher.

Step 5:   Feeding the results into the system

When the interlock diagram stops changing, or slows down sufficiently, the researcher and other network members can collaboratively write a series of papers or articles dealing with the integration of specific parts of sub-systems, for example, energy production from agricultural waste, or district heating using power station reject heat. The ideas will be respected since they are 'endorsed' by professionals working within each specialisation, who will probably also be able to assist in getting the paper into the appropriate professional journal.

Part of this programme for interlock research and network action has been put into practice in the experiment I carried out at the Open University. Professionals and researchers, about 80 in all, representing the agriculture, water, waste and energy areas, and the related ones of irrigation schemes and health in the Third World, attended seminars and filled in profiles.

The essential feature of the network that arises from such a procedure is that it behaves dynamically. Any proposed innovation can be fed into it and it will respond by producing the relevant likely effects. If our original researcher, for example, considered using straw for fuel, the appropriate agriculture gatekeeper could give an immediate telephone estimate of the amounts involved, and perhaps a warning that a significant amount is used in certain building materials. This could lead to another conversation with a gatekeeper from building, who could supply information on the effects on his sub-system of altering the supply of straw.

Once the ball has been set rolling, the network really assembles itself. If a particular sub-system is missing, it will be brought in by a gatekeeper in an adjacent area, who will see its relevance. Interaction between gatekeepers will ensure that new factors are brought to bear. The informal nature of the contact between them means that dialogue takes place through which cosmological barriers can be surmounted. Nor is the use of the network any longer confined to the purposes of its instigator. Each gatekeeper can and will use it to get accurate feedback on ideas, possibilities and courses of action he is considering, and in so doing will provide feedback to other members.

The significance of the lateral medium so generated is that the interactions between members come to resemble the potential interactions between the sub-systems. Decision-making in an area of any complexity involves the assessing and weighing of data with which the decision-maker is more or less unfamiliar, conventional channels of communication being either limited to one particular specialisation, or too general to be helpful. But a network provides a collective model of reality with in the jargon of cybernetics 'requisite variety', that is, as much variety as the reality being dealt with. By means of the network it is possible for any member to talk with a key person from any of the relevant sub-systems, across the boundaries of institutions.

The mass of links that has been created provides a form of dispersed control that satisfies Ashby's Law. The links control decisions arising from network members simply by influencing their view of reality, their internal map. This recalls the slime mould and its ability to perform synchronised choreography by the simple expedient of each element transmitting and receiving the right signals.

Networks similar to the one described can assemble themselves in any large organisation. Much information is passed very effectively through grapevines or the old-boy networks, and organisations depend on such informal channels of contact. But, as we have already seen, boundaries tend to form within sub-groups which inhibit their information and the flow of informal knowledge between them. This means that large organisations have models of the world they are dealing with which lack requisite variety, and this leads to bad decisions being made, or, at best, decisions that could have been better. If countries are seen in this respect simply as large organisations, governments are subject to the same problem.

We can conceptualise a failure of dialogue between sub-systems as open loops on the interlock diagram. In this chapter's original example of the agriculture, water, waste and energy sectors, the diagram shows that pollution occurs when output from a box is not fed usefully into another box, meaning that every time a waste product is not used, it becomes a source of pollution. There are, of course, qualifications to be made – many open loops are for instance too expensive or impractical to close – but in general the principle applies. Every time a loop is closed, energy is saved and pollution is reduced. Indeed, the advantages may be even greater: if a material which was previously a polluting waste material can be used instead of a natural raw resource, the use of that resource is also saved, and so is the energy used in processing the raw material in the first place.

There are numerous examples of the plural advantages of taking action which closes loops. Children are currently paid a small sum for returning used cans. Materials from these are recycled, which saves both the original ore from which the cans were made, and all the energy used in smelting the metal. Asda Superstores have recently installed a system to use the heat from their refrigerators to heat one of their stores. In the past the heat was disposed of by radiators mounted on the roof, which is what a cooling tower is; the heat is now recovered and used to heat the store, saving some of the gas previously used. Again, in the United States, in California's China Valley, a plant has been set up which takes the dung from numerous dairy units and converts it to a valuable compost. The animal waste had previously been a considerable pollution nuisance to the valley. And Sweden has gone as far as to classify all refuse as fuel. It is intended that in future it will all be incinerated, which would greatly reduce the amount of rubbish while assisting the fuel problem.

But perhaps the best example of closing loops comes from China. A small village called Xinbu, which five years ago faced a crisis due to a shortage of energy and fertiliser, could today be considered the world's first integrated energy village. The consequent web of integrated processes is truly remarkable. Family and community digesters have been constructed, and energy crops planted on previously unused land. 'The digesters operate mainly on nightsoil plus waste from the pigs, the kitchen, the napier grass and the bananas. Biogas generated from the family units is burnt for cooking and lighting, whilst the gas from the communal digester powers a motor to drive a generator . . . This electric power is used to operate electric lights and a pulveriser. Waste heat from the motor is channelled into the silk-worm cocoon drying sheds. Banana waste is fed to the biogas digesters, and the consequent slurry helps to fertilise the fields that are growing bananas. Mulberry leaves are fed to silkworms which are kept warm during the cold season by biogas heaters. Silkworm droppings are fed to fish as well as to the digesters. Napier grass is fed into the biogas digesters in raw form, or after mastication by pigs. Leaves from 135 tonnes of sugar cane, produced each year, are fed to carp in fishponds. The sludge at the bottom of the fishponds in turn serves as fertiliser, not only for the napier grass but also for the sugar cane, mulberry and the banana fields.'[3] The economics are very good too. The payback period is calculated to be two to four years, about a third of the time it takes to build a large power station or sewage works.

Exactly the same concept that I have been describing applies to non-technical areas. Where decisions are taken from the partial viewpoints of separate organisations there will be unforeseen or unavoidable negative effects via open loops. I have already mentioned the example of cuts in local spending on services for the elderly, the result being more old people in expensive hospital beds. The example cited in Chapter 4 showed that children taken from an institution and put into the sole care of a retarded adolescent girl in another institution did far better than those who remained in children's homes. This not only saved part of the cost of caring for the children, but also no doubt led to longer-term savings. Numerous studies have also shown that children from institutions are more likely to be involved in crime, are less able to form relationships, and are more likely to become drug addicts or alcoholics. The personal satisfaction and enrichment for the children and the girl is another factor.

Interlock diagrams can be drawn for these situations, and interlock research could throw up many solutions which would save money and produce better solutions for the benefit of society. During the 1960s, when the tower block building programme was at its height, an interlock diagram could have been constructed for local authority housing. The first stage might have looked something like Fig 11.

Over time, it would of course have become much more complicated, as it educated the people involved about the issues. No such procedure was followed, and the disastrous results are familiar. In some countries tower blocks have been much more successful, for a greater awareness of the factors involved in living in them and some of the adaptations that can be made, have made them much more suitable. But in Britain, channels of communication to facilitate such a wider awareness did not, and do not, exist.

Within many large organisations, of course, tacit interlock diagrams do exist. People interact in a way which establishes their relevant roles, who they should listen to, who they should instruct, and who they should liaise with. This vast informal tacit interlock diagram is what actually enables any large organisation to operate. The common conception of such organisations is that they are hierarchies, with orders coming down from above, and each level reporting back to the top. But the reality is different. Although hierarchies do exist, there are alongside them, and bearing little resemblance to them, informal networks which facilitate the smooth running of the organisation.

The problem is, however, that the information flow across boundaries within organisations, and, to a greater extent, between them, is inadequate. And without interlock diagrams which cross boundaries most of the formal knowledge stored in the educational system, in the vast libraries, in the computer data bases and teleinformation systems, is completely useless. People cannot look for information they don't know they need. No amount of cross-indexing and interlinking can help, since the number of potential interlinks is too vast. People simply cannot cope with such systems. Seen in this light, the new society we are promised of technological information presents serious problems. The only way to ensure that people get the information they need to take correct decisions, taking into

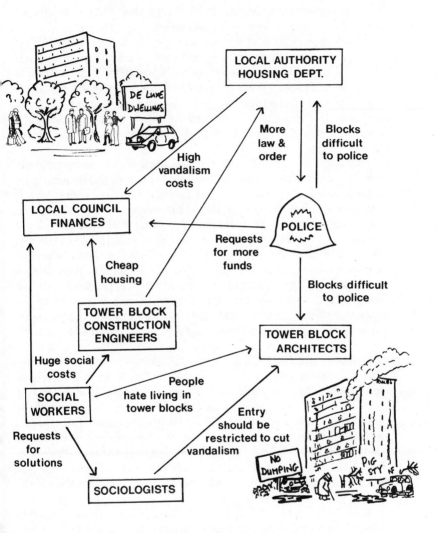

Fig 11   First stage of possible interlock diagram for tower block
building programme

account all relevant factors, is to ensure that there are relevant networks crossing information boundaries.

A colleague of mine in a northern water authority reported to me that many firms discharge poisonous metals into the authority's sewers. This metal is very expensive to dispose of, and the industry is charged accordingly. What many of the firms do not realise is that it is now economical to recycle the metals in private treatment processes, and that the capital costs for such an operation are insignificant when compared with the savings. In effect these firms have to be *forced* to save money.

We could describe this example as 'passive' information failure. People are made to look silly for not knowing everything they might be expected to know, and many put in more effort or money than is required to achieve some object. This seems to be so widespread throughout the Western world that it must inevitably cause national economies to run at lower efficiency than they would otherwise. We do not have to look too far, however, to see that the results of similar misunderstandings can be more serious, and that unwitting victims may take actions that actually exacerbate the problem they are addressing, or minimise the effect they are trying to achieve. In the following cases, ill-conceived policies have caused great social dislocation as the original problem has merely been made worse.

The Aswan High Dam
This huge project was intended to make available over a wide area of Egypt both hydro-electric power and irrigation, with attendant economic benefits. In fact, in the long run the negative effects of the dam may well have far outweighed the positive. Prior to its introduction, for example, the annual flooding of the Nile deposited rich alluvial silt on the flood plain, ensuring the fertility of the region. When the dam was built this flood stopped with the result that soil fertility dropped significantly. Much of the electricity that the scheme produced is now used to make chemical fertiliser to replace lost natural fertiliser which now has to be bought. This alluvium is now dumped in Lake Nasser reducing the lake's capacity and shortening its life, whereas much of it used to reach the Mediterranean. The large population of plankton and other aquatic micro-organisms in the Mediterranean which the silt once supported has now diminished, which in turn has led to the destruction of anchovy and sardine fishing, with major economic effects for the local population, and a rise in the price of sardines. The policy of spreading the water as far as possible has led to inadequate irrigation, which causes soil salinity. In the past

leaching, due to excess irrigation, prevented this. In addition, the year-round irrigation created by the dam has led to a dramatic rise in the level of bilharzia in the region, and as already mentioned in Chapter 5, one-third of the population in Egypt now suffers from this debilitating disease.

The dam builders, therefore, ultimately got their feedback in the form of these negative effects, many years later. If they had performed an initial interlock study, however, most of these negative effects would have surfaced earlier, and the scheme would either not have gone ahead, or would have done so in a modified form. For in effect, the interlock network models the effect of any action, giving feedback to the decision-makers before reality does.

The Green Revolution

The logic behind the Green Revolution was simple: people all over the world are short of food, it was argued, therefore it follows that if we develop strains of high-yield crops there will be more food and less hunger. So about fifteen years ago high-yield strains of grains were developed, by genetic selection. But the applications of this simple theory turned out to be much more complicated than the originators thought, as a recent study elucidates.[4] Subsistence agriculture uses draught animals, as tractors are too expensive. In a typical Indian village a large part of the food for the animals comes from crop residues. Any reduction in these will result in their having to eat more food obtained from pasture land, at the expense of food for the villagers' own consumption. Land is scarce, however, because of high population densities, so the minimum acreage is allocated for grazing. The villagers are now no better off because there are fewer crop residues, and in some cases small farmers and communities have gone bankrupt and have been forced to sell their farms to rich landowners, in the long run actually exacerbating the poverty problem.

The study describes the delicate balance which has evolved over time in the village: 'Since both humans and cattle must depend on crops and on different components of the biomass, *all* components of crop biomass are vital to the functioning of the ecosystem. Thus as long as agriculture is achieved through such ecosystems, a traditional strategy has been to produce all the various biomass components, and not only the grain, in precisely the ratios required to sustain the populations of humans and cattle. This is in sharp contrast to the Green Revolution strategy which exclusively emphasises the grain in its dwarf varieties. By yielding a lower percentage of crop residues the fodder output of the dwarf varieties is reduced, and this either necessitates a separate production of fodder or more pasture land, or a replacement of animal draught power with mechanised equipment which then creates a demand for fuel.' The study also found that the grains were not as high-yielding as they could have been because the villagers did not use water, fertiliser and pesticides scientifically.

The study goes on to make practical suggestions for helping the villagers. It found, for example, that a lot of firewood was used for brick-making. But this demand could be eliminated, since unburnt mud bricks are just as good. Conserving trees could also make a real contribution to a village like the one studied since this would conserve the scarce soil resources. But useful information like this can only come from a close on-the-spot study of a community. The village, over thousands of years, had acted as a tacit interlock diagram which linked the minds of people carrying on different tasks in it and enabling it to reach an optimum interplay of agricultural resources. When the researchers from the Indian Institute of Science in Bangalore lived with the villagers and studied the ecosystem in great detail, they mathematically modelled the interactions of all the systems, even down to the level of how much grain was stored by rodents in burrows, and from this theoretical basis they produced a model showing the interactions between sub-systems, which demonstrated that the village conformed very closely to theoretically ideal maximum production.

In another case[5], researchers remote from the situation devised high efficiency stoves for use in developing countries. These well-intentioned people had a model of how traditional villages work and what they are short of. They noticed what they thought was a shortage of cooking fuel, hence their idea for new wood-burning stoves. In fact, they were addressing the wrong problem, since twigs are in any case the usual source of fuel for cooking, and incidentally are not contributing to deforestation. But the researchers were also unaware of the conditions under which most cooking is done, with smoke curling up through a hole in the roof of the huts, at the same time percolating through the thatching material, with a powerful drying and insecticidal effect. Where high-efficiency stoves have been introduced to the huts, there has been a big increase in insects and bacteria in the roofing, with a consequent rise in disease.

I have attempted to show that an interlock diagram provides a way of examining and visualising how complicated systems and sub-systems interact. Information flows from node to relative node in a decentralised operation, and such flows match the resource flows or policy interactions. In natural systems such as ecosystems, and to some extent in mature and effective organisations, these lines of communication are inherent within the system. In new organisations, or large hierarchic organisations, the links have not yet formed, or are prevented from forming. But in all man-made organisations and groups of related organisations, there are flows of resources, or policy interactions, between the sub-systems. For each system to work properly there must be lateral communication between people or groups involved in different sub-systems. If this is lacking, people in the different sub-systems are either unaware of possibilities for integrating activities, causing unnecessarily high levels of effort or resource-usage or the activities of one sub-system may have a negative effect on another.

7 HIERARCHIES AND THEIR PROBLEMS

There are numerous anthropological records of societies composed of small autonomous tribal villages in which institutional hierarchies are unknown. As we saw earlier, the daily activities of these villagers are largely dictated by membership of the tribe as a whole, and the network of relationships within it. The stock of myth and folklore which exists among the people also plays a role. In this respect the villagers are like an amoeba from the slime mould, the control of their activities being dispersed among them, so each controls his neighbour. Such villages survive side by side with the more complex institutions of the modern West.

Institutional hierarchies are in fact a very recent phenomenon in the history of Man, only appearing during the last 10,000 years or so. They date, presumably, from the time when tribes first grew large enough to start expanding territorially, bringing them into conflict with tribes with rival claims to the land, and the establishment of warrior classes who were initially able to hold or take territory, and later to form and defend dynasties. Warrior dynasties supplanted tribal chiefs, who had been elected to their positions, and whose main role had been to adjudicate in disputes and provide a form of social service.

Once it has begun, the process of hierarchisation appears to be almost unstoppable. Its culmination is found in 'advanced' bureaucratised modern society, where the majority of people work in some form of institutional hierarchy, a pyramidal organisation in which people at the top tell the more numerous people below what to do.

In sixteenth-century England the village was the primary unit of organisation for the vast majority of the population. Until then the Church, which provided a convenient means of explaining and justifying the existing order to the masses, was the only significant institutional hierarchy. But for the majority of English people, who still lived in villages, an institutionalised hierarchy did not loom large in their daily lives. From Elizabethan times onwards, however, the English village was in slow decline. The force for change was the new middle classes, who were gaining in numbers and influence as they congregated in the towns, gradually intruding into the traditional lord and peasant relationship. Greater ease of transport and the development of central media, forged these new elements into a class that looked after its own interests.

The source of much of Britain's wealth, the wool trade, had depended on water power, then an inherently dispersed source of energy, and small villages tended to be sited on rivers, where the wool was converted to cloth. With the onset of the Enclosures, the peasants were progressively forced off the land, ultimately to be employed in factories in the neighbouring towns. Although the early Industrial Revolution was based on the small villages, its full development in the burgeoning towns was made possible by the invention of the steam engine, which in contrast to water power was an inherently centralised energy source. The growth of towns, the influx of dispossessed villagers, the rise of the middle classes and the Industrial Revolution, brought about the destruction of the old system of dispersed social control, and the basic tribesmen-chief relationship that underlay it. The new city-based industrial society eventually gave rise to the first large, modern, secular bureaucratic hierarchy on which all other modern hierarchies are modelled: the Poor Law Commission, founded in 1834. What was different about this new form of administrative institution was that until its setting up, political office, like most others, had been settled by a system of patronage. People such as Newton, who ran the Royal Mint, or Allen who ran the Post Office, did so because they were favourites, friends, or relatives of influential people, or as a result of the exchange of favours, or marriage, and a large part of the high-level administration of England was carried out by such means. Architects such as Wren, landscape gardeners such as Capability Brown, and composers such as Handel, were also appointed by a system of patronage operated by the informal networks of the aristocratic ruling classes.

The new middle classes were in the main excluded by such a system and resented it. So when they gained sufficient power to do so, they gradually, over the course of a century or more, changed it. Entry to the lucrative, powerful and prestigious posts in the new hierarchy was not on the basis of personal favour or relationship but on that of merit, as assessed by examination results: a striking innovation. As a result of the bold establishment of the first modern institutional hierarchy, closely followed by others, the public schools, too, changed their role. They were now called on to educate the sons of the middle classes, those who had prospered in manufacturing or farming or commerce. Their education was completed at either Oxford or Cambridge. This concept of the well-educated civil servant, made by public school and Oxbridge, has survived to the present day.

Once established, the modern form of the administrative hierarchy flourished. It spread through central and local government, affecting taxation, the police force, the armed forces, education, planning, health, the supply of water and so on. Most large business firms, unions, societies, environmental groups and political parties have since also come in some ways to resemble institutional hierarchies. At the international level, super-bureaucrats now run super-hierarchies such as the EEC or the United Nations.

No one would disagree with the view that much of what is called progress has taken place because of the existence of bureaucratic organisations. Indeed, hierarchical systems have become so ubiquitous that it is difficult to imagine how most of our organisations could be differently structured. Nevertheless, it is not sufficiently recognised that there are features endemic in institutions structured exclusively hierarchically, which can impair their efficiency. Generally speaking the larger and more monopolistic the institution, the more hierarchic it will be, and the more subject to the problems I am about to analyse. Modifications can be made to take account of these features, which would enable hierarchic organisations to function better, and these will be discussed in the next chapter.

It will be recalled that Ashby's Law states that if there is to be a well-controlled system, its controls must have a complexity at least equal to that of the system being controlled – or requisite variety. Many hierarchies are in themselves control systems for dealing with part of reality: health, water supply, education, criminal behaviour and so on. But the problem is that in a pure hierarchy it is almost impossible to satisfy Ashby's Law. By definition, the further you go up a hierarchy the fewer the people, and individuals can only grasp a certain amount of information at any one time. The flow of information upwards takes the form of people feeding situation reports and information to those above them. As these move up the hierarchy, new and shorter memos and reports are compiled from the originals. So the information becomes more and more abbreviated, which means that models of lower and lower variety are being constructed, as the top, the seat of ultimate executive power, is approached. As an illustration we can take the difference between the amount of material collected by GCHQ, the Government's spy centre at Cheltenham where analysts wheel trolley-loads of information about, derived from their continuous monitoring of Russian, and other foreign telephone conversations. A minuscule proportion of this ends up on the Prime Minister's desk. British Intelligence staff at Cheltenham have in principle a very high-variety model of the Soviet Union, derived from their communication. But after it has been sifted and filtered for matters judged to be of national import, the detail of information arriving at Downing Street is consequently very simplified.

This feature of hierarchies is of course in some respects what makes them function effectively as decision-making organisations. Generals and Assistant Secretaries and Managing Directors need to construct a general overall model without getting bogged down in detail. But the simplicity of that model, brought about by its distance from reality, and the process of filtering information upwards, can also lead the person at the top to make wrong, irrelevant, or unnecessarily expensive decisions. The people at the top of the Aswan Dam-planning hierarchy, for example, clearly had models, or interlock diagrams, lacking in requisite variety. A higher-variety model, existing lower down the hierarchy, might have said, 'We are short of water for agriculture and electricity, therefore we will build a chain of small dams, as Austria has done, as this will not disrupt the movement of alluvial silt. Then we can use some of the electricity to pump water to new field systems. Intermittent flooding will reduce the risk of bilharzia and salinisation, etc.'

Hierarchical institutions also have an inherent tendency to favour large-scale, broadly-based solutions to the problems that confront them. When a hierarchy selects a course of action, the spectrum of choice usually has a few very large solutions (coarse-grained) at one end and a larger number of small solutions (fine-grained) at the other. If a country has a housing problem, for example, it could theoretically build either one vast house for everyone, lots of blocks of houses in each city, or very large numbers of individual houses. People at the top of large hierarchies tend to favour a few large solutions in preference to a large number of smaller ones. They are both easier to conceive and to administer. It is less trouble to deal with one designer, one architect, one contractor and one site, than with a multiplicity of them. A case in point is the formation of the British water authorities, as J.D. Hunter, recently retired from the Severn Trent Water Authority, makes clear: 'From the point of view of government, who decide the borrowing limits of the water authorities, it is easier to control ten water authorities, most of whose members they appoint, rather than several hundred locally-elected bodies.'[1]

This tendency of hierarchies to give coarse-grained output is also seen in the case of the US Army Corps of Engineers, which is responsible for many of the large-scale public works in America. According to one journalist, it is 'A body which neither Congress nor Courts seem able to stop once it gets moving. The money continues to flow in and out of its coffers in a golden and apparently uncontrollable stream.'[2] One of its planned projects is a scheme in Chicago costing some $12\frac{1}{2}$ billion, which aims to rebuild most of Chicago's sewers because they flood every time it rains. The expenditure of this vast sum would only marginally improve the situation, and enable the system to withstand, 'brief, accidental exposure to storm water'. It has been pointed out that a much cheaper solution would be simply to enforce more strictly existing housing regulations, which demand that house roofs hold back up to six inches of rainwater; this would prevent the surge of water which causes the flooding.

The effect of this kind of sweeping approach, can also be seen in British cities. Most European cities were originally 'fine-grained', in that numerous small decisions occurred at local level – 'Shall we use thatch or tile?' 'Shall we make it three storeys or two?' The environment changed very gradually as a result of small, locally-made decisions, so that seen from a distance there was no obvious sudden change, but a gradual evolution over a period of years. Change in most modern cities, by contrast, has now become a very 'coarse-grained' affair. A few big decisions are taken centrally, by bureaucrats. These involve the periodic razing of large areas, the building of large areas of identical housing and so on, and, seen from a distance, the landscape changes in blocks, drastically and suddenly. The contrast between the look of our cities up to 50 years ago, and now, illustrates the point.

In the real world, as distinct from the paper world of most bureaucratic hierarchies, small, local solutions are frequently best. No matter how cheap and effective they are, these solutions are unlikely to be produced by hierarchies, because they are more difficult for them to administer. Of course, there are economies of scale to be gained from some large-scale enterprises, but as we have seen in the case of power stations, there are also diseconomies. If we compare the large monopolies set up to run the generation of electric power in Britain and the United States with the policy adopted in West Germany and Scandinavia, where public utilities are frequently operated by town councils and where power stations are generally much smaller, it can be seen that large is not necessarily more economic.

One of the essential internal features of hierarchies is that people at the top of the hierarchy have to tell people further down what to do. But the question is, how do you get people further down to do what you want without giving continuous instructions? Earlier, I used an example of a police commander, in control of a large number of men, organising a search of open land. What he does is delegate. But he also has to retain control of the situation. So he introduces a set of rules.

And if the number of men below him is too great to control personally, he brings in intermediate levels of command, to whom he can give more responsibility. A pyramid structure, with sets of explicit rules for underlings to follow, is what develops when large numbers of people have to be co-ordinated to achieve certain tasks.

But this structure, which is the very nature of all hierarchies, contains the seeds of its own inefficiency. If the people at the top are to get the people lower down to do what they want, they have to persuade them to do so against what may be conflicting local pressures. People with whom the underlings are dealing may in fact try to stop them carrying out their instructions. So a system of rewards and punishments has to be introduced in order to get subordinates to do what is required. Rewards are usually related to money and status – powerful incentives. People like both, so there is every reason to stay in the hierarchy, safeguard one's own position, and promote its growth. By the same token each member will try and avoid penalties for breaking rules, or more importantly for not doing what he is supposed to do, since this may mean loss of influence, prestige or money.

Let us now look at the way this affects the exchange of information within the hierarchy. At any particular moment a person in a hierarchy is likely to know more about a given situation than his superior, since he is actually involved in it, whereas the superior will, by definition, be occupied supervising more than one subordinate. If anything goes wrong, it is quite hard for the subordinate to explain exactly what is going on, because the superior is occupied with other problems, dealing with other subordinates and trying to keep his own boss happy. The tendency, therefore, is for subordinates to begin to distort information going upwards to suit what they know is demanded by superiors. They want to be seen by their superiors as doing what is expected, following the rules, and the ethics of the organisation.

Coupled with this possible distortion of information flowing upwards, there is also a tendency within hierarchies for superiors not to listen to the advice, suggestions or criticisms of subordinates. One reason for this is suggested by the theory of cognitive dissonance. This is the uneasy feeling experienced by someone who is faced with information that conflicts with a decision he has already taken. Smokers, for example, experience dissonance when faced with the evidence that smoking increases their chances of dying from lung cancer. The theory says that individuals tend to act so as to lower feelings of unease brought about by cognitive dissonance. The smoker tends to relieve his feelings of unease by ignoring, or in some other way discounting, anti-smoking propaganda. People in positions of authority may also suffer cognitive dissonance when it is pointed out to them that, say, they have been building the wrong type of power station, or providing the wrong type of health care. Since any acceptance of the new information from subordinates is likely to bring blame or criticism for wrong decisions in the past, the easiest thing to do is to ignore or taboo the counter-information.[3]

Another reason for superiors ignoring the contrary views of their subordinates is that they are trying to maintain their own position of supremacy within the organisation. When people of different levels try and communicate, they all come armed with different maps of reality, in part corresponding to their level in the hierarchy. A person in a position of authority, anxious to maintain his credibility and prestige will often refuse to revise his own map in the light of a subordinate's message. This may make the subordinate look stupid, or confuse him, or force him to give up and go away, thus demonstrating his superior's power over him. A good example is the boss who says: 'I don't want excuses – I just want it done.' He is refusing to alter his map of the situation to take in what the subordinate is trying to tell him, and simply reasserting the views he already holds, and his power. Essentially power is communicational incompetence.

An excellent example of what happens when two parties refuse to adjust their respective maps of reality, and therefore fail to communicate, is provided by Britain's ill-fated attempts to negotiate trade terms with China in the early nineteenth century. The two sides had totally different notions about international intercourse. Britain promoted the concept of a family of nations with matters arising dealt with between ambassadors on a more or less equal footing. The Chinese 'map' of reality on the other hand, allowed only for the concept of an empire and subject peoples. Instead of meeting the British delegates on equal terms, the Chinese therefore regarded them as bearers of tribute. This clash of views led to the suicide of the British Ambassador, the Opium Wars and Hong Kong.

Within a hierarchy, much the same thing can happen. This is what lies behind the common complaint, 'You just can't communicate with him' or 'You just can't get through to her'. The boss who won't listen and the subordinates who tell him only what he wants to hear are both victims of their hierarchical environment. Neither can properly share his experience with the other. Yet without a willingness and ability to share experience, true dialogue and effective communication cannot take place. This becomes clear if we contrast a hierarchical institution with a more relaxed and informal social situation: a group of friends, say, or a tribal village. Here, communication is, or can be, centred around the activity of determining the truth – that is to say, an internal map of reality with requisite variety – because people are less likely to have a vested interest in distorting it. When this is the case, communication tends to converge; that is, each person will get his message across and the participants in the conversation will form a joint internal map of reality. In a hierarchy this rarely happens, since people are too busy trying to maintain their credibility with their colleagues above and below them in the pecking order. In other words, communication is centred around the activity of maintaining esteem, rather than establishing the truth.

To illustrate the difference in end-product between true dialogue and the kind of information-tailoring that goes on in most hierarchies, let us take a simple example from industry. In the past, the various hierarchies in charge of the water, coal, steel, electricity supply and nuclear industries all predicted a demand for their products which turned out to be way in excess of the actual figures. On the basis of these forecasts, huge sums of public money were invested in capacity which is now redundant. It has since emerged that disinterested groups of people *outside* these various hierarchies predicted the demand far more accurately. Those whose careers were not at stake did not come under the same pressure to distort information as those within them, and were therefore free to examine the facts more objectively.

In Fig 12, the left-hand table is the official 1977 forecast. The one on the right is from a small independent research institute, Earth Resources Research. Both sets of figures relate to a future of high economic growth in which UK GDP approximately triples between 1976 and 2025. The latest official figures, while not actually forecasting a reduction in energy demand like the ERR figures, show much more gradual growth.

Such forecasting information is presumably doctored so that those at each level in the hierarchy can please their superiors and ultimately so that those at the top of a hierarchy can give palatable information to governments. For these generally, at least conservative ones, support big business, and big business likes expensive generating capacity. But numerous unofficial studies have shown that money spent on insulation rather than capital-intensive generating plant would be far better for energy conservation, and much cheaper. A recent report[4] estimates the cost of thoroughly insulating the housing stock of Britain and compares the cost of saving a unit of energy by these means with the cost of providing energy. It shows that conservation is at least three times cheaper. It is a direct substitute for gas, and one-third of the cost. This study is one of many unofficial ones that have come to the same

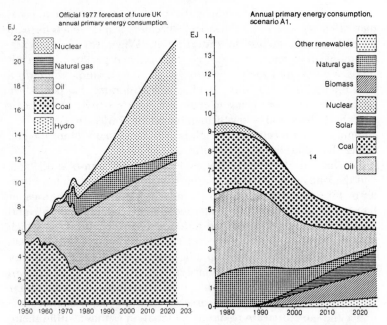

Fig 12   Various estimated figures for total UK energy demand, 2025. Source: David Olivier, Hugh Miall, Francois Nectroux and Mark Opperman, *Energy Efficient Futures: The Solar Option.* Available from Earth Resources Research, 258 Pentonville Road, London N1 9JY. £38

conclusion: that it is better for the country as a whole to conserve energy and money by spending a small amount of capital on large numbers of individual houses and offices, rather than a lot of money on a few big energy supply plants. Governments much prefer the latter course, since it is simpler, benefits big business, and keeps political power in the hands of a few – the nature of hierarchies. The official government response has been to duplicate these studies, but to suppress the reports which broadly agree with the conservationist, fine-grained approach, for example, one from the Building Research Establishment, and, more recently, one from the Department of Energy. The conclusions of the latter were so unpalatable to the then Energy Secretary that he ordered the report to be suppressed and had a new one prepared under his close supervision. Unfortunately for him a copy was leaked to the press and other interested parties.[5]

During the time that such reports were being suppressed, I had occasion to telephone a senior civil servant. When our business was over, and the conversation turned to more general matters, he assured me that, despite appearances to the contrary, there were individuals within government departments who supported the views of those in the energy debate who were calling for government support for conservation, rather than greater expenditure on power plant. He described, with increasing bitterness, how they either had to produce reports saying what their superiors wanted to hear, or they were shunted into dead-end jobs with no promotion prospects.

To turn to government hierarchies, in the case of Prime Ministers, who wield enormous power, the pressure on subordinates to distort, select, or even withhold information to order, can be considerable. The result is that it becomes increasingly difficult for them to arrive at any true picture of reality. Take the case of Margaret Thatcher, whose view of the world comes either from her advisers or in the following way: 'Whisked between official residences in official cars, Prime Ministers soon become sealed off from the real world and begin to place exaggerated store by their meetings with ordinary people, whether across a factory bench or a gin-and-tonic. But nobody, introduced to the Prime Minister, is going to start by attacking her. Reality soon begins to disappear, like a shape half-glimpsed in the mist, discerned only through short, haphazard and misleading encounters. Which is more real, which (if any) tell [her] more about the British people: a girl in a chocolate factory, mumbling politely into the fondants; Jimmy Savile, paying one of his frequent visits to Downing Street to talk about Stoke Mandeville hospital, or a crowd of yelling demonstrators? "You see, they all go mad, they all start hearing voices," says an MP who has studied several Prime Ministers. "They are cut off from the world, so they rely on their gut instinct, and of course it is very often wrong." '[6]

There is widespread evidence to support the view that the systematic distortion of information to suit superiors occurs in all kinds of administrative hierarchies. Laurence Freedman, in a book about the history of American intelligence operations[7], suggests that the pressures on any intelligence analyst to conform to the views and assumptions of his peers are very great. Moreover, he argues that officers in military intelligence, who are serving officers already in a rigid and formal hierarchy, are under *extra* pressure to present their data in a way that appears to support the point of view known to be held by superior officers. The implications for world peace are obvious.

As with other examples, the main concern of the subordinate is not to supply his superiors with an accurate picture of reality, but rather to protect, and, if possible, to enhance his own position, often regardless of the inconvenience or long-term harm this may cause. An example of the doctoring of information to suit superiors occurred during the British nuclear bomb tests at Maralinga in South Australia, in the 1950s. Health teams monitoring the tests issued film badges and radiation meters to those working in the blast areas. Unfortunately the radiation meters, which measure an individual's total exposure to radiation, did not work, because their batteries were flat. Rather than admit this to their superiors, plausible estimates were made and submitted. The person who made these estimates now admits that they were wildly inaccurate.[8]

Another mechanism used in hierarchies to suppress or thwart the free flow of information is the taboo, whereby people within the hierarchy tacitly agree not to mention subjects, however relevant, which might threaten the prevailing power structure. This mechanism, as we saw, operates powerfully within the CEGB, where use of the term 'combined cycle plant' was in effect suppressed.

Studies of the experience of people within institutions such as mental hospitals, prisons, local authorities, who 'go public', that is, publicly expose cases of abuse within their particular institution, reveal how powerfully sanctions are brought to bear on those who refuse to tailor their information to the demands of their superiors. In most cases studied the institutions fail to respond to the internal complaints and warnings of dissidents, and so-called public 'whistleblowers' either lose their jobs or are demoted.

Just as members of hierarchies are penalised for stepping out of line, so conformity and orthodoxy are rewarded. In the 1940s, Lysenko won rapid promotion in the intensely hierarchical society of the Soviet Union because he managed to produce a new and spurious form of Darwinism, one more suited to the ideology of the ruling élite. He 'fought his way to recognition not by laborious experiment and careful logic, but with the weapons of the mediaeval schoolman: appeal to the authority of official philosophy, and zeal against heretics.'[9]

In time, what begins to happen in most hierarchies is that, other things such as competence being equal, those who are most assiduous in tailoring information and observing taboos tend to get promoted. Thus the hierarchy slowly comes to be packed with conventional, orthodox thinkers, all of whom share the same increasingly inaccurate view of the world. As a result, it becomes steadily more resistant to change, and the policies it pursues become less and less appropriate. To make matters worse, of course, as we have seen, hierarchies *already* have an in-built tendency to favour inappropriate coarse-grained policies. If internal dissent grows, it has to be suppressed; if criticism mounts from people outside the hierarchy, a crisis eventually develops. Instead of merely accepting distorted information from their juniors according to tacit rules, members of the hierarchy may then actually start *demanding* distorted information, behaving rather like the Russians in the battle of Port Arthur, in the Russo–Japanese war of 1904–5. The Russian Officers used to do a verbal drill with their men: 'Front Rank, tell me why the Japanese are fools?' In chorus, the soldiers would reply: 'Because when attacking, their firing line extends widely.' Yet ultimately the Russians lost the battle *because* the Japanese extended their firing line when attacking: the Russians were still locked in a military doctrine made obsolete by the invention of the magazine rifle, making sure their men were locked into it too.

Hierarchies can react just as aggressively and irrationally when they come in for what may be perfectly valid criticism from outside: 'After a senior member of the Science Policy Research Unit at Sussex University questioned planning forecasts by the Electricity Council during a debate on nuclear power, the Chairman of the Council and an influential adviser to the government, Sir Francis Tombs, cancelled a £3,000 annual grant to the Unit. He then banned from the Council's offices editions of the Electrical Review which carried an article by the Unit critical of the electrical industry's forecasting methods. The decision to cancel the grant, he told the Unit – one of very few groups conducting independent research into nuclear policy – was dictated by financial considerations. Yet a few months later the Council's annual report showed that it made an operating profit last year of £16.8 million and spent £4.8 million on publicity and exhibitions.'[10]

In addition to displaying intolerance of criticism, a hierarchy which has become detached from reality will also start carrying out a form of 'positive vetting' on its own members, constantly checking to make sure that they share the 'correct' ideology. This process can be seen at work in the 1982 Thatcher government. As the gap widens between what monetarism is supposed to achieve ('real' jobs), and what it actually achieves (no jobs), a strain is placed on the loyalty of members of the government, so more loyalty is examined for and demanded. A recent article[11] describes how senior civil servants, as well as being screened for anti-Muscovite zeal, are also being vetted for their commitment to the Thatcherite monetary policy in a way reminiscent of McCarthy's declarations of loyalty demanded in the United States at the height of the cold war period of supposed Communist threat.

Apart from having a profoundly negative effect on individual members, this distracts hierarchy members from their function within it. Instead of furthering the aims of the institution, it forces them to spend more and more time protecting themselves from possible retribution from their superiors. This process has been well described by Professor Chris Argyris of Harvard University: 'The result of such action, on the part of the superior, is to create defensiveness in the subordinate. The subordinate now finds himself constantly checking on all details, lest he is "caught" by the superior. However the activity of the organisation is not carried forward with such behaviour. The result is simply one of making the subordinates, (and usually their subordinates) more defensive. Their response is to build up organisational defences in order to protect themselves. For example, in one case where executives were managed by detail, the subordinates created the "JIC" file, which stands for "Just-in-case" some superior asks. This file was kept up to date by several lower-level managers working full time, and countless other people working part-time. The JIC file is an organisational defence to threat experienced by individuals at various levels.'[12]

The defensiveness described here tends to make worse an already bad situation. As people within the hierarchy become more anxious to defend their positions, they begin to form themselves into factions and alliances, each one committed to particular views and courses of action. These hinder the flow of information even more by interfering with the informal networks which, as we saw earlier, are so essential to the gathering of reliable, accurate and relevant information.

As the hierarchy becomes more and more sensitive to criticism, both from within and from outside, its members are forced to waste more and more time and energy in generating information which has no other purpose than to bolster their own position. This can be seen very clearly in the case of the CEGB. Between 1970 and 1979, it was involved in an intensely acrimonious internal debate over what type of nuclear power station to build, a British or an American model. As time went on, people became identified with certain camps, and the CEGB was split at board level, which led to resignations, and people being forced off the Board. Glyn England, the former Chairman of the CEGB, had earlier produced a report with an economist demonstrating the 'clear' economic benefits of the AGR over the PWR and other types of power station. The current Chairman, Sir Walter Marshall, is, however, a PWR man. Inside the CEGB, this debate over AGR versus PWR has had the effect of generating vast amounts of paperwork, designed to support each of the two camps in their diametrically opposed views and diverting them from their proper task - effectively running the

CEGB. Outside it, there has been much time and energy devoted to lobbying on behalf of both sides.

Over the years, the CEGB has come under increasing attack from outside bodies. The latest and most well-informed of these attacks came from the Monopolies Commission, which referred to 'seriously defective policy' and drew attention to an 'atrocious record on building power stations'. Two years have passed since this appeared, and the CEGB has still not replied to it. The chief reason for the delay is thought to be the fact that the CEGB has been too busy preparing literally tons of documents for the Sizewell B enquiry, in which it has to defend its decision to build a new PWR.[13] The result is that just as the CEGB is engaged in a fruitless and ineffectual debate *internally* over the AGR/PWR controversy, it is also bogged down in a sterile debate with its *external* critics.

Of course, the CEGB is not the only hierarchy to find itself in this kind of dilemma, and there is evidence to suggest that many very different institutions can fall victim to the same pattern of faction-fighting and internecine battles. To a greater or lesser extent, these splits and battles occur in most hierarchical institutions at periodic intervals. In the case of the CEGB, when such periodic crises do occur, huge amounts of largely irrelevant information and argument are flung back and forth by the participants as they fight to protect their position. This in turn places an enormous strain on the information-gathering and processing resources of the institution, which responds in a number of alarming ways. These have been highlighted in an interesting experiment entitled 'Information Input Overload' carried out by James G. Miller, Director of the Mental Health Research Institute of the University of Michigan.[14] It looked at five different information processing systems: cell, organ, individual, face-to-face group, and social organisation. A suitable signal was fed into each of the information processing systems and the output observed. In the case of the human subject, for example, a pattern of five lights in the shape of a person's outstretched fingertips was illuminated in various patterns. The subject had to mimic the pattern of illuminated light. Similar inputs were fed into the other systems. The experimenters gradually increased the rate at which the information was fed in for processing, and recorded how well the subjects did. They found that at low information-handling rates all the systems gave relevant responses – pressed the correct buttons in the human case. At higher rates the responses became increasingly irrelevant and unrelated to the output. In the human case, for example, the subjects pressed the wrong buttons, although they did not stop pressing buttons.

The various ways in which the systems studied dealt with this information input overload were omission, only some of the information being processed; error, the wrong response to the input being made; and filtering, systematic omission of certain classes of information.

Such processes are precisely what we see in many hierarchies today: censoring of information, either tacitly by subordinates, or explicitly, by superiors; the operation of taboos; the suppression of dissent, both internal and external; and witch-hunting. These are all means of cutting information input and allowing the hierarchy as such to cope with the information overload. Similarly, ideologies such as Marxism, Conservatism, Monetarism, and so on, are all filters, which process information input and enable it to be handled by the groups concerned.

In the experiment just cited, the researchers dealt with very simplified systems and fed in very simple information, so we should be very cautious about extrapolating to real institutions and real situations. Nevertheless, it is the common experience of most people that institutions do tend to pursue policies unrelated or inappropriate to the problems they are dealing with. These then provoke further public criticism, which puts the institution even more on the defensive. The entire process could be represented as in Fig 13.

In institutions which are under information input overload there is little attempt to examine and deal with its causes. Just as in the examples studied by Miller, the subjects carry on processing incompetently, and producing irrelevant output, so do hierarchical institutions. If we put all these ideas together, the variety-attentuation of information, coarse-grained policies, distortion of information and information input overload engendered by internal warfare, we should not be surprised to note that many of our institutions are producing 'irrelevant output'.

We can clearly see this process at work in the medical profession, a hierarchy which produces many examples of irrelevant output. In this case, inappropriate or counter-productive policies are aimed at enhancing the status of medical practitioners, with benefit to the patient coming a poor second. Vast amounts of money have been poured, for example, into glamorous and status-enhancing heart transplant operations, but the NHS has made only feeble attempts to implement preventive medicine, which is widely accepted to be a more cost-effective way of reducing deaths caused by heart disease.[15] One study, for instance, indicated that spending $1-2 million on preventive medicine, counselling people to change their habits, has saved $4

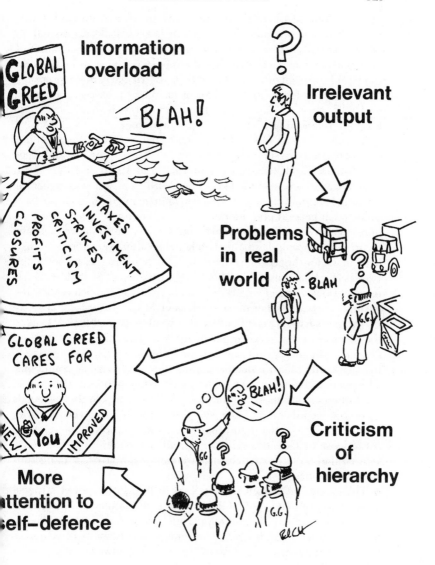

Fig 13   An institution suffering information overload

million alone in disability payments in an area of Finland. Other research has shown that the victims of heart attacks do as well, or better, at home, in comparison with treatment in intensive care units.[16]

It is also widely accepted that the medical profession has become more and more intrusive in its methods, particularly in the process of birth. Twenty-five years ago half of all births took place at home, under the care of a midwife, whereas most births these days are in hospital, often under the care of an obstetrician.

Marjorie Tew, a medical statistician, has analysed the published data of two national perinatal surveys carried out by the Royal College of Obstetrics and Gynaecology in 1958 and 1970, and the official annual statistics of still-births. Crude death rates were far higher for births in hospital with active obstetric management, than for births at home or in general practitioner maternity units with the supportive, non-interventive care of midwives and GPs. Analysis showed that the death rate in hospital remained higher even after every allowance had been made for the greater proportion of births in hospital being at high risk before the onset of labour. The evidence is that obstetric interventions, none of which were scientifically tested before their use became general, do not make birth safer in the majority of cases.[17]

Another survey, carried out by Dr David Stewart,[18] looked back to the nineteenth century, comparing midwife birth then with obstetric delivery. The survey contained a bias, of course, in that in the past only the rich could afford a doctor, a good diet, and hygienic conditions. The poor, who tended to be undernourished, in poorer health, and in less sanitary housing, could only afford a midwife. On these grounds alone the records might be expected to show that midwife deliveries were more dangerous than obstetrician ones, simply because of the conditions. In fact, the evidence revealed the contrary. The study showed that obstetrician deliveries were more than twice as dangerous as midwife ones.

This irrelevant output can be seen in terms of a power struggle between obstetricians and GPs. In the true manner of hierarchies, parts of the medical profession have adopted practices which offer no practical benefits and which consume a vast amount of resources which might be better spent elsewhere. They do, however, improve the status of those in power in the hierarchy.

Much academic research has been carried out into organisations and the people who work in them which supports what I have had to say in this chapter. The type of behaviour which I have described as tending to be produced by hierarchies, for instance, Professor Argyris calls 'Model 1 type behaviour'. 'People programmed with Model 1 theories of action produce Model 1 group and organisational dynamics that include quasi-solution of conflict, uncertainty avoidance, mistrust, conformity, saving face, intergroup rivalry, invalid information for important problems and valid information for unimportant ones, misperception, miscommunication and parochial interests. These, in turn, produce ineffectual problem-solving and decision-making. Under such conditions, top administrators become frustrated and upset with results and react by seeking to increase control, by increasing secrecy about their own tactics and strategies, and by demanding loyalty of subordinates that borders on complete agreement with their views.'[19]

This view is similar to one of the Civil Service in Britain put forward by one of Margaret Thatcher's senior advisers: 'The typical civil servant devotes himself to survival not to action. He is a drudge and a pessimist, lacking both faith and energy. Having presided over Britain's 30-year decline, the bureaucracy thinks it cannot be reversed: few, if any, civil servants believe that the country can be saved. Additionally, they are marked by occupational deformities. Survival burns them out, so that when they get to the top and have to act, they are exhausted.'[20]

The processes I have identified in institutional hierarchies which impair their efficiency are the following:

1 Information exchange is governed by the desire to maintain or increase personal status rather than to determine the truth of any matter; this leads to distorted information flows.

2 Superiors are initially fed information censored by subordinates who anticipate the required censorship. In time the superiors come to specify how information is censored.

3 The allocation of blame or praise becomes the most important activity, rather than simply establishing how a failure arose. More and more time is spent by individuals in protecting themselves, and producing memos and reports justifying and recording the reasons for any decision, to guard against future retribution.

4 Lateral communication between members is inhibited, due to the initial hierarchic structure, the development of cliques, secrecy, factional alliances, and inter-departmental rivalries; information progressively loses variety as it rises through the hierarchy. This accentuates the tendency to produce outputs based on models without requisite variety.

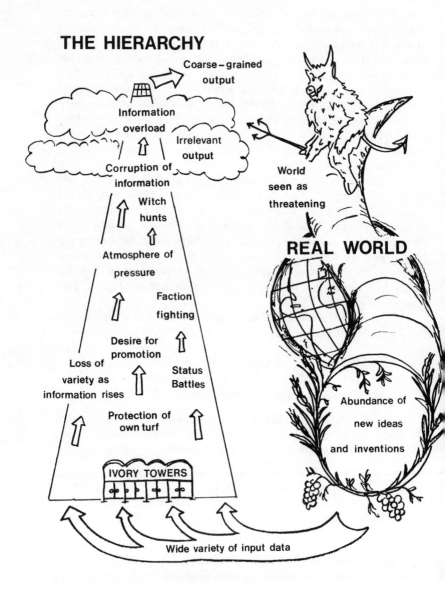

THE HIERARCHY

Coarse – grained output

Information overload

Irrelevant output

Corruption of information

Witch hunts

Atmosphere of pressure

Faction fighting

Desire for promotion

Status Battles

Loss of variety as information rises

Protection of own turf

IVORY TOWERS

Wide variety of input data

World seen as threatening

REAL WORLD

Abundance of new ideas and inventions

Fig 14   A hierarchy

5 In the atmosphere of pressure and crisis which inevitably develops, members spend more and more time and energy processing and generating information related to attempts to protect their own positions. This inevitably leads to information overload, and irrelevant output, from these people themselves and from the hierarchy as a whole.

6 As the inevitable crisis develops, orthodoxy and its associated witch hunts – attempts to simplify and deal with the crisis – become more pronounced. Unorthodox views are seen as heretical, if they come from insiders, and mischievous trouble-making if from outsiders.

7 Insiders pointing out valid discrepancies between ideology and reality are disciplined rather than rewarded. Outsiders become the object of propaganda attacks, impugning their methods and personalities, rather than dealing with issues.

8 Private goals develop which are different from the stated aims of the institution, and are basically attempts to maintain or enhance prestige.

The main elements of this process can be illustrated as in Fig 14. The outputs of institutional hierarchies will tend therefore to be:

1 *Irrelevant*: decisions and policy are not related to the stated aims of the hierarchy.

2 *Coarse-grained*: not necessarily appropriate, optimal, or even productive as related to the problems in hand.

3 *Out of step*: the length of time it takes to process information within the hierarchy, and the coarse-grained nature of any output (with long planning and completion times) causes the hierarchy to be out of step at any moment with the real world in terms of plant, manpower or policy. In time the hierarchy becomes increasingly inefficient, requiring more and more resources to achieve the same result, or even acting in a counter-productive manner.

8 *ALTERNATIVES TO HIERARCHIES*

If the situation in all our large hierarchic organisations is as bad as I have implied in the previous chapter, we may wonder how anything gets done at all. It is clearly not the case that all hierarchies produce bad decisions all the time. The lives of most people who live in countries with such institutions is undeniably better than it was 150 years ago. We are better fed, better clothed and have better health. But can we identify the reasons why some of our institutions work better than others?

In Chapter 6 I introduced the idea of an interlock diagram, a network which provides lateral access to gatekeepers and tacit knowledge. I looked at how such a self-assembling network could be conceived of as a control system with requisite variety, because it is capable of accurately modelling the full complexity of reality, even if each individual cannot. In Chapter 5 I considered the vital role played by networks in transmitting both the formal and tacit knowledge that is essential for getting things done. In Chapter 7 I showed that, in theory, institutions, always hierarchic to some degree, do not have requisite variety, because there are too many barriers to lateral communication between different parts of the hierarchy, and variety is lost as information is fed upwards. So in many institutions the policy-making models are woefully inadequate.

Putting these elements of my analysis together indicates where the key to the success of hierarchic institutions is likely to lie. I have indicated that institutions function better where the degree of lateral communication between members of the hierarchy is high, allowing internal interlock networks to form. Since these networks possess requisite variety, adequate solutions can be proposed, accepted and acted upon. Where they do not form, people in hierarchies tend to be working with wrong information, or wrong models, with nobody listening to them, even if they are right.

Donald Schon describes the phenomenon like this: 'There are formal networks within established organisations, eg. the networks, related to command, information or distribution of goods within a large firm. And there are the informal or "underground" networks connecting persons, groups and organisations. These are used to circumvent, supplement or replace the operations of formal organisational systems.

'Informal networks have long served to enable people to get things done when the formal network has failed. The Russian *tolkatch*, for example, created through his own person informal relationships of exchange between units of Soviet industry. Functioning illegally, he compensated for errors in planning and enabled industrial systems to work which would otherwise have been hopelessly paralysed. All large organisations, military and governmental bureaucracies are famous for having their interpersonal networks for exchanging favours on which much business depends. The very life of social systems has depended on the operation of informal networks.'[1]

It follows from this that institutions operate more successfully when the rigidity of their hierarchical structure is relaxed enough to take advantage of the initiative of subordinates. Superiors must delegate and allow their subordinates to act on their higher-variety models. What appears to happen is routine rule-bending or breaking, in which the subordinates seem to do what they are told, but in fact systematically deceive their superiors, not for any personal gain, or through negligence, but simply in order to get things done. When a catastrophe occurs, the lurid headlines read, 'Vital Safety Rules Ignored' or 'Standing Orders Ignored in Horror Incident', the implication being that in this particular case the neglect of the rule was an exception. In fact, rule-breaking is commonplace. It is simply not possible centrally to control all the actions that take place in an organisation, and attempts to do so are counter-productive. People facing the realities of the situation are usually better able to discover ways of doing things than their superiors, who are too remote from what is going on.

A recent example comes from the well-publicised case of an RAF pilot who accidentally shot down a £7-million RAF Jaguar. The initial press reports, including headlines such as, 'I Forgot I was Armed – Missile Pilot', implied stupidity and forgetfulness on the part of the pilot. But as the court martial unfolded it became clear that the accident happened because it is standard procedure to break the rules, otherwise few RAF flights would get off the ground. For the rules state that, firstly, 'any missile carried on the aircraft should be secured against being fired by means of links, locks, or plugs'; secondly, bright yellow notices saying 'Aircraft Armed' warn the pilots that they are carrying live missiles; and thirdly, 'the master arming switch has to be taped and secured in a safe position.' These safety devices, in fact, could not be fitted to the relevant planes, Phantoms, and a Squadron Leader testified that it would also be too dangerous for planes to fly with them in place. Various members of the squadron testified that they had never come across either the safety links and plugs or the statutory warning notice.[2] The pressure on both pilots and officers to flout the rules is indicated by the comment of a Falkland veteran pilot who said, 'Officially, you could quote the rules and refuse to take off, but you wouldn't have much of a career left.'[3]

Any large hierarchic organisation such as British Rail, British Telecom, bus companies and airlines, have a set of rules which have evolved over a period of time, and which are usually gathered together into a book or chart and displayed on walls or distributed to each employee. These have usually developed in response to organisational failure. When the railways were being developed, for example, if a train broke down another engine was sent out at full speed to investigate, often at night, without lights. After the inevitable fatal crashes, rules were introduced forbidding this, and stating exactly what was to be done instead. Crashes have continued to occur, however, due to unforeseen circumstances or new eventualities, to be followed by new and more complicated rules. After a while any rule book will contain some obsolete rules which it is pointless to follow, and some rules which have unintended effects. If all these are obeyed to the letter, the system will not be able adequately to function. If a driver, for example, is supposed to check that his train carries a full set of safety equipment, detonators, flags and so on, and if any of these are missing, if any of the gauges are not working, or if the screen is at all dirty, he can legitimately refuse to take his train out. A responsible driver does not take the train out if the defects he finds are serious, of course, but in the minor cases, he merely reports the irregularity at the end of his shift.

Research shows that a work-to-rule, used as a form of industrial action, means essentially that a group of people work exactly as their management has instructed them to. The organisation concerned might therefore be expected to function better than usual. In fact, things grind to a halt. If everyone followed their instructions to the letter and worked to rule simultaneously, the country would collapse overnight. What can be understood by this is that the country is only kept going by a large part of the working population systematically ignoring or bending the instructions of their management, and organising their work as efficiently and as competently as only they know how to.

A good example of what happens when people are not prepared to break the rules was described recently in the *Daily Telegraph*.[4] One Sunday, a number of passengers at Hamble station moved towards an incoming train, expecting to get on it, unaware of British Rail's decision to save money by reducing the number of stops on Sunday trains. 'We only stopped to tell you that we don't stop here on Sundays,' said the guard. 'If you want to catch a train, you'll have to walk to the next station at Netley, where we do stop on Sundays.' Passengers then watched in disbelief as the train pulled out without them, and they had to trek the mile or so to Netley.

A BR spokesman described the action of the guard as a 'little over-zealous', saying that he was carrying out his duties to the letter, but that his common sense should have told him that he might have allowed the passengers onto the stopped train.

Generally speaking the higher one goes in a hierarchical organisa-tion, the less one finds formal written rules to be followed, their place being taken by a system of tacitly understood rules. Such rules, like riding a bicycle or learning a language, are so complicated that they cannot be formalised, and have to be picked up through experience. Those who pick them up the quickest get on the fastest. Alongside these rules are others indicating how and when and how far one can break the first kind.

To show how rule-breaking aids an organisation, let me take an example from a large British industry, with an annual turnover of several billion pounds, which delivers a certain commodity to most households and businesses in the country. Let us call this industry British Trokken. British Trokken is divided into about six regions, each run by an executive board comprising heads of various functions such as finance, engineering, marketing, distribution, safety, personnel, research and development. Within each region there is a corporate planning department, whose job it is to undertake long-term planning into alternative Trokken supplies, distribution methods, markets and so on. Within Trokken, as in most hierarchies, people only deal with their immediate superiors, or with people on the same level in different departments. Corporate planning is an exception, in that its head, although at least two levels below the board, deals directly with the heads of each function.

Corporate planning does a lot of operations research and in so doing uses many computers. They also need to be supplied with the most up-to-date equipment, so every few years they order new and better computers. This, however, can cause problems at board level since it is they who vet purchases. Their attitude tends to be, 'Haven't they got enough computers already? Didn't we buy them one only a couple of years ago?' Such a question results from a low variety model. The actual official system, the formal rules for vetting and authorising the purchase of computers, is very complex, but in simple terms requires that a proposal be written which is sent to a financial officer, below board level but above the corporate planning one. If the value is below a certain figure, the 'signing limit', this man can sign the authorisation. The financial authoriser is, however, a timid man who does not want to put a foot wrong, meaning that he sends all applications on to the board. He thinks that because an amount is below the signing limit, the board will 'nod through' the application. The board, however, has usually taken the opposite view: 'Why hasn't he signed it? Must be something suspicious here', and has tended to turn down such proposals. With experience of failing to get computers in this way, the head of corporate planning decided on an unofficial strategy. Exploiting his unique access to all the heads of functions at board level, he now individually sees each one and lobbies them. He indicates to each that they are unique in being approached in this way, and points out the advantages to their particular department of the new computer and its facilities, also emphasising the value of corporate planning to them. This activity of course breaks certain tacit and formal rules, such as the tacitly agreed status of the head of corporate planning being that he only has access to the other heads to discuss official business, not for the discussion of purchases. If his boss found out about this unofficial activity, he would be very angry. This unofficial method of achieving ends, and the rule-bending involved in it is typical of the way things really get done in all effective hierarchies, to the benefit of all concerned.

But while it is true that informal networks and rule-breaking are to some degree what make institutions work, they can only function if the authorities turn a blind eye to them. In especially rigid hierarchic situations, subordinates are too frightened to engage in unofficial activity for fear of official reprisals if they are caught out. This is, of course, what happens in totalitarian regimes of both the Right and the Left. In the Soviet Union the rigidity of the state bureaucracy is perhaps one reason why the country is far behind the West in some technical developments. The rulers are so aware of the power of lateral communication and so determined to prohibit it, that the use of Xerox machines, for instance, is restricted to higher party officials, and the use of the telephone is similarly curtailed. For both the telephone and the Xerox are enhancers of lateral communication. Unofficial networks that function do so by means of the 'samizdat' circulation of subversive typescript, using typewriters and carbon copies.

A spectrum of institutions can be envisaged, with, at one extreme, the rigid, rule-bound, bureaucratic ones, where lateral communication is discouraged and rules are strictly adhered to; and, on the other, more relaxed institutions, where lateral communication flourishes and a blind eye is turned to rule-bending, so long as it achieves the organisation's aims. The 1970s reorganisation of the Health Service has tended to create a more rigidly bureaucratic and hierarchic organisation than the original. The increased use of committees, reports, memos, and monologue communication have replaced informal groups and dialogue. More and more formal systems, such as the use of Authorising Committees, have been introduced, ostensibly to control expenditure, but the system has in fact required increased amounts of money to do less and less. The paradox is that the more formal systems you introduce, the less effective the system as a whole seems to become. If the man at British Trokken were either too timid or too restricted by bureaucracy, or pressure of time, or geography, to engage in his unofficial liaison, he would not get his computers. That is exactly what is happening within the Health Service. One consultant, however, has told me how he has tried to bring a semblance of order into the enormously complicated bureaucratic structure. Together with other colleagues he has organised an unofficial dinner club, which meets at varying intervals, and at which methods of implementing policy and desirable action are facilitated. The members find this approach much more effective than official committees and procedures.

People at the top of hierarchies, as I have said, tend to end up with an inadequate, low-variety model of the situations they are dealing with, based on the wrong data. The only way this can be overcome is for someone lower down, or outside, the hierarchy, who is immersed in a higher-variety network, to talk to someone at the top, thereby increasing the variety of the top person's models. In strictly hierarchic organisations this cannot be done, as it threatens the status of the subordinate's boss: only he can feed on the royal jelly of his superiors. In the Police Force, for example, constables do not have direct, casual access to commissioners, except when they are being reprimanded or receiving medals. By contrast, Robert Jungk tells the story in his book *Brighter than a Thousand Suns*[5] of how the atomic bomb was developed as a result of an informal network circumventing the official hierarchic system. A group of refugee scientists from Nazism had access to Roosevelt's ear, through the friendship of one of his top advisers. When the same group realised that the Germans were not developing the bomb, however, they tried, without success, to get Roosevelt to drop the project by the same channels: they don't always 'work'.

The question to be asked is this: if informal networks, rule-breaking and short-cuts to the top are some of the features of successful action in organisations, would it be possible to facilitate the development of these features in less successful organisations? In most of the examples I have given, the features seem largely to have arisen by accident rather than design.

Consider the possibility of encouraging informal networks to form. If you were a bureaucrat charged by a higher authority to 'get everyone in your department on friendly terms', what steps could you take? A career bureaucrat might issue a memo, instructing his subordinates to 'indulge in frequent informal social contact in accordance with the attached schedule supplied by the Personnel Department. Any failure to carry out such informal contact in the amount specified will lead to disciplinary procedures.' But someone with more common sense would organise a programme of activities – parties, outings or flower-arranging lessons – to attract people without official compulsion. A colleague of mine who once worked at Guy's Hospital told me that there are numerous bars near it which are always full of medical staff discussing informal hospital business. Good firms supply facilities for their staff as perks. But more can be done.

Regular reorganisation

I once worked for a civil engineering consultant, whose 50 or so office staff were housed in three Georgian houses linked by new connecting passages. Teams of three to five engineers and draughtsmen worked in the formerly elegant rooms, each team working on several projects at once. What was remarkable was the speed with which the teams formed into amoeba-like organisms, with their own private cosmologies, language and aims. 'Outsiders' from the same firm coming into the room were subjected to concerted ridicule and barracking. Up to a point this worked very well; it encouraged team-work and a strong desire to succeed in the projects in hand, since group honour was at stake. But if the teams had become too entrenched it would have severely restricted lateral communication, the informal exchange of information between them and other groups. So it was a matter of deliberate policy on the part of the senior partners to shift people around regularly, usually at the end of each project. The policy worked very well. It was very common for a new member of a team to lean over someone else's drawing-board to ask why he was doing that detail in that way, since they had done it differently on the previous project. There would then follow an informal drawing-board conference. This system helped undermine the relevance paradox, and keep the organisation functioning as a whole, rather than as fragmented component parts.

Quality circles

These have flourished in Japan for nearly 20 years. About 100 British firms have adopted the technique in the last few years, and most are very enthusiastic. Basically, groups of workers are set up, and their task is first to identify, and then to solve, any problems that exist in the firm. They meet at regular intervals, an hour a week, for example, and pursue solutions in a rigorous way, tracking down, say, alternative solutions and providing costings. Their solutions are then presented to management. At Wedgwood, for example, handles had been falling off cups for as long as anyone could remember. As a result of two months' investigation by the relevant quality circle, it was discovered that the reason lay in faulty storage; the handles were falling off because they were being kept at the wrong temperature. When this was corrected Wedgwood were able to save £20,000 a year. Then Abbey Hosiery Mills was unhappy with the yarn supplied by Courtaulds. One of their 12 quality circles went to Courtaulds' mill in pursuit of the source of the problem, and found, among other things, that Courtaulds and Abbey workers were using different terminology for the same things in connection with the yarn.

The practical benefits of quality circles are obvious: they save money and improve quality. Marks and Spencer, for example, are so impressed that they are encouraging all their suppliers to introduce them. They are also very successful in motivating workers. 'Members say it gives them true job satisfaction and makes the workplace seem like a second home. Taking part in a quality circle discussion can boost the confidence of even the most timid worker.'[6] An article by a quality circle consultant which appeared recently in the *Health and Social Services Journal*[7] reports three cases where the circles achieved ratios of investment cost to savings of 3:1, 5:1 and 8:1. The same article also gives two case studies of quality circles in hospitals where in one case accident rates dropped by 50 per cent as a result of their introduction, and use of space and personnel were also improved. There was better communication between nursing groups and planning groups in the other. Some managers, of course, are not enamoured with the technique, for it is inevitable that in more rigid hierarchic structures those higher up should feel threatened by lateral communication between their subordinates which might show up their own shortcomings, or make some of their tasks redundant. This does not seem to have deterred the Japanese, however.

Quality circles offer, then, a good way of improving lateral communication, by the setting up of formal networks which inevitably engender a good deal of informal contact. Improvements are made by ordinary workers with high-variety models, who then have direct access to management.

Theatrical mechanisms

One of the underlying tendencies of hierarchies is, as I have said, for the people in them to become more concerned with processing information in such a way that it merely enhances their position in the hierarchy. One information-processing strategy that does this is the taboo on negative comment on the performance of a superior. If the members of a department, for example, do not feel that their head is fulfilling his duties, there is little they can do about it, other than going above his head.

One way round this problem is the frivolous-sounding expedient of giving a party. Every Christmas, instead of going to a posh hotel for a formal dinner, the departments of some institutions organise private parties, an essential feature of which is a revue, usually put on by the most junior staff. In these, all members of staff can be ruthlessly lampooned and their shortcomings mercilessly caricatured, to the merriment of all concerned. It is invariably the powerful who get lampooned the most mercilessly on these occasions, although everyone's idiosyncracies and shortcomings are pointed out. Because of the generally relaxed atmosphere, people do not generally take offence, since the information about their behaviour reaches them in a way which is not threatening. If in everyday life you were to go and tell a superior that he was always embarrassingly drunk at meetings, he would discipline you for insubordination, and then block out the information by denying it or producing 'evidence' to the contrary. But the revue allows the presentation of otherwise unpalatable facts in rather the same way that dreams allow the presentation of unpalatable fears and events to the mind, which in the conscious state may be blocked out.

A revue such as this is, of course, nothing more than a variant on the informal mechanisms considered in Chapter 1 – Skimmerton riding, blood and bread riots and so on. Through these means villagers were able to operate a considerable degree of self-government, and give feedback to their superiors, the local lords.

That such a frivolous-sounding mechanism could seriously be considered an aid to organisational function may seem a little far-fetched. And yet as serious and dedicated a body as the Parachute Regiment incorporates a revue as part of the training of their men. Recruits dress up in bizarre costumes, frequently drag, and perform skits lampooning parts of army life, including the foibles of their superior officers. Men were specifically told that unless they took part in the performances in a wholehearted manner, their chances of being selected for the regiment would diminish.

Worker directors

It would clearly be valuable if it were accepted that employees at low levels in a hierarchy could go over the heads of superiors, right to the top. The indication would seem to be, therefore, that every large institution, government bureaucracy or large private company, should have some form of lower-level representation at board level. The point is not so much that the 'worker director' so created should represent the grievances of workers to senior management, or that he should convey the feelings of the management to the workers, but simply that someone from the bottom should be given the *status* of board member, so that if the need arose he could approach the senior management informally.

When I was working at the Open University we used to have a joke that as mere research students we were effectively invisible to those higher up the hierarchy. If and when you got a higher degree you became semi-transparent, but only when you became tenured did you become fully visible. Of course, the man at the top cannot afford to have every Tom, Dick or Harry dropping in on him whenever he feels like it. So if a small number of people are elected to meet regularly to discuss the workings of any large organisation, conditions and output should improve. In Japan and West Germany worker directors have long been part of the scene. Such a system also apparently improves industrial relations.

Lateral information routes

So deeply ingrained in modern societies are the concepts of hierarchic organisation that, when faced with a bureaucratic malfunction, the only response of the bureaucrat is to apply more bureaucracy, in turn frequently creating more problems. An example of bureaucratic blindness to reality is provided by the way one educational establishment approached the problem of audio-visual equipment. A great deal of such equipment was being used, but different departments were buying different makes and types of slide projectors, cameras, videos and so on; these were mostly incompatible and required a large number of different spares to be stocked. The problem was addressed by the bureaucracy of the institution in time-honoured fashion: by the setting up of a committee of senior academics to vet all purchases of equipment.

It is very hard for a would-be purchaser to explain exactly why he wants a particular piece of equipment. Only he thoroughly understands the conditions for its use, and these will often be very hard to transmit via a written request to the vetting committee. For the vetting committee does not possess the right tacit knowledge, and has low-variety models. Frustration and time-wasting will be the result, as requests are shuffled backwards and forwards, with requests for further clarification. For the committee members, too, this is also a very boring and time-wasting process.

The problem would be better seen as a failure of lateral communication within the system, and the simplest solution would be to ensure that the relevant people in each department were thoroughly familiar with the audio-visual technician and with others with particular expertise, so that they were free to approach each other to discuss purchases. It would be much more productive to take steps to improve the flow of information at the appropriate level, instead of thinking bureaucratically about putting superiors in charge, setting up committees and generating more paper.

I have already mentioned how the firm of engineering consultants overcame the type of problem where individual sections work independently to the detriment of the whole organisation. There were numerous opportunities for the engineers at the consultant's to design or make specifications, oblivious of the fact that someone in another office a few feet away had done a similar job in a better and cheaper way. But the problem was not tackled by setting up a committee to vet designs with forms for requesting use of a particular design; the system worked by moving staff around from team to team, and by encouraging an atmosphere in which they felt free to wander up to other people's drawing boards and poke their noses in.

My suggestion is not, of course, that all formal procedures should be abolished, merely that those in charge should think very carefully before they introduce more of them, and always ask the question, Is the problem I am attempting to solve a symptom of something else? Can it be solved by promoting lateral communication, by altering the physical layout of the building or by organising quality circles or social events with revues? For there is no doubt that increased informal contact improves the functioning of an organisation.

A recent article in the *International Herald Tribune* extolled the 'brilliant record' of the Cavendish Laboratory at Cambridge, the world's foremost molecular biology laboratory, which has produced six Nobel Prize winners.[8] What clearly interested the journalist was the 'overcrowded and undistinguished-looking' place that housed the lab.

'Until 1962, the unit was housed at the Cavendish, the Cambridge University physics laboratory where scientists and technicians were separated according to rank. Dr Perutz changed that when he moved the unit to its present site. He introduced the egalitarian atmosphere that, his colleagues agree, is largely responsible for their unusual scientific fecundity. There are no grand offices. Dr Brenner sits in a cluttered little room. Senior staff members have tiny cubicles, managing research in the laboratory itself rather than ordering teams around from behind desks. Dr Perutz perceived overcrowding to be a virtue; as commonly happens now, a biologist and a chemist standing in a corridor may discuss a difficult synthesis or the problems involved in breeding bacteria.' In addition, the Director 'makes it a point to keep the administration of the laboratory informal. "I don't know how much anyone spends," he said. "If things get tight, I tell people to take it easy. If spare cash is available, I let them know. They really do respond to appeals to their sense of community." '[8]

Even if there were few direct benefits to be derived from reducing the amount of bureaucracy, and encouraging lateral links, even if it only saves paper and committee time, there are subtler benefits stemming from the fact that such links make people happy. A sociologist friend of mine who studied a British car factory, with the brief of finding out how many people, on average, each worker at the plant knew well enough to chat to regularly, found that each worker only talked to three others, the person up-line from him, the one down-line, and one other. The plant run by the Swedish firm Volvo at Kalmar has replaced the conventional production line invented by Henry Ford with an arrangement of workers in teams of about ten, who build entire vehicles as a team, working out their own labour schedules and days off. Although no great economic case can be made for the scheme, being about as economic as existing methods, it is apparently far better for the workers, absenteeism and days off being far lower than with the conventional system.

In the previous chapter I gave some of the reasons why purely hierarchic organisations are inherently dysfunctional, and so far in this chapter I have indicated how successful hierarchic organisations are never purely hierarchic, and I have also suggested ways in which hierarchic organisations can be improved. I will go further, however, and propose the more radical thesis that in some cases hierarchic structures should be abandoned altogether.

It will be no surprise that my first candidate for this is the CEGB. My view is that the provision and operation of power stations should not be in the hands of a single hierarchic structure. If the single hierarchic institution were supplanted by numerous smaller and less hierarchic ones, communication and hence efficiency would improve.

Let us consider the developing countries. The stereotype of the shanty towns that cluster around many large Third World cities is of filthy hovels inhabited by criminal gangs and prostitutes, which, worse still, are breeding grounds for Communism. But studies have shown that in many cases this image is largely inaccurate. Mangin and Turner made a study of Peruvian shanty towns or *barriadas*,[9] and found that they represent highly-successful solutions to the housing problem presented to their people. Because of administrative costs and builders' profits, government housing can cost as much as twice the equivalent *barriada* dwelling. In addition, the official houses have to be identical, and built and paid for all in one go. *Barriadas*, on the other hand, are built very much as required. A family will illegally invade land on the fringe of the city, and build a temporary structure. As soon as possible this is converted into a permanent brick or concrete one, initially just a roof and four walls. As more money becomes available, internal walls, and perhaps more floors are added. Eventually, each family gets the individual house it wants. As the fringe of original *barriada*-type dwellings moves out, the inner, more durable dwellings are connected to services, schools are built, community councils elected, and so on. Official housing, by contrast, consists of fifteen-storey blocks of identical flats, with services that no one can afford to use. Mangin and Turner cite the case of a family with a goat on the fifteenth floor. They also found that crime and vandalism rates are in fact far lower in the *barriadas* than in the 'official' housing for poor people.

A similarly fine-grained, dispersed solution has quietly been put into action in Britain by Liverpool City Council.[10] 'It funds the people who need new housing to organise the design, construction and management of it themselves, through self-generating, self-reliant co-operatives. Liverpool's first new-built co-operative scheme of 61 homes was funded by the Housing Corporation and is now two-thirds occupied. Nine more, involving 341 families, have been approved, and are at various stages of design and construction.

'It works like this. Local authority tenants living in slum clearance areas or deteriorating tenements organise themselves into groups – so far ranging from 19 to 61 family units – and obtain the management services of one of Liverpool's co-operative development agencies: Cooperative Development Services (CDS), Merseyside Improved Houses or Neighbourhood Housing Services. With its assistance they register as a 'non-equity' housing co-operative with limited liability, locate a suitable site and negotiate to buy it. (So far, nearly all the land has come from Liverpool City Council or the Merseyside Development Corporation.) They then select a firm of architects with whom they design a scheme which is submitted to the DOE for subsidy and yardstick approval, as on all local authority-funded housing association schemes.

'When the houses are built, the co-op members become tenants in their homes, paying standard fair rents, but they are also, collectively, the landlord, responsible for management and maintenance.

'The full significance of events in Liverpool has not yet been grasped nationally. The need for participation by tenants in public housing has been talked about for years. There have been endless research studies and experiments. Occasionally, as at Byker in Newcastle for instance, architects for new schemes have worked closely with the tenants, but they have always remained accountable to the local authority.

'But the Liverpool new-build co-ops are totally different. The tenants are not being asked to participate or be involved – they are actually and firmly in control: they choose the professionals they want to work for them, they choose the site, the layout, the floor plans, the elevations, the brick colour and the landscaping . . . when built, they manage and maintain the estate.

'The implication of all this for architects and other professionals is immense. Only a handful of firms are involved in the work so far but already they have developed a unique new style of working. Instead of being accountable to council committees or housing association managers, they are accountable to the consumers, who are making very different demands on their talents. The architect's vision, technical expertise and design skill are as important as ever, but, in addition, a new range of knowledge and skills has to be learnt.

In place of riots[10]
'The venue is a church in Toxteth, Liverpool 8, Wednesday 14 July 1982 at 20.30. One section of the church has been cleared of pews, and grouped around trestle tables covered with house floor plans are over 70 men and women of all ages. Reflecting the area's 35 per cent unemployment level, many of them are unemployed, the remainder mostly in low-paid manual and service jobs. All of them are currently living in some of Europe's worst housing, crumbling six-storey municipal tenements, often without hot water.

'This is the Mill-Street Co-operative and its members have met in the hall two or three nights a week for over three months, designing their 54 new 'dream houses' with architect Martyn Coppin of Brock Carmichael Associates. Even when the World Cup match between

England and Spain was shown on television, there were no absentees from the co-op meeting.

'Tonight they are finalising details of their floor plans. Some people are opting for a combined kitchen/diner, others a combined living-room/diner, while some want three separate rooms. Coppin moves from table to table, pointing out problems and suggesting ideas on each person's layout:

'"If you want a carpet in your dining room, the last thing you want is French windows into the garden, as that's your only access."

'"Why not switch the sink round so that you can reach the drainer better?"

'"You'll get more space in the living-room if you turn the staircase round the other way."

'Mostly his advice is heeded, occasionally ignored, – it's up to the future occupant to decide – unless the co-op as a whole considers the chosen design so bad as to seriously jeopardise future lettability. In the end, the Mill Street Co-op opts for six basic house types with 16 variations.'

There is no reason why the same principles could not be beneficially applied to supplement or supplant numerous other hierarchic institutions in this country. In both the Netherlands and Denmark, for example, any group of parents, subject to certain conditions, can open a school. There must be a minimum number of pupils, and the mother-tongue and a minimum of maths must be taught, but apart from these and a few other basic stipulations, the schools can be run much as parents want and, unlike our public schools, the fees are fixed at a low rate. The state pays the school a proportion of what it costs them to provide an equivalent school place in a state school, between 85 and 100 per cent of the state's figure, including capital and running costs.

The same principle could be applied to the National Health Service or any other hierarchy. In a homeostatic system, the NHS would have to publish the cost of carrying out its various functions: the cost of a tonsillectomy, an injection, a community health programme, and so on, in much the same way as under homeostatic control the CEGB would have to publish the costs of producing power and pay equivalent private producers, or as the education system in Denmark already has to publish the cost of teaching each student. Private facilities offering the same services could then be set up, and could be paid by right 85–100 per cent of its official price. The public could then choose which service it preferred, NHS or private. Again, maximum charges could be set, to limit élitism. Compulsory health insurance could be introduced, much as motor insurance is mandatory. This would have another homeostatic effect, in that people who did unhealthy things such as drinking or smoking excessively would get lower premiums. Insurance companies might even come to pay for community and preventive health programmes.

The essential feature of the types of initiative described is that a rigid institutional hierarchy is replaced with a much looser network, or smaller institutional hierarchies. This has the effect of allowing competition between various small hierarchies, and winnowing out the least appropriate. In effect, the centre no longer has to have an overall 'theory' or formal knowledge, about how best to organise itself; it simply sets up criteria of performance which small groups try and fulfil, using whatever strategies they think will succeed. Dispersal of control to the 'sharp end' also means less recourse to the rule-breaking and disobedience that occurs in a rigid formal hierarchy. Rules have been replaced by realistic specifications of the results required.

9 COMMUNICATION, LANGUAGE AND BEHAVIOUR

I should like to return to an earlier theme, language and communication, and expand my ideas on it in relation to the behaviour of hierarchies. In Chapter 4 I attempted to establish the overwhelming importance of speaking as the basis of later development. Without continuous communicative interaction throughout childhood, a person's language and personality will remain impoverished. What I am interested in now is not the amount of interaction that takes place, but its quality and type.

A serviceable way of describing the functioning of the human brain is that essentially it is a pattern-recognition and pattern-relating system. A recent theory[1] postulates that the brain, and indeed any nervous system, can extract patterns from the reality to which it is exposed, which are useful for its survival. The patterns which are recognised create corresponding patterns in the brain making up a person's cosmology. Such patterns cannot be seen or located in any one part of the brain; they exist, according to the theory, in the same way as holograms, three-dimensional images which one can study like a piece of sculpture, but which are formed by shining laser light through a two-dimensional film. Just as the patterns formed in a person's brain cannot be located under a microscope, so a holographic image cannot be seen in the two-dimensional film, or be associated with a particular bit of it. This view of the brain's behaviour is known naturally enough as the Holographic Theory.

Clearly, the question of *which* electrical patterns are formed by *which* aspects of external reality depends not only on the individual's brain structure, but also on his cosmology. For example, the sight of children squabbling may trigger very different mental responses: one person may interpret it as bad behaviour and wish to stop it, while another may see it as perfectly normal, and all part of growing up. Similarly, when we see snow, we see little more than something white and cold; an Eskimo, however, will be able to distinguish between several different categories of snow, and will be able to describe the properties of each one.

The point here is that these internal models, once they have been formed, actually determine to a large extent what we perceive and what we don't; since we have fewer models for snow than the Eskimo,

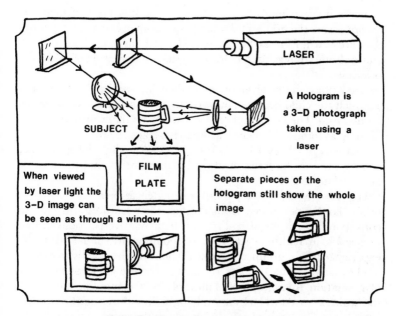

LASER

A Hologram is a 3–D photograph taken using a laser

SUBJECT

FILM PLATE

When viewed by laser light the 3–D image can be seen as through a window

Separate pieces of the hologram still show the whole image

Fig 15   The holographic theory

we will actually fail to notice aspects of it which for him could be a matter of life or death. Furthermore, these models are culturally determined to a degree one doesn't appreciate until one starts to contrast and compare our own with those of other cultures. In the West we view our mothers' and our fathers' brothers as basically the same class of relative, ie., 'uncle', and treat them in a broadly similar way. In Saudi Arabia, however, it is the custom to treat the mother's brother as a friend, someone with whom one can indulge in jokes and horseplay; the father's brother, on the other hand, is a figure of enormous authority and is accorded far greater respect.

Differing internal models can even make us *feel* in different ways – a fact which can make life very difficult for British doctors working in areas with large immigrant populations. Indian and Pakistani notions of how the body functions and what it is composed of, differ markedly from the prevailing Western view, and lead to an entirely different way of experiencing and describing pain. While Western patients are used to distinguishing between 'sharp pains' and 'dull aches' and can usually locate them, an Indian, when asked by a British GP where it hurts, may frequently shudder and say 'All over, doctor'. This naturally considerably complicates the process of diagnosis.

These internal maps or models do not simply grow of their own accord inside the brain, in the same way as an organ or a set of limbs: they are learnt from earliest infancy onwards, as part of every child's cultural inheritance, each culture having a different set of values and priorities.

A key phase in the development of these internal models is the point at which the child begins to fit words to the objects and people he sees around him. The Holographic Theory suggests that words involve the forming of some kind of electrical pattern triggered by the perception of whatever or whoever it is they happen to describe. This in turn acts as precursor to the series of muscular movements that produce the appropriate sound.

We can envisage these patterns or models as being rather like an urban landscape viewed from the air, their features and patterns corresponding to bits of reality, and their relative positions to their *relationship* in reality. Patterns corresponding to similar ideas and experience will be grouped together. When one idea is activated, it will tend to activate adjacent ones, by linkages corresponding to our notion of association. An example of a failure of lateral communication within the brain occurred when I was studying civil engineering. The lecturer introduced Coulomb's Law, which relates the pressure forcing water through soil, the resistance to the flow, and the flow. At the end of the explanation he asked, 'Does anyone see any similarity between this and another well-known physical law?' Nobody could answer him. In fact, the law is essentially the same as Ohm's Law, which relates electrical pressure, electrical resistance, and the flow of electricity. Yet none of the 90 engineers in the room, all of whom were familiar with Ohm's Law, saw the connection, because only their civil engineering landscapes had been activated, and these did not include Ohm's Law.

The patterns in the landscapes of people's minds correspond with the notion of the interlock diagram already described. Every time you think of doing something, such as, 'I must go to Sainsbury's on Friday', an internal and unseen interlock route calls up a node in the diagram which comes back with, 'You can't do that, you're going to be in London all day. Oh yes, and don't forget to tell Fred he's driving.' Floating above the internal landscape barrage balloons can be imagined, with words on them corresponding with the patterns below them. Every time a pattern is activated by reality the appropriate words light up. Thinking is then simply a matter of manipulating the interlock diagram, from reality to the condition you want, with no open loops. Then you simply speak the string of words that are illuminated in the sky above the new diagram: 'Well, go to Sainsbury's on

Saturday, then.' Floating above the barrage balloons will be some other system for getting the words in the order preferred by the culture concerned – a sort of aerial vacuum-cleaner: 'On Saturday we shall visit Sainsbury's.' 'Sainsbury's on Saturdays will be visited,' etc. Of course, I have conceptualised thinking and speaking using a three-dimensional analogy in time. In the holographic theory, the analogous process occurs within a hierarchy of interacting holograms.

It would appear that from a very early age, even before birth, the child is forming these tentative landscapes of the external world within his or her brain. Not long after birth – six months to a year – he or she is trying to fit words to the models. What makes this such a crucial stage in the child's development is the fact that words enable him to communicate and thus check the validity of his models with his parents, and to do this, the parents must listen and respond to him. For the child's words are specifically addressed to them, not to thin air, and it is vital if he is to adjust and refine his models, that the parents take part in the process, correcting and encouraging. When the words and models involved are relatively simple, the kind of feedback demanded of the parent is itself relatively simple, but as the child's models develop in complexity to include feelings and emotional wants as well as more basic object-word relationships, the need for feedback becomes more acute.

Depending on how his parents, and later others, respond, so will the child's models of what communication is develop. For him or her to develop useful models of communication, that is, ones which will enhance his sense of well-being in life, feedback of a particular type is required from his parents. This, although apparently occurring in many daily interchanges between child and parent, is in fact often lacking. The exchange between Johnny and Mummy – 'What time is dinner?' 'Seven o'clock' – is superficially satisfactory. But on a deeper level there may be a misunderstanding. She may be thinking to herself, 'He is wondering if there is time to go outside and play.' But he *may* mean that he feels hungry. Communication has in effect broken down, though neither party is as yet aware of it. In a case like this it may not seem very important, since no doubt the misunderstanding would have emerged later, but in the long run, the accumulated experience of this type of failure has serious effects on the parent-child relationship.

In his dealings with his parents, the child is not only learning daily about the world around him, he is also slowly acquiring a picture of how he fits into that world: cosmology is being developed. If his parents fail to listen to him and give him the feedback he needs, he will not only be prevented from correcting his internal models to fit reality, he will also, over a period of time, come to feel shunned and rejected by the world around him, and the result will be frustration and unhappiness. In addition, as we shall see later, he will form a distorted model of the process of communication itself which he will unconsciously impose on others in later life.

Dr Thomas Gordon, an American psychologist, has done a good deal of work on child-rearing related to this aspect of learning. The result is a large organisation in America that attempts, using seminars and counselling, to train parents and teachers to respond more effectively to children, in itself an indication that there is something wrong with prevailing American methods. According to Gordon, there are twelve typical ways in which parents respond to their children:[2]

1 *Ordering, directing, commanding*
   Telling the child to do something, giving him an order or command, such as, 'Stop complaining!'
2 *Warning, admonishing, threatening*
   Telling the child what consequences will occur if he does something: 'If you do that, you'll be sorry.'
3 *Exhorting, moralising, preaching*
4 *Advising, giving solutions or suggestions*
   Telling the child how to solve a problem, giving him advice or suggestions: 'I suggest you talk to your teachers about that.'
5 *Lecturing, teaching, giving logical arguments*
   Trying to influence the child with facts, counter-arguments, logic, information, or your own opinions.
6 *Judging, criticising, disagreeing, blaming*
   Making a negative judgement or evaluation of the child: 'You're not thinking clearly.'
7 *Praising, agreeing*
   Offering a positive evaluation or judgement, agreeing: 'Well, I think you're pretty.'
8 *Name-calling, ridiculing, shaming*
   Making the child feel foolish, putting the child in a category, shaming him: 'You're a spoilt brat.'
9 *Interpreting, analysing, diagnosing*
   Telling the child what his motives are or analysing why he is doing or saying something – communicating that you have him figured out or diagnosed: 'You really don't believe that at all.'
10 *Reassuring, sympathising, consoling, supporting*
   Trying to make the child feel better, talking him out of his

feelings, trying to make his feelings go away, denying the strength of his feelings: 'Don't worry, things will work out.'

11   *Probing, questioning, interrogating*
Trying to find reasons, motives, causes; searching for more information to help solve a problem: 'Why do you suppose you hate school?'

12   *Withdrawing, distracting, humouring, diverting*
Trying to get the child away from the problem: withdrawing from the problem yourself; distracting the child, kidding him out of it, pushing the problem aside.

Dr Gordon finds in his seminars that 90 per cent of parents habitually respond with one of the above. But these 'typical twelve' are in fact all attempts to deny or ignore the child's model, and, in particular, the emotional content of the child's message. The adult interprets the communication using his own model, and then attempts to force not only the interpretation, but the model itself, on the child. This strategy, in time, leads to a serious breakdown in communication, with neither side getting what it wants or needs – on the part of the child, a coherent model of the world and how to be in it, and a feeling of being loved and understood. The implicit rejection of the child's model, and his feelings about it, is experienced by him as a rejection of himself, since in a real sense he *is* his model. The emotional outcome is that both parent and child feel frustrated.

As a way out of this obviously deteriorating relationship, Dr Gordon advocates an approach he calls 'active listening'. The technique is that the parent feeds back to the child what he understands the child's message to be, not at first sending a message of his own, but simply trying to establish exactly what the child is feeling or what his message means, and lets the child know that he is being heard. The following two dialogues used by Gordon illustrate the difference in approach. In the first, the mother uses the 'typical twelve' and in the second active listening.

The Typical Twelve[2]

JOHNNY: Tommy won't play with me today. He won't ever do what I want to do.

MOTHER: Well, why don't you offer to do what he wants to do? You've got to learn to get along with your little friends. (*Advising, moralising*)

JOHNNY: I don't like to do things he wants to do and besides I don't want to get along with that dope.

MOTHER:	Well, go find someone else to play with then if you're going to be a spoilsport. (*Offering a solution, name-calling*)
JOHNNY:	He's the spoilsport, not me. And there isn't anyone else to play with.
MOTHER:	You're just upset because you're tired. You'll feel better about this tomorrow. (*Interpreting, reassuring*)
JOHNNY:	I'm not tired, and I won't feel different tomorrow. You just don't understand how much I hate the little squirt.
MOTHER:	Now stop talking like that! If I ever hear you talk about one of your friends like that again, you'll be sorry! (*Ordering, threatening*)
JOHNNY:	(*walking away and sulking*) I hate this neighbourhood. I wish we would move.

Active Listening

JOHNNY:	Tommy won't play with me today. He won't ever do what I want to do.
MOTHER:	You're kinda angry with Tommy. (*Active listening*)
JOHNNY:	I sure am. I never want to play with him again. I don't want him for a friend.
MOTHER:	You're so angry you feel like never seeing him again. (*Active listening*)
JOHNNY:	That's right. But if I don't have him for a friend, I won't have anyone to play with then.
MOTHER:	You would hate to be left with no one. (*Active listening*)
JOHNNY:	Yeah. I guess I just have to get along with him someway. But it's so hard for me to stop getting mad at him.
MOTHER:	You want to get along better but it's hard for you to keep from getting mad with Tommy. (*Active listening*)
JOHNNY:	I never used to – but that's when he was always willing to do what I wanted to do. He won't let me boss him anymore.
MOTHER:	Tommy's not so easy to influence now. (*Active listening*)
JOHNNY:	He sure isn't. He's not such a baby now. He's more fun though.
MOTHER:	You really like him better this way. (*Active listening*)
JOHNNY:	Yeah. But it's hard to stop bossing him – I'm so used to it. Maybe we wouldn't fight so much if I let him have his way once in a while. Think that would work?
MOTHER:	You're thinking that if you give in occasionally it might help. (*Active listening*)
JOHNNY:	Yeah, maybe it would. I'll try it.

In the first example the whole discussion stalls and both parties feel frustrated. The child does not feel he is getting through to his parent, and becomes increasingly incoherent. In the second case, with the parent simply feeding back what she thinks the child means, he becomes increasingly coherent, and in the end, he unexpectedly solves his own problem. The parent was in effect letting her son use her brain temporarily to augment and enlarge his model, to the point where it was effective enough to solve the problem.

Actively listening to children in this manner brings more obvious benefits, which Gordon describes. In the first place, expressing troublesome feelings instead of trying to suppress them or forget them often helps to get rid of them. In addition, when a child sees that an adult accepts his feelings, he learns that they are legitimate and 'friendly', even if they are negative. If, on the other hand, the feelings are blocked by the adult he will learn that some feelings are bad and not acceptable. Active listening also encourages the child to talk his way through his problem, which is usually an effective way to start reaching a solution.

The dialogue above in which the mother actively listens also shows how the child can learn to be more responsible for himself and more independent. Trust in the child conveyed by the listener gives him the confidence to begin dealing with his own problems. The kind of conversation that takes place when an adult is trying to give full attention to the child's thoughts and feelings also tends to increase the bond between them. The child feels warm towards the parent, who seems more receptive to his point of view, and the child is more likely to listen to his parents.

In the end, the parent may well have to say, 'OK, I've heard what you have to say but I don't agree – you'll do what I say because I'm bigger than you and I'm telling you!' But as Gordon illustrates in his book, with numerous examples from his sessions, the chances of this kind of confrontation are much reduced and the two protagonists generally feel better, if they have both had a chance to express their views.

I would also add that the atmosphere conveyed in Gordon's book by the 'active listening' dialogue is one of sweetness and light, rather like an American soap opera. I would guess that effective communication of the type Gordon is advocating is not necessarily like this: much more feeling may be expressed, and emotions may reach a higher pitch. A more realistic model of healthy communication may be the robust and vigorous lampooning and chastising that tends to go on in groups of adolescents, and between some adults.

The type of communication that Gordon describes, however, is really an amplification of the dialogue concept of language that I have already outlined. I indicated that unless two people share the same language and cosmology, effective communication, leading to the establishment of shared meaning, can only take place when there is continual feedback. Gordon has elaborated on how this is frequently absent. Many of the exchanges that take place between child and parent, even the most conscientious and loving, are disguised attempts to impose the parent's model of the world on the child via the 'typical twelve'. There is a monologue concept of language behind this kind of upbringing, which holds that all you have to do is tell the child what you require, and he will absorb it and turn into the sort of adult you want.

Neil Smith and Deirdre Wilson have written about the resistance of children to explicit language correction. 'It seems clear . . . that neither explicit teaching nor direct imitation plays a primary role in first language acquisition.'[3] What really is crucial, however, is the fact that a child might feel insecure or a social failure if continually, explicitly corrected. Instead of paying attention to and exploring a child's problem, a mother might try merely to teach him to speak the language in a socially acceptable way.

Other examples of non-communication between parent and child are easily found in our everyday experience. I recall having a conversation with several adults, including the mother of a young family, from a distinguished academic background. When the conversation mentioned photographers, the little girl of about six who was listening said, 'Mummy, what is a photographer?' To which her mother replied, almost without hesitation, 'Mary, a photographer is someone who knows what is going to happen just before it happens.' She then dived back into the conversation, ignoring the little girl's blank look.

I have noted numerous similar examples. While being generally loving to their children, the ingrained models and expectations of most well-meaning parents lead them to inflict a very frustrating environment on their children. Once I was watching a friend cutting grass in his garden, while the other parent raked up the cut grass. Their two small children started to imitate them with their sand rakes, spreading the grass around again, rather than putting it into a neat pile. The reaction from their mother was, 'Oh, for goodness sake, try and behave sensibly, can't you?' The children, who had believed they were helping their mother, burst into tears. Another parent had been painting her hall, and went into the living-room to discover that her two-year-old had been painting the furniture. This child, too, received a good ticking-off, leading to tears. A young child cannot distinguish the complicated motives and priorities involved in such acts, and will tend to experience the actions of the parent as arbitrary and unloving. The parents usually work, albeit subconsciously, on the basis of Pavlov's and Skinner's theories – the stick and the carrot – punishing bad behaviour and rewarding good. But the child may not be able easily to distinguish what is good and bad.

In these examples, the response offered by the parents is almost as bad as no communication at all. I have already discussed in Chapter 4 what I see as the threat posed by television in removing the child from contact with the world around him, including his parents. This, as we saw, has the effect of impoverishing not only his linguistic development but also his development as a person. It further seems that when parents actually do switch off the television and find time to talk to their children, they frequently fail to listen properly to what the child has to say, having long-term emotional effects on the child which are just as serious.

One hesitates to lay a large number of the ills of Western society at the door of poor parent-child communication or television, but it does seem that these attitudes to child-rearing can have far-reaching consequences. I would suggest, for example, that lack of 'active listening' or real communication contributes to a feeling of 'unreality' in the child, which in certain circumstances can grow to become intensely destructive later on. In effect, it turns the child into an existential 'outsider'.

Take the case of the radical 'Weathermen' of the 1960s, the American group committed to the violent overthrow of 'the system'. A former friend of theirs is quoted as describing them as follows: 'I saw them as particular victims of that strange *angst* that overcame young Americans in that period, an element of which was the feeling that the only way you can know you are *real* is if you can provoke the wrath of the State.'[4]

This source reported that the favourite movie of the Weathermen he knew was *Butch Cassidy and the Sundance Kid*, and their favourite moment in it, which they kept repeating to each other, was the moment when Butch and Sundance realise that they are being pursued by a posse of the most expert law enforcement officers in the country. They keep asking each other in wonderment why they could be thought so important: 'Who are those guys?' The Weathermen wanted to provoke a similar large-scale response, says the source, 'then they would know that they had made it'. This state of feeling unreal and unnoticed, and needing to provoke a reaction, is a persistent theme in recent American literature, from Kerouac onwards. The article on the Weathermen also mentions that Dr Spock was a family friend of the parents of one member of the group, and his book *Baby and Childcare* could be seen as the Bible of post-war American parents. There is a thread running through it of management and confrontation, with sections on discipline and spoiling, and words such as 'tyranny' and 'submission' used. Spock also favoured such ideas as letting a child cry itself to sleep. All these would be strange concepts to most traditional societies, where infants are usually kept in continuous close physical contact with their mothers and other members of the extended family. Autism, a strange disorder involving non-communication, often affecting the children of highly intelligent Western parents, may in some cases be the result of extreme impoverishment of a child's need for physical closeness, in the same way that not handling a new-born baby even though it is fed, will cause it to die of a wasting disease called marasmus.

Many Western children are, then, growing up with a degree of physical or communication isolation which may jeopardise the quality of their lives as adults. Clearly, it is difficult to establish a direct link between this kind of isolation in childhood and the more extreme forms of adult maladjustment. In the case of the Weathermen, poor parent-child communication was only one factor among many, including social factors. It is interesting to note that these forms of destructive *angst* are generally unheard of in the few societies still in their traditional state, where relations between parents and children may be closer. Of course, it may be argued that such societies also lack the hundreds of other factors that go to produce psychological maladjustment: ugly sprawling cities, dehumanising factory work or chronic unemployment, vast impersonal bureaucracies, and so on. While this is undoubtedly true, it is also the case that even in stressful, highly industrialised societies like our own, mental and emotional maladjustment is less evident where close family bonds survive. This is the situation which exists in Hong Kong, for instance, where stress levels are as high, if not higher than in Britain, but where members of each family live in far greater physical and mental proximity to one another than we do.

Even by the standards of societies broadly similar to our own, it can be seen that parent-child communication and family relations in Britain are poor. John Ardagh confirms the strength of French family life:[5] 'Daily social relations in France have always been dominated, more than in Anglo-Saxon countries, by family ties. The family has appeared as the focus of the individual's loyalty and affection, of his economic interest, and even of his legal duty, for the rights and obligations of the family were defined in the still operative Code Napoleon of 1804. Many an older Frenchman has spent his youth in a world where . . . the family's needs and demands were put before those of the local community or even of the state: "I cannot pay my taxes, you see, I've a duty to support Aunt Louise," has been a common French attitude.'

The development of the particularly oppressive style of child-rearing found in Britain from the nineteenth century onwards is described in Susan Lasdun's book *Victorians at Home*. 'Children had once mingled freely with adults in the public life-style of the Middle Ages, but now they became more and more excluded from adult life. Both the growing concept of class, which by the eighteenth century precluded mixing outside one's own, and the strict moral code by which many parents sought to raise their children prohibited the free intercourse that children had hitherto enjoyed. They had at all costs to be protected from undesirable influences. This led to their continual sequestration, and, in the home, this meant greater confinement to areas designated for their own use. As the nineteenth century marched on, architects' plans, whether to improve old houses or build new ones, included "the children's wing", "the children's floor" or "the children's quarters". Cloistered more and more in these areas and cared for variously by nurses, governesses or tutors so "that they might never fall into the hands of servants", as Fanny Drummond wrote, children emerged from their nether regions at regular and regulated intervals . . . A common punishment was to withdraw their after-tea visit to the drawing-room.'[6]

The Victorian maxim that 'children should be seen and not heard' is still widely observed in this country. The relatively repressive attitude to children may also have a great deal to do with Britain's longer and more developed history as an imperial power, and with the earlier hierarchisation of our institutions. In the educational system in Britain, and in our hierarchical society as a whole, it is the handing down of packages of knowledge, like the repressive parent, which prevails in many schools and institutions.

To illustrate this point, let us look first of all at how well our educational system meets the needs of our hierarchical society. The phenomenon of the majority of the population working in large pyramidal organisations, is something that has emerged only over the last two hundred years, and it is only during that time that there has been any need for a formal, centralised educational system. Prior to the emergence of large organisational hierarchies, most people learned all they needed to know by doing a work job alongside their fellow-workers, usually their parents. No formal teaching was required, except for the acquisition of extra social accomplishments. But the demands of a hierarchical, centralised society such as ours are more complex, and education has had to alter dramatically in order to meet them.

An educational system always reflects the needs created by the economic one, and a prime requirement for a hierarchically-organised economy is discipline. Hierarchies require that at every level employees accept the orders of their superiors and act on them; they in turn will expect the same from their subordinates. The concept of discipline has, therefore, to be firmly instilled in the population as a whole if society is to function as required. The educational system, as well as teaching specific subjects, which are often of secondary importance, having no direct relevance to the child's possible working life, has to see that the children who once wriggled and talked and shouted at each other are organised into orderly groups who listen to the teacher, do as they are told, and interpret the world as the teachers see it. In order for this to be achieved, lateral communication has largely to be replaced by central communication, or monologue.

Late eighteenth-century reformers noted the beneficial effects of education on children, 'beneficial' meaning that it made them more suitable for long shifts in factories. Powell, in 1772, also saw education as a training in the 'habit of industry'; by the time the child reached six or seven it should become 'habituated, not to say naturalised to Labour and Fatigue'. The Reverend William Turner, writing from Newcastle in 1786, recommended Raikes' schools as 'a spectacle of order and regularity'. Once within the school gates, the child entered a new universe of disciplined time. At the Methodist Sunday Schools in York the teachers were also fined for unpunctuality. Once in attendance, they were in effect under military rule.[7]

John Fletcher describes the implementation of the Poor Law of 1834, saying that this, 'in its implementation, required the construction of the first large modern administrative pyramid, [and] was also the cause of the invention of a new and dreaded literary form – the memorandum. The memorandum is a mass-produced communication; its purpose is to be able to go anywhere and be understood by anyone. It demands uniformity in language, uniformity in its readership. No centralised, industrialised society can function without it.

'A few minor social changes had to be engineered before England could succumb to the victorious dictatorship of the memorandum.

Mass education had to be imposed on the masses to numb their intelligences sufficiently to enable them automatically to obey those memoranda aimed in their direction, while the upper orders had to be taught the art of memorandum composition. The ideal method chosen was the examination. It is a lie that the examination measures originality (since anything original, by definition, cannot be measured against anything else), but what it does do, superbly, is to calibrate how effectively a candidate can take a ragbag jumble of other people's opinions and theories and arrange them in a neat and orderly memorandum. This is superb training for his future life as an administrator, or manager, since management consists of being able to reduce and channel the whole glorious, riotous chaos and spontaneity of everyday life into a neat and orderly production process.'[8]

By the time the child has left a modern school with his examination results showing how well he has conformed, taken a job in a hierarchical institution and raised a family of his own, a positive feedback loop will have come into effect. The concepts he has tacitly taken on board will reinforce the effect of his upbringing, and he will impose the same mode of communication on his children. As society centralises and becomes more complex, education is seen as being more and more necessary in order to 'get on'. People who have 'got on' tend to treat their children hierarchically, imposing their models more inflexibly, and at the same time pressing them so that they get further than they themselves did. So in time, people may well begin unconsciously to see communication and relationships in a more and more hierarchic fashion, and there will be a gradual shift to a wholly monologue concept of communication.

The distorted view of communication which is being too widely imposed by parent on child has interesting implications for the teaching of a language. In a hierarchical society, language tends too often to be seen not as a means of communication but as a means of social advancement, a set of rules which, when mastered, will help the child to 'get on' as his parents may have done.

In a hierarchical society, too, a great deal of store is set by 'talking properly', in other words, talking like those who have 'got on'. It has often been noted how the lower classes often try and ape the speech of those they consider their 'betters' (until the upper orders change the rules again!). This is one of the reasons why language changes over a period of time. A modern example is quoted by Jean Aitchison, concerning a study carried out in New York into the pronunciation of certain words by different social groups. It seems that an 'r' sound is increasingly being inserted into such words as 'beard' and 'bear' by language-conscious lower middle-class women, in imitation of a 'prestige feature' found in the speech of the upper middle class.[9]

The emphasis placed by British parents on correctness of speech adds to the somewhat chilly atmosphere often found in middle and upper-class homes in this country, which contrasts so strongly with family life elsewhere in Europe. A friend of mine once stayed as a guest in the house of a Spanish family in a backward and rural part of Spain: they could speak no English and he no Spanish. He said that for the first few weeks he thought that at meal-times, they were continually arguing and screaming at one another with real hatred. But he gradually realised that in fact there were merely far fewer restrictions on the expression of emotions than in more 'advanced' Western countries. In this country, such behaviour is simply not acceptable to parents.

I have mentioned a grave social consequence related to this environment: a widespread feeling of unreality and alienation, which can take many destructive forms. Another outcome is the classic authoritarian personality, the person who, faced with cold disciplinarian parents, has adopted the monologue concept of communication, and who blindly accepts authority and seeks to impose it on others. He has learnt from his parents and his teachers to accept their authoritarian models, and he re-imposes these on his own subordinates. He cannot properly listen to other people, and rejects what they say unless it is backed by some sort of greater authority.

Norman Dixon, Professor of Psychology at London University, has made a study of the authoritarian personality,[10] and states that 'the hierarchical structure complete with rules, rituals and conventions . . . will attract more than its fair share of authoritarian personalities.' He quotes a study[11] which found that 61 per cent of Prime Ministers between 1800 and 1940 lost one or both of their parents in childhood, with the figure for the rest of the population being 1–7 per cent, and postulates a link between this experience and an insatiable urge to achieve. The significance of losing a parent could well be described in terms of the loss of even the potential for that person to achieve emotionally close interaction. Other shared traits observed in these Prime Ministers were loneliness, depression, and contrived *bonhomie*. Professor Dixon goes on to list the hazards associated with the authoritarian figure in modern organisations.[10] 'The first is that when recruiting newcomers or effecting promotions within the firm they will tend to go for people like themselves. For obvious reasons they feel threatened by original thinkers and the unconventional. The last thing they want is boat-rockers. Mavericks and those who might question existing practices make them anxious - even though it is just such people which the organisation may desperately need if it is to triumph over its competitors.

'Their second and related shortcoming is that they tend to be notoriously bad at human relations. Whereas a high level of motivation and morale are the very life-blood of a successful industrial organisation, these people - cold, hostile, cavilling, negative and abrasive - are peculiarly adept at extinguishing any signs of warmth or enthusiasm in colleagues.

'The third special hazard of authoritarians is that, because they often have considerable administrative skills - "the so-called anal triad of being orderly, obstinate and mean" lends itself to careful housekeeping - they run the risk of being promoted to positions for which they are quite unfitted.

But people who tend to do well in hierarchies are those who tend to have such authoritarian tendencies. At each level in a hierarchy, as we have noted, the boss really only wants to issue instructions, based on his low-variety view of the world, downwards, and to receive the kind of information he expects, couched in terms of the model he is using. Any subordinate who delivers these 'goods' will be noted as someone who gets results: 'We don't get any problems from so-and-so'. This is the type of person who will be promoted, even though his subordinates might find it hard to communicate with him. He may be the boss *because* he cannot communicate. In order to be in charge of other people, he has to be able to isolate himself from their feelings. He has to discipline them, order them about, even sack them, without letting his feelings intrude. Similarly, an officer in one of the services has to be prepared to order his men to attack, knowing that they may be killed. If he can talk with them in the manner described by Dr Gordon and the children, he would automatically become vulnerable to his subordinates' feelings, and do his job less well *in the eyes of his superiors*. For effective communication brings about a convergent area which makes separation of interests less easy. The person who gets on well in hierarchic systems is, among other things, the one who can think rationally, and isolate himself from the feelings of those below him.

We may see more clearly why a subordinate so readily distorts or tailors information to suit a superior's desires. On the one hand, on a personal survival and promotion level, he knows what is good for him. But on a more immediate one, he is frightened by the thought of annoying his boss, risking being put in the position his parents or schoolteachers put him in when they were not using active listening. This will have powerful associations of insecurity, anger and frustration for him. If his boss gets really angry, he may get a vigorous dressing-down, which takes him back to when he was severely disciplined by his parents or teachers. This is a degree worse than the 'typical twelve', for it involves the parent or teacher smashing his model into the child with such violence, that the child's model temporarily disintegrates. In a very real sense such anger really does destroy a child's fragile personality.

The most experienced proponents of the debased form of 'communication' I have been describing are politicians. They are politicians precisely because they have developed the ability to cling so rigidly to their particular world view that they can successfully block any communication which might endanger it. They are masters of the art of trivialising, mis-stating, and misunderstanding their opponent's point of view. We have all seen the performances of a Margaret Thatcher or an Arthur Scargill on television, and wondered how they always manage to come through such gruelling experiences unscathed. Their tactics confuse and bewilder any inexperienced questioner.

The art of parrying unwanted questions and information is, of course, given great emphasis in British public schools, generally the training ground for those who occupy the top rungs of British hierarchies. As Evelyn Waugh pointed out, the main thing you learn at public school is the ability to win arguments. What is of interest is not a discussion to arrive at the truth of a proposition, merely the ability to state your model and the conclusions arising from it in such a way as to confound your opponents. Civil Servants, politicians, and those at the top of the armed forces, of business organisations, the law, and the churches, all tend to come from public schools. The positive feedback loop that I have identified between oppressive upbringing, leading to positions of authority, leading in turn to more repressive upbringing, would suggest a reason why the public schools have survived for so long, despite egalitarian efforts to abolish them.

In a hierarchic society, then, there will be a tendency for parents to treat their children in such a way that they will rise in the existing system. This involves instilling in them a distorted view of communication, as a process of superiors imposing models on subordinates. As time passes, a self-perpetuating élite of incompetent communicators will establish itself, tending to be impervious to alternative world views, and in turn repressing *its* children.

This pattern may have an effect on the actual language we use – the raw material of our communication, as it were. As we saw earlier in the chapter, language evolves to suit the needs of a particular society. In traditionally hierarchic and imperial societies, then, we would expect to find differences reflected in the structure of the language. There is some evidence, again rather speculative and anecdotal, to support this point of view. The New Tribes Mission is apparently having great difficulty in converting the Panare Indians of Venezuela to Christianity, as they have no words (or concepts) basic to a religion such as Christianity, such as 'sin', 'punishment', 'redemption', and, in particular, 'guilt'. Such words are associated with discipline and control, and are necessary for centralised hierarchic societies.[12] The Panare congratulate God if it is a nice day; we humble ourselves and thank Him for being so decent as to send us worthless sinners a nice day.

In British society, research has shown that those occupying higher positions speak a different language from those in lower ones. Essentially, upper and middle-class children use more words from the Graeco-Latin tradition than working-class children, who use shorter, simpler Anglo-Saxon words.[13]

The British also developed English in order to run a large Empire, involving the co-ordinated movements of armies and navies, planned a long time in advance, together with the operation of huge administrative structures, where massive co-ordination is required across the base of a pyramid. One result is a high degree of sophistication as regards the description of time. Skill in using various tenses, in addition, is useful in the allocation, or avoidance of blame: 'We would have attacked the French had it not been for the bad weather delaying our landing, and the fact that we would have been overwhelmed by their superior numbers.'

The emergence of modern hierarchies is, of course, a relatively recent phenomenon, while the language we use today is the product of many centuries of development. Nonetheless, comparisons between our language and that of other non-hierarchical societies suggest that English is in fact a remarkably appropriate medium in which to express the world-view of a centralised, hierarchical state. Indo-European languages such as our own are essentially noun-verb ones, based on a three-dimensional concept of space and a longitudinal view of time. The prevailing sentence structure uses those with an actor, an action and a goal. The chief effect of such usage is always to place the speaker or thinker apart from the world, acting on it. For example, in English we say: 'I love you; I talk to you; I see you; it rains', and so on. We are always doing something to someone, or something or someone is doing it to us. We tend not to say: 'We have love for each other; we dialogue;' or simply 'rains', as some other groups of people do.

This kind of language, in which the subject acts on things or people, is a fitting medium for a society which is geared to the manipulation or exploitation of nature, and the management and control of large numbers of people, just as our own centralised, hierarchical society is. Indeed, so fitting is it that it is difficult for us to envisage any possible alternative to this basic noun-verb structure and the world-view that seems to go with it.

According to Benjamin Lee Whorf,[14] who studied the subject in great detail, many of the American Indian languages do not have the same basic noun-verb structure as we do, nor do they share the view of space as being three-dimensional and time as being longitudinal. Their world-view, though perfectly coherent, is thus diametrically opposed to that which prevails in Western industrialised society.

The Hopi Indians, for example, have a language which makes no distinction between present and past, and which divides reality into two categories which Whorf terms 'manifested' and 'manifesting'. The 'manifest' category embraces all the phenomena accessible to the senses in the historical physical universe, both present and past, while the 'manifesting' category includes all that we might call 'mental or subjective', ie., everything that exists in the mind not only of man but of the animals, plants and things around him. This second 'manifesting' category also comprises everything that we would call future. Whorf describes this second category as follows: 'The subjective realm (subjective from our viewpoint, but intensely real and quivering with life, power and potency to the Hopi) embraces not only our future, much of which the Hopi regard as more or less predestined in essence if not in exact form, but also all mentality, intellection, and emotion, the essence and typical form of which is the striving of purposeful desire, intelligent in character, towards manifestation – a manifestation which is much resisted and delayed, but in some form or other is inevitable.'

Of course, the problem here is that the actual experience encased in the Hopi language cannot be expressed by means of our own noun-verb language – we can only approximate to it. However, I believe it is possible to see even from the brief description above that the relation between the objective and subjective realms is far closer in the Hopi language than it is in our own. Among the Hopi, mental and spiritual activity – hoping, wishing, striving, praying – is constantly impinging on the manifested, or objective realm – hence the constant hopeful praying of the Hopi community, 'assisted by their exotic communal ceremonies and their secret esoteric rituals in the underground kivas.'[14]

The point of making this comparison is to show that language, as well as being a means of describing the world, also shapes the way we perceive it. The Hopi language is radically different from ours, and so too, argues Whorf, is their vision of reality. The significance of this is that in Western industrialised countries, we seem to be locked into a language, and therefore a way of thinking, that predisposes us to see, and hence to try and solve our problems, in a hierarchic centralised way. Our entire thought mode may have become encased in an inflexible mould which prohibits us from seeing the world any differently. We do not see ourselves as part of a homeostatic relationship with each other or the world, but as establishing mastery over nature – which we manifestly cannot do – at the same time increasing the control of our institutions over individual people.

But we can only survive in co-operation with nature and one another; if we destroy the earth's natural ecosystems, then we will destroy ourselves. Similarly, if we go on increasing the control of institutions over people, then we may also destroy our humanity. Having evolved a language and cosmology that is inherently expansive, centralist and exploitative, we cannot break out or change direction.

It is legitimate to ask whether Western civilisation and culture are successful in terms of people's happiness and well-being, or even their very survival.

At present few governments have the vision to see any alternative to a course of continued development along the same lines, despite the fact that there are, for example, clear environmental limits to further growth. But there *are* alternatives. The way to change the behaviour both of institutions and the people in them is not to exhort or cajole them into acting differently, but to change the information conditions in which they operate. As I hope to show in the Chapter 12, the new information technology, although open to misuse, offers the possibility of bringing about precisely the right kind of change.

10 CENTRAL MEDIA AND THE CORRUPTION OF INFORMATION

We considered in the last chapter some of the modern parental and educational factors in Western upbringing, and British upbringing in particular. But parents and teachers are not the only influences affecting an individual's development. So far we have not considered the role of the peer group, that band of contemporaries whose apparently haphazard social interactions provide a growing child with vital tacit knowledge that cannot be acquired elsewhere.

The process can perhaps be envisaged by imagining a long platform on a disused underground railway. Every ten feet or so, although wider apart towards the end, there are barriers running across the platform separating it into zones. At one end are small children, and at the other old people. So each zone contains children or adults within a year or so of the same age. The small children are playing with special toys, which are continually passed around from child to child, each being shown by another child how to play with them. If he learns properly a particular part of his brain is unlocked which makes him ready to go on into the next zone. He will in any case proceed to the next zone after a certain time, but if that part of his brain remains unlocked he will not be able to play with the new and more complicated toys there, or have so much fun with other children.

In this analogy the 'toys' are really the games, rhymes, turns of phrase, jokes, gestures and ploys which children pass from one to another. Most of the original work identifying the more explicit currency of catch-phrases, songs, rhymes and street games was done by Peter and Iona Opie in *The Lore and Language of Schoolchildren* and *Children's Games in Street and Playground*.[1] What emerges from their work is not only that some sayings survive for centuries, but that when new sayings emerge, they arise simultaneously all over the country. As Keith Waterhouse put it: 'Since children do not operate fleets of long-distance lorries, have no access to radio wavelengths and are not in possession of clandestine printing-presses, there can only be one logical explanation. Word of mouth.

'But the implications of that are mind-boggling. Are we to understand that from Penzance to Perth, from Liverpool to London, from Cardiff to Colchester, a great commonwealth of children are invisibly holding hands and in defiance of all the parents who want

Fig 16   The underground railway of life

them to speak nicely, all the teachers who want them to learn their songs from books, all the playgroup leaders and organisers and social workers and qualified child specialists who want to purify and process and package their culture like Swiss cheese segments, are secretly passing one to the other like an Olympic torch, their mutinous anthems and Rabelaisian verses and private, haunting rhymes?"[2]

This 'lore and language' remains in the age zones through which children move, the 'toys' of each stage being by and large inaccessible to younger or older children. But the cumulative experience of each stage creates the necessary shared experience for communication to occur. Without it an individual will be excluded from much of the tacit knowledge that he needs in order to be successfully socialised. Moreover, if a child's ability to enjoy himself is not activated, exercised, stretched and given context by learning and passing on seemingly trivial and incomprehensible children's games – in other words, by playing with other children – he will find any sort of social enjoyment in later life very difficult to achieve.

The Opies stressed the more sophisticated and easily collectable artefacts, such as games and rhymes, but clearly all sorts of social skills are passed around in the same way: when to be aggressive, or dominant or submissive; how to make friends, and alliances; how to intimidate other children; how to be liked; how to believe in the rules of a game, how far to carry cheating; when to lie; when to be honest, and so on. Such skills and sub-skills all belong to the realm of tacit knowledge, and are picked up from other children. They cannot in fact be formally taught. Most parents, for example, attempt to teach their children to be honest, and yet social life depends on a degree of selective dishonesty. If all adults were scrupulously honest all the time society would collapse in a morass of antagonism and hurt feelings. So although children may be taught formally to be honest, they also have to learn when to be dishonest.

The way in which children exchange information is of course through lateral media, a network of potential or actual links which transmits information from person to person. Lateral media are distinct from central media in that at each stage in the transmission of a message it can be distorted, modified, re-combined with others, fed selectively to certain nodes in the network, or not transmitted at all. Lateral media are essentially concerned with the transmission of messages through dialogue, so everyone is continually receiving different messages. A children's rhyme may spread unchanged through the network, but it may also become altered and embellished. Other examples of lateral media are small village communities, private networks in organisations, the CB network and professional groups. Just as children swap jingles and snatches, these groups circulate jokes, stories, gossip, anecdotes, rumours, fears, views on life and useful tips. And each item contains a piece of tacit knowledge from the model of the part of life it embodies. It indicates something about how society works, what is important, and what is and is not done – information which cannot, in principle, be formalised. And just as with children, belonging to such an informal grouping is intrinsically enjoyable. I would claim, in fact, that men and women communicate most successfully when they are standing around grumbling, telling stories and gossiping.

Central media, however, transmit the same message simultaneously to large numbers of people. The media, most notably television, newspapers and radio, are essentially monologues. Magazines and professional journals also belong in this category. I have already described in some detail the potentially serious consequences of the intrusion of television. If the average American has spent 22,000 hours watching television by the time he graduates from high school, twice as many as in school,[3] then he has to some degree missed out on years of interaction, participation, conversation and play. In the same way, time spent going to films, reading the newspaper, listening to plays on the radio, all relatively recent pastimes, is not spent on talking to someone, writing a letter, or playing a game.

I am concerned here, however, with a more insidious impact of central media – the inhibiting effect on lateral communication of the sheer amount of information from them that daily bombards almost everyone in our society. It is often said that the only thing people can talk about these days is what was on television last night. But as far as I can see this is not quite true, for if two people saw the same programme the conversation usually turns out to be extremely limited. It is only when one person saw something that the other one did not that a real conversation can get going. For another feature of lateral media is that they operate because, besides the common shared experiences on which communication is based, the people participating are all individuals, with varying experiences and perceptions. It is these differences in individuals' maps which are passed around, so that the gossip, chatter and grumbling which goes on in any group is a mixture of comparison, agreement, disagreement and attempts to place in context news and events. In other words, lateral media operate by virtue of some members knowing more than others. Central media, by contrast, give identical, simultaneous messages from a position of real or apparent superior knowledge, so the process of passing on information laterally is disrupted. The person talking about a television programme to another viewer no longer has something that the other does not already have, because central media have informed them both.

The type of conversation that takes place, uninhibited by handed-down information with official status, is what Desmond Morris originally called 'social grooming'. Sitting around picking things out of one another's fur is not only good for the biological health of monkeys, it is also good for their mental health. Monkeys that are deprived of it start behaving abnormally. Similarly, standing around talking about the weather and the like is beneficial for humans. It makes them feel good, it binds communities together and gives them a sense of purpose. The corollary is that as people spend more and more time watching television or reading solitary magazines, they experience increasing feelings of alienation, loneliness and pointlessness in their lives. In the same way that they need food, drink, fresh air, and so on, people need a quantity of communication. Eric Berne, in his book *Games People Play*,[4] pointed this out. He calls social intercourse 'social stroking' and says that without it 'the person's spine shrivels'. His therapy is based, in part, on the idea that so strong is the need for stroking that if people cannot get it in the normal way, by being interesting, sought-after people, the more they will contrive to get it in more harmful ways. Berne says that most maladjusted people who seek therapy have similar problems, such as getting beaten up, stood up, put down, or jailed. He sees these as a result of the 'victim's' need for deep social interaction. He creates a problem since he is unable to satisfy his need for social stroking in other ways. A habitual criminal, for example, gets a social pay-off every time he goes through the process of being arrested and tried.

The function of social grooming in binding groups together into organisms is a fundamental theme of the present book. I have already described how people brought into social contact with one another by membership of any group develop feeling for it, their togetherness and shared experience generating a private language, that carries slang, humour, mythology and a cosmology. When such groups form within organisations they can inhibit the effectiveness of the organisation as a whole, but the phenomenon can also be used to advantage by an organisation such as an army, to create a group of people willing to die for one another.

The pervasiveness of central media today has, I would claim, deprived people to a considerable extent of the experience of belonging to their community. It does this in two ways. In the first place, time spent with central media is obviously time spent away from lateral media – you cannot properly converse and watch television at the same time. Secondly, if central media provide everyone with the same information, then lateral media cannot function, since their main formal function of passing on information has become redundant. If there is important news to be passed from one member of a community to another, then conversations transmitting that news play a recognised role in that group. If, for example, a flood threatens a neighbourhood, and the minute-by-minute developments outstrip the local news bulletins, then there will be a surge of communication between the neighbours. Their group will temporarily come to life as vigorously as any rugby club, with all the attendant informal links and feelings of friendliness. But without such events there is no real function for lateral media in a community, and correspondingly few opportunities for the interactions that give rise to a feeling of belonging.

At a child's level it is not so much news and information that circulates as the games, rhymes and songs that I have already referred to. 'Television, linked with other less important social factors, has done something in only 30 years which the Black Death and the Industrial Revolution failed to accomplish in the previous 1,000 years. According to the Assistant Mistresses' Association, it has almost stopped the transmission of nursery rhymes between generations. Leaders of the 5,000-strong teachers' union [have] said . . . that these old songs, which have previously survived the roughest of country soil, were largely unknown to the generation of children now entering primary schools.'[5] The association went on to point out that a large number of children were entering primary school with a vocabulary of only 50 words, whereas children who had learnt, nursery rhymes had a much wider vocabulary.

Until the advent of printing, fairy tales circulated as part of a vast lateral network covering most of Europe, with slight geographical variations. What the famous Grimm brothers did was merely collect particular versions of some of these tales together and print them, thereby solidifying them. Since Grimm, instead of circulating as an oral tradition, they are now passed on, if at all, from parent to child, usually at bedtime. Some research from Germany[6] provides evidence of what is lost if fairy stories are replaced by picture books and television: 'Children who are told fairy tales are more intelligent, calmer, mentally more balanced, and more open-minded than those who are not.' Moreover, 'fairy tale children' have better memories, concluded H.G. Wahn, Walburga Hesse and Ursula Schaefer in their study involving 76 children.[6]

They examined the stage of development of the children and the effect of fairy tales and stories told to them. Of the 26 children aged up to three-and-a-half years only 15 per cent had reached a stage of development below their calendar age; 40 per cent equalled the calendar age; and 45 per cent had developed beyond their chronological age. All listened to fairy tales regularly. In a control group lacking fairy tales, those children who absorb primary visual and audible impressions through picture books or television, two-thirds were below the development age in calendar age, while one-third had reached a stage of development corresponding to the chronological age. Only one child in this group was ahead of his calendar age.

The three researchers recently also reported on the background of these findings in the *Medical Tribune*.[6] 'They held that the ability of the brain to store impressions is much greater during early childhood than at any other stage. As a result, this phase of development has a major bearing on emotional and intellectual maturity in later years. In pre-school age, knowledge is conveyed primarily through speech. Imagination, vocabulary and manner of speech improve in proportion to the audible and visual impressions the child receives from its environment. This is why fairy tales and other stories are so important.

'While listening, the child projects vivid images, it practises the ability to concentrate and remember, learns new words, terms and interactions, and thus improves its own style of expression to a greater extent than normal dialogue permits.

'Moreover, the fairy tale is a magic mirror in which the child sees reflected its own thoughts, fears, inhibitions, hopes and expectations.

'The happy end of most fairy tales is particularly important here. The child frequently identifies itself with the characters of the tale and the dramatic struggle between right and wrong, good and evil, craftiness and stupidity. The happy end lends confidence and hope in overcoming the child's own problems.

'Old fairy tales are usually more true to life and fascinate the child with their timeless symbolism much more than modern stories with their false idyll. The importance of fairy tales is demonstrated in the different ways in which children react to a threatening situation.

'For instance: a child stands on a rock, surrounded by constantly rising water which threatens to wash him away. A child seeing this situation on a TV screen experiences it as a real threat, it is frightened and cries. The same situation when read or told to the child causes him to take on a serious and attentive mien but does not make him cry.'

It appears to be essential that the story is told to the child in person, even if it is read from a book. The replacement of the person by a television screen or a picture book is alienating.

In addition to the tendency of central media to disrupt lateral media simply by carrying the information which they would normally carry, central media are inherently disintegrative. I have concentrated in earlier chapters on why and how things tend to go wrong as a result of lack of integration between individuals in a community, between departments of an institution, or between institutions themselves, and I have shown how information networks, where they exist, create lateral media that tend to carry out an effective integrating function. Central media, on the other hand, tend to disrupt this process.

The following has been said of newspapers in Britain:

The *Times* is read by the people who run the country;

The *Guardian* is read by the people who think they ought to run the country;

The *Financial Times* is read by the people who own the country;

The *Daily Mail* is read by the wives of the people who run the country;

The *Daily Telegraph* is read by the people who remember how the country used to be run;

The *Daily Express* is read by the people who think it is still run that way;

The *Daily Mirror* is read by the people who work for the country;

The *Sun* is read by the people who don't care who runs the country so long as she's got big tits.

I think there is more than a little truth in this. People select their particular branch of the central media to suit their particular world view. By and large they buy newspapers in order to have their world view confirmed; in other words they buy newspapers which distort reality in the way they want it to be distorted.

Each newspaper tends to print the type of news that its readers want to hear, and to present it in the way they want it presented. This frequently gives rise to diametrically opposed statements over a period of time, depending on what the readers are presumed to want at any particular moment, reflected by circulation figures. This is a clear case of positive feedback.

The sort of emphasis that causes the *Daily Telegraph* to treat a story involving the shooting of a suspect by police in order to save a hostage's life as an example of police bravery, and *The Guardian* as a reason to query the circumstances under which the man was shot and call for an enquiry, is common. The most extreme example of distortion I have come across occurred in Northern Ireland in 1979. The British and Loyalist papers were carrying stories about the auctioning in the United States of a machine gun that was alleged to have been used to kill four British servicemen, using a tone of outraged moral indignation at the callousness of the IRA's supporters. In the Republican press the story was presented just as convincingly as a particularly nasty piece of propaganda devised by the British secret service to discredit fund-raising in America. Whatever the objective facts of the matter, the various central outlets had transformed the event into something which confirmed readers' prejudices.

The inevitable tendency of the kind of central media we have at present in Britain is to fragment society into camps which do not trust or understand one another. In Britain we have a few large-circulation daily papers based in London, which carry the important political news and national stories, and local newspapers, which show a marked inclination to concentrate on jumble sales and weddings (with, of course, some notable exceptions). In Germany and the United States, however, the provincial and local newspapers carry far more weight, and respectable political comment, than they do here, giving rise to greater diversity of view and possibly less fragmented social groupings.

When covering international events newspapers tend to be globally disintegrative, owing to their attempts to satisfy their readers' insular prejudices. The classic example of British ethnocentricity is the apocryphal *Times* headline for a weather story about the disruption of cross-channel ferries which allegedly ran, 'Fog in Channel, Continent cut off.' In a similar vein, a headline in the *Stornoway Gazette* in 1912 allegedly read, 'Local man lost at sea.' The ship in which he had sunk was the *Titanic*! In the long run this reinforcement of national and parochial prejudice can have harmful effects, since it leads people to make decisions on situations based on misleading perspectives, the result of years of distorted information. Whenever there is a Third World disaster, for example, people in the West like to imagine that the disaster-struck people have lost the ability to cope, and can only be nursed back to normalcy by huge injections of Western aid and know-how. We get reports of dazed, demoralised people not knowing what to do and of looting and chaos.

In fact, this sort of scenario is usually far from the truth. Ian Davis of the Disasters' Settlement Unit at Oxford Polytechnic's School of Architecture says that frequently a Third World disaster, and its impact on people, is not nearly as bad as it is made out to be in Western media. The dazed, corrupt or incoherent behaviour of the local people is usually exaggerated or invented. Local networks inevitably form and spring into action, generally far more able to cope than imported aid teams, which may misinterpret the operation of local networks as 'insubordination', 'lack of co-operation', 'irrational behaviour' or 'lack of discipline'.

Distortion in the information carried by central media occurs for reasons similar to those applying in hierarchies. Newspapers, television and radio are not so much about scrupulous reporting and reality as about attracting readers, since this increases the power of the operator by increasing revenue from sales and advertising. Consequently, information has to be presented in such a way that it increases the desire of the consumer to have it.

Another feature inherent in central media is lack of requisite variety. By their very nature, newspapers, for instance, have to extract a few big stories from a day's total reality, and compress them into the small space available. This inherent loss of variety is also illustrated by radio traffic news. In 15 years of driving and listening to the radio I have never yet heard a bulletin which applied to my current journey, or indeed to a road anywhere near me. By contrast, CB radio is lateral media *par excellence*, and can give very detailed information. Experienced users can receive a constant stream of information about road conditions ahead, the position and state of transport cafés, where police cars are lurking, people who have broken down, and so on. The messages are picked up and diffused laterally from user to user, and in total give an extremely high-variety model of the traffic situation. To see these lateral media in operation is astonishing. A colleague of mine once travelled with a CB user who was late for his plane from Birmingham airport. He radioed ahead to CB lorry drivers, who were able to force traffic over to let him through, so that he was able to speed through rush-hour traffic and catch his plane.

The coarse-grained nature of the information given in central media is unavoidable. If the same message is being transmitted simultaneously to large numbers of people it is impossible to cater for special interests. They can only carry big stories which will interest a large number of people – big crimes, big arguments or big fights (wars). In the real world there are in fact many more small things than big going on, but the effect of central media on the people exposed to them tends to make their internal models eventually coarse-grained. So that, in addition to the other pressures towards centralisation and gigantism, there arises a tendency to think in large, coarse-grained terms. In order to get any press coverage, a PR man knows his hierarchical firm will have to take large, coarse-grained actions, building large power stations, or large dams, or setting up large aid schemes.

So central media emphasise the abnormal rather than the normal. To an extent, then, they are anti-homeostatic, in that homeostatic systems tend towards the norm. Very few people, for example, actually witness a rape, a mugging or a murder, but these events are frequently reported in the press. As a result people are frightened by what they see as a lack of 'law and order', and are sometimes frightened to leave their homes despite the fact that, due to domestic accidents, home is a far more dangerous place to be, statistically, than the street. Newspapers rarely carry stories on how to make homes safer, certainly not with the same regularity as stories about violent crime. This contributes to the erosion of mutual trust and respect between people, and allows law-breakers to feel that their behaviour is not so aberrant after all.

Another distorting effect of central media occurs in the reporting of the mistakes and shortcomings of organisations. Anyone with any practical experience of working in one of the hierarchic institutions I have discussed knows that decisions are continually made based on inadequate information, with too little time for reflection. That things go wrong, is, as I have indicated, frequently an inevitable outcome of hierarchic structures rather than a reason for blaming individuals. In fact, we should feel surprised and grateful that buildings do not fall down more often and that more people do not die on operating tables. For engineers, doctors, pilots, and the rest, do remarkably well in operating so successfully in the conditions they have to contend with. When the inevitable failures do occur, they are reported in the press as aberrant: 'Vital Safety Rules Ignored in Horror Disaster' sums up the usual response of central media, as I have mentioned. The willingness of central media to seize on any dysfunction which becomes public knowledge, exacerbates the problem by raising the level of tension, increasing information overload, secrecy in other organisations, setting up witch-hunts and the search for scapegoats, and causing demands for the allocation of blame.

Central media are often more concerned with pillorying someone for alleged negligence than explaining the full background to the situation, as the latter makes much less exciting reading. There is also quite simply not enough time or space to go into all the details of a particular story. News editors are interested, essentially, in short, sharp, interesting stories, rather than detailed, boring explanations of the inevitability of most mistakes.

These features of central media – low variety, coarse grain, emphasis on 'big shots' and the pillorying of scapegoats, so far considered in relation to mass-circulation media – are equally pronounced in the specialist central media, professional and trade journals and magazines. Here, though, the disintegrative effect is more marked. The tendency for these coarse-grained hierarchies, and the people who work in them, to have fragmented world views, is compounded by the education system, which creates blinkered specialists who cannot see outside their own specialisation. When they finish their training they join restricted professional lateral media, associated with each particular division of reality, which have their own particular taboos. If there are specialist magazines and journals for every conceivable specialism, very few attempt to transcend them. *New Scientist* is of course a notable exception, but is chiefly read by (generally powerless) academics.

Because of the pressure to carry stories of general interest to their specialist readers, professional journals will tend to focus on items of interest within their particular areas. Architectural journals tend to carry stories about top architects, rising young architects, large prestigious buildings, architectural methods, competitions, and so on. Each profession offers many potential interactions with other professional areas, but each of them will tend only to be of interest to a limited number in the profession. So the tendency is for those areas either not to get covered, or at best only infrequently. So in time the concentration on the central concerns of any professional group, rather than its interactions with others generates and compounds tunnel vision. Interaction and integration with related areas never become part of the specialist's cosmology.

The fact that the professional and the specialist sit at the centre of their own secure and well-defined areas is implicit in their 'meta-world', their subconscious, idealised internal map of how their part of the world is. Some up-market women's magazines nicely illustrate the nature and power of meta-worlds, but the same could be said of architects' journals, medical journals and so on. Cheap colour printing has enabled the men behind women's magazines to create an entirely non-existent world, peopled by beautiful, amazingly young, slender women with perfect complexions and figures, and tall, handsome, rugged-but-sensitive men. The women in this meta-world live in detached houses, have fine, healthy children after marrying Mr Right, and probably a discreet affair or two. The women reading women's magazines, visible on any train, are in general not a bit like the women depicted (nor are the men). The pages of these magazines are packed with advertisements telling these women how to enter this particular meta-world: by buying and using the right products. Advertisers monitor which advertisements generate most sales, and editors have a vested interest in attracting advertising and revenue, so in time a type of journalism evolves which merely complements the advertising. The articles tend to focus on people and situations which make the reader feel inadequate by comparison, thereby creating a need for advertised products. 'Debates' are also conducted which attempt to delineate the meta-world, along the lines of "Where is the modern marriage going?" 'Does feminism mean loss of female mystique?' and so on. Such articles attempt to formulate what being a woman is, based on a coarse-grained, low variety model. One of the reasons women have felt unhappy with their role in life is that it has been stolen by central media, and hived off to a group of slick professionals in the same way that health, law, and education have been stolen and marooned in their various meta-worlds. By contrast, women who go to women's groups, the small informal ones which have been set up all over the country as a spontaneous result of the feminist movement, are better-informed. These women's quality circles, as we might call them, generate tacit knowledge about being a woman that is as diverse as the situations in which they find themselves. There is no attempt to extract a sort of intellectual elixir, glamorise it, and hold it up before all the women in the land.

Together with private meta-worlds, specialist central media tend to assist the development of private languages, or jargon. In a society without central media everyone has the same general shared experience, the same cosmology, the same language. As that society evolves and changes everyone keeps more or less in step. But if there are specialist central media operating, then the different shared experience they generate, via words and pictures simultaneously transmitted, can create discordant languages. This means that communication between members of different professions, architects, engineers, teachers, becomes virtually impossible on any specialist level, because the parties speak slightly different languages. Specialist central media accelerate the development of multiple private realities, and the words which express them. These are experienced by outsiders as jargon, and are not understood, since they refer to concepts on the user's map, but not on the listener's. In effect, the buildings of modern architects are not understood by the general public; they are seen as visual jargon because they only have beauty, context and relevance in the eyes of those who have the appropriate meta-worlds, and not the public's.

The remaining category of central media is books. They do not transmit an identical message to large numbers of people simultaneously, in the same way that newspapers, television and journals do; but they are, nevertheless, a largely monologue form of communication. As information systems, books suffer from many of the defects which I have so far outlined. In the first place, because thousands of children spend a lot of time devouring story books, the content of such stories is important. The best-selling children's author is still, as she has been for many years, Enid Blyton. In her books, well-mannered white middle-class children have exciting adventures, take jobs, catch criminals, have kindly understanding parents and get rewarded for good works by kind but firm authority. But the qualities of Blyton's children are nowhere to be found in real life, where children are made of a richer mixture of dishonesty, laziness, unreliability and so on; they also frequently experience adults and authority as unkind and unresponsive. Few children have exciting adventures, catch criminals, and get rewarded by adults, or belong to an exclusive dependable group of unchanging friends. The appeal of all this to children is undeniable, but those fed on too much of it can have a hard time of it with real life if they begin to confuse the two, since the story world is more beguiling. Polly Toynbee describes her disillusionment:[7] 'Enid Blyton was responsible for my five less than delightful years in a boarding school. Her Mallory Towers and St Clare's books had me begging to be sent away to one of those blissful institutions – dishonest advertising if ever there was. Here, for instance, is Darrell Rivers' arrival at Mallory Towers: "Darrell looked. She saw a big square-looking building in soft grey stone standing high up on a hill. The hill was really a cliff, that fell deeply down to the sea. At each end of the gracious building stood rounded towers . . . It looked like an old-time castle." Would boarding schools still flourish were it not for the propaganda in school stories like these, and the Chalet School books?'

The lingering effect on people of absorbing such meta-worlds from childhood reading is that parts of their internal map are from then on wrong. They respond to people and situations with inappropriate expectations and actions because the meta-worlds do not coincide with reality. In societies with purely oral narrative traditions, stories either coincide with reality, or are obviously imaginary and therefore have a different status. The problem with printed fiction – especially bad fiction – is that it creates plausible meta-worlds that children take on board as the truth.

Books also tend to be a poor substitute for lateral media in areas of tacit knowledge. Take child-rearing, for example. Various writers have, over the years, appointed themselves as experts on how to bring up children. In traditional societies, those with extended families, or communities where the relatives lived close by, or where neighbours were in constant and close contact, there were ready-made lateral media offering advice and example to guide on problems as they arose.

Such knowledge was largely tacit; people simply copied the un-consciously-acquired habits which they observed. If you enquired of a traditional society what the guiding principles were in their methods of child-rearing, they might have been able to make vague statements referring to 'respect for elders', but they would not have been able to give you a definitive list of situations and how to deal with them, any more than they could explain, by reciting a complete list of the rules, how to speak their language.

Even where people *can* state their methods they may not actually practise what they preach. Many people, for instance, could quite sincerely say, 'I believe in being firm but fair', but observation of their actual behaviour might reveal quite a different story. Nevertheless, throughout most of history, cultures have successfully raised children who behaved more or less like their parents, with very little awareness of method. The matter was never considered to be the province of formal knowledge. These days a young couple on a new housing estate composed of similar young people do not have lateral media to call on and learn from. Most people do not live in extended families, nor are they 'in and out of one another's houses', or continually meeting in informal situations, so child-rearing books, of which Dr Spock's already mentioned is probably the best known, have replaced lateral media.

These books are, in the first place, inevitably very coarse-grained. They cannot offer specific enough information to enable the parent to respond smoothly and optimally to every situation. They are also of doubtful authority when compared with experience embedded in a community. In fact, the concept of 'expert' in this field is somewhat spurious, as no one can really see the results of their advocated methods for thirty years or so – and by then it is too late to start again with a revised method. Penelope Leach's loving approach to child-care represents the current popular ideal as surely as Dr Spock's represented the 1950s'. By attempting to extract and formalise one approach, and promoting it in book form, speculative ideas are given the status of authority, and whole generations may be influenced. Each book implicitly creates a meta-world, and the promise that if you follow the author's guidelines then you will get the kind of child you want – happy, obedient or responsible. The implication is that if your children are not like the family depicted in the pictures and text then you have failed. In a lateral media situation such ideas are automatically modified and qualified by first-hand experience, so cannot develop to such an extent. The adherence to such regimes, arising from lack of confidence on the part of the parent, must surely create blocks in communication with the child, and so contribute to blocks in communication between generations.

Libraries of course contain collections of books, together with journals, papers, magazines, and newspapers. My general comments about central media apply to libraries but as information sources they are potentially more fine-grained and to some degree interactive. But the relevance paradox greatly limits their value to the unwary information seeker. He may go to a library as an information source, and look, but his search will of course be guided by his internal model of any situation, so he will look only for the information which he thinks is relevant to him. This leads to the paradox that there may be other information relevant to him, but because he is not in possession of it, he cannot see its relevance.

To take an example, evidently one of the reasons why the loss of life was so high when the *Titanic* sank was that the radio of the *Californian*, a ship 20 miles away, had been shut down for the night, so the *Titanic*'s distress calls were not picked up. After the disaster it was made mandatory for large ships to install automatic receivers, operating on certain prescribed emergency frequencies, which would ring an alarm bell on the bridge. At that time transmitters were weak, and relied on good aerial design, and early textbooks had whole chapters on aerials, or antennae, as they were called, and the associated insulator design. But within a relatively short space of time, as one correspondent wrote to *Wireless World*,[8] 'textbooks ceased to dwell on "what everybody knew" and gave the space to other aspects of a rapidly-developing technology.' As a result, knowledge which was familiar after the First World War disappeared from books, and eventually from the stock of tacit knowledge. For example, 'since modern "sophisticated" manuals on radio technique fail even to recognise the existence of the wet insulator problem, it is necessary in seeking an explanation of the nature of the "leakage", to turn to the fundamental literature on the physics of electrolytes. Most of these books have been long since removed from library stocks as "obsolete", but can still occasionally be found in backstreet second-hand bookshops.'[8] The result is that much of the art of good aerial design appears to have been forgotten. Designers concentrate on high-powered transmitters, which are always tested in harbour in good weather. The fact that they are inadequate in a gale, when the ship is sinking, with salt spray surrounding the badly-designed aerials, has been advanced as an explanation for some of the large numbers of ships that simply disappear without trace every year, apparently without giving a distress signal. The limitation on knowledge from libraries is that they can only respond to requests for specified information. They cannot perceive gaps in the seeker's map and provide the information that he is unaware he needs, or that which has become 'obsolete'.

In some cases written sources of extremely valuable information have never even existed, let alone been available through libraries. Whilst NASA scientists were designing space suits, they made a special visit to the Tower of London in order to look at suits of armour. I obtained the following details from Ian Eaves, Keeper of Armour. 'It seems that when NASA were working on the design of their spacesuits, and were considering the various ways in which all the normal movements of the astronaut could be allowed for, someone, a member of staff or a visitor, asked why they did not look at old armour, since its makers must have been faced with similar problems, and it might be helpful to investigate the solutions which they had already come up with. Apparently no one had thought of this before, but the idea seemed such a good one and so sensible that it was taken up almost immediately. They spent only a day or two at the Tower, and for the most part they concentrated on the examination of one particular suit of armour, the foot-combat armour made for Henry VIII in the Royal Workshops at Greenwich, about 1520. This armour is exceptional in that it covers every part of the body, including buttocks, groin, the insides of the elbows, the armpits and the backs of the knees. The way in which each plate links to the next, and the wearer's movements are allowed for, is marvellously ingenious, yet simple and effective. When the NASA team saw this armour they observed that they wished they had seen it earlier on their development programme, since it would have saved them a lot of time and money.

'From what I have been able to gather,' Eaves continues, 'the NASA team who visited the Armouries came specifically to look at this unusual armour of Henry VIII. If I am correct in this assertion, it seems likely that someone knowledgeable about arms and armour directed them to it.'

It is very hard to see how a library, or even a computer data base, could be organised to yield the suggestion of looking at old suits of armour in connection with space travel. Most literature searches would be guided by the various specialist models of the situation, and it is only with hindsight that the connection with armour is obvious. What is important is the manner in which the link was forged, simply by caprice, by a chance, unplanned recognition of ignorance. In this sense, libraries, data bases and central media are not interactive, whereas lateral media are.

Electronic libraries aim to convert all books, journals and scientific papers into electronic form, store them in a central computer, and enable them to be retrieved by a user equipped with a suitable terminal. Ultimately it is envisaged that every home in the industrialised countries will have a terminal. The advantages to be derived from such a system are obvious, but I consider it essential to be aware, too, of its inherent limitations.

In the first place there is the problem of the sheer bulk of information that can be retrieved. How do you pick out what you want? How do you know if it is credible or not? In reply to an article of mine in the *Guardian*, raising some of these issues,[9] Eric Liggett, a lecturer in politics at Glasgow University wrote in praise of centralised computer-based systems. He said, 'I spent half-an-hour with Gordon Anderson of Glasgow University Library. We discussed my research and produced a short list of key words. My colleague dialled a number, pressed a key and teleprinted our words – interdisciplinary, multidisciplinary – via satellite to California. In seconds we had sample titles of relevant articles, and promises of delivery by air mail of a further 492 titles. The operation cost £19.'[10] Impressive. And yet, has he really got the right information? Has he used all the right key words? Is he suffering from the relevance paradox? How does he select from the 492 papers? Has he got time to read them all? Are they worth reading? Had he been a general purpose radio designer, would the computer have old textbooks on radio aerials in it? Would the librarian have pointed the problem out to him? Would he even have gone to a library in the first place? Similar questions could be asked of engineers on Third World irrigation schemes, the designers of housing, the producers of Green Revolutions, the designers of temporary shelters for disaster areas, and so on.

The chief limitation of all information systems, electronic or otherwise, is that essentially they confirm pre-existing ways of looking at the world, simply adding more detail. These models may be inappropriate or faulty, but that can only be discovered by talking to other people with superior or different models.

Another letter responding to my article in *The Guardian* was from an information officer at the Library Association. She defended the role of librarians, saying, 'Librarians are trained both to find and to transmit information. We do not simply respond to requests – we also supply any material which we would consider relevant to the user's interests. So if, to use Mr Andrews' example, his "designer of an irrigation system in a developing country" had gone to the library and asked, he would probably have been nearly buried in the mountain of information with which he would be supplied.'[11] Of course librarians can be very helpful, but they cannot, as a rule, know enough about all the related areas of every subject – particularly the unconventionally related areas – to be infallibly useful. The result would indeed be a mountain of material, but much of it would be irrelevant, and it would not necessarily include all that was relevant.

This point is recognised in a letter appearing in *New Civil Engineer*.[12] The former head of the information service of a major firm of consulting engineers wrote protesting about the Institute of Civil Engineers' idea of setting up an information centre. 'There exist already in, and on the fringes of, the construction industry a number of excellent sources of information – in all the institutions, in research establishments and, as your article rightly stresses, by personal contacts.

'There is no case for a central information centre, except perhaps in the minds of lazy and badly-informed civil engineers, since such a centre could not handle the breadth and depth of information needed, even with electronic retrieval.

'Practising civil engineers do not require full literature surveys of innumerable and often third-rate papers, many of them not readily available. They need only one or two good immediate references and these are usually found by personal telephone contacts.' The fact is, of course, that if you want to know, for example, the effect of silage on concrete, the best course of action is a phone call to the Cement and Concrete Association, who would refer you to someone who knows about the problem, can discuss it with you, and tell you of any relevant sources. Consulting a computer data base containing all the papers ever printed on the deleterious effects of certain substances on concrete, although appropriate in certain circumstances, would be a far more cumbersome and expensive procedure.

The fact is, of course, that all the multi-faceted activities of central media are an inextricable part of the twentieth century, and have played a vital role in disseminating social, political, technical and other information: the advantages are obvious. But if a society, or any part of it, is interested in optimising the success of its policies, including the well-being of its members, then it is as well to be aware of deficiencies in the way information is handled by existing central media. For the means are now available to replace these deficiencies by the creation of additional forms of electronic lateral media.

11 PROBLEMS OF CENTRALISED SOCIETIES

Throughout this book I have drawn a distinction between centralised and dispersed control systems. I described some dispersed control systems such as the slime mould in some detail, because for most of us, living in a highly-centralised society, it is an unusual concept. I also said that it is virtually impossible for hierarchies, the organisational expression of centralised control, to operate successfully without adequate dispersal of control to lower levels, and with lateral communication across the base and lower levels of the pyramid to co-ordinate the different members. The law of requisite variety means that only by having large internal networks, forming interlock diagrams, can policies be formulated at a lower level that remedy the deficiencies in central policy caused by the low-variety models of those at the top. The mind of an individual can be visualised as functioning in the same way, in that it contains models of reality that together form an interlock diagram. If an adult is to act successfully to deal with all the situations life presents to him, he must possess models with requisite variety.

Societies can also be treated as organisms with minds of their own. It may be easy to accept that an ant-eater is an organism, despite being composed, essentially, of millions of cells living as a colony, just like the slime mould. It may be less simple to realise that an ant-hill can also per-fectly well be regarded as such an organism. For the ant colony as a whole acts as a large nervous system or brain. It forms patterns equivalent to interlock diagrams, with requisite variety, and these enable the colony to function as a whole, the patterns being the groups of ants that carry out co-operative tasks. It is in fact, a perfect example of dispersed control. Even if the queen is removed the nest will go about its business of being an ant-hill much as before.

Before going on to consider in more detail how entities such as an ant's nest, a brain, slime mould or a country, react and communicate without purely central control, we need to look at the idea of meta-levels. Let us suppose that there is a James Bond book open on a table. If we have no knowledge of writing, then it would just look like some paper with curious squiggles on it. If we ask ourselves what the squiggles are, to discover the answer we would have to learn an alphabet. So we have to apply some learning, some appreciation of the outside world in order to answer the question. But what words do the letters spell? To answer this we would have to master spelling, and could probably do with a dictionary as well. More learning. Next, what kind of sentence do the words make up? To answer this we need to know a language and some grammar. Suppose this particular version of the book is in Portuguese. We could probably spell words from letters without understanding the language, but sorting out a sentence requires some knowledge of Portuguese. Finally a question *about* the sentences: what kind of book do they make up? For this we need to have a good reading knowledge of Portuguese. It is a James Bond book, not an encyclopaedia or a car maintenance manual. We need to be sufficiently widely read to tell the difference.

As we climb the ladder of questions, we need more and more complex information about the world in order to operate, for each question is pitched at a certain logical level. Every time we ascend a level we ask a question about the level below, and go up one meta-level. It takes children about two years to learn to shift from one level to the next. Hofstadter,[1] pursuing the Turing Test to design an artificial intelligence machine indistinguishable from human intelligence at a particular logical level, points out that computers can already decipher squiggles as letters, correct bad spelling, and make recommendations for good grammar in business letters.

Every question we might ask about our James Bond book implies a certain logical level and a certain amount of external knowledge. Godel's Theorem says that at any particular level there are always questions that can be asked that are not answerable by the information to hand at that level. If, for example, we are at the 'letter' level of looking at our book, we cannot ask questions about the words.

Getting confused over the meta-level at which a problem is being dealt with can be very serious. It is no good, for instance, trying to discuss the relative merits of James Bond and Simon Templar books if the conversation is limited to the quality of spelling. Mastery of meta-level confusion seems to be a prerequisite of being a good evasive politician, and is the technique behind their successful interviews that I have already referred to. When asked a straight question by a journalist, requiring him to confirm or deny a particular statement, a politician will often shift his reply up at least one logical level. This is to get the discussion onto wider ground, requiring more knowledge from the opponent. The reply might be, 'This document is secret/stolen/only a discussion paper', or along the lines of 'only a Communist/Fascist/gutter journalist like you would ask such a question.' Similarly authoritarian bosses baffle and terrorise their subordinates by changing meta-level in mid conversation.

Essentially, in order to communicate effectively with another individual, both parties must be on the same logical level, or meta-level. People who can communicate effectively – jointly solve a problem, for example – have learnt certain tacit conventions which enable them rapidly to synchronise their meta-levels. Politics, of course, is not usually about the determination of the truth of an issue, the arrival at a consensual representation of reality in an agreed frame of reference at an agreed meta-level; meaning that effective communication in politics frequently involves deliberate misinterpretation of what an opponent means. On a personal level this is essentially what arguments are, and at the 'highest' level, it is warfare. So arguments, politics, and arms-racing can be seen as attempts to proliferate variety at such a rate that the opponent is reduced to impotence, irrespective of the truth of the matter.

I have already described how the same effects manifest themselves in the kind of child-rearing which prevails in the Western world, the typical parent ignoring the child's internal models and the meta-level at which he is operating. I mentioned earlier the case of the little girl who was punished for trying to help her parents sweep up the grass. In her frame of reference she was doing the same as her parents, but at a higher logical level she was not actually sweeping into a central point as they were. Unless the child's own model is first confirmed, and then extended, she will experience herself as the *victim* of arbitrary correction in her interactions with her parents. This leads not only to intense frustration and unhappiness, but also to a delay in developing a coherent, logically-ordered intellectual framework.

It is precisely people who are the product of authoritarian upbringings who have an overdeveloped craving to rise in hierarchies, who succeed in doing so. In Chapter 9 I have already referred to Professor Dixon's study of the authoritarian personality. In another of his books, *On the Psychology of Military Incompetence*[2] he describes this phenomenon in connection with the army. He acknowledges that some commanders get to the top because they are outstanding at their job, and rise naturally through the hierarchy; Montgomery is one of his examples in this category. But there is a second type, the incompetent, who reaches the top through an all-consuming passion to get there. One of Dixon's examples of the latter type is Haig, who managed, despite plenty of warnings and good advice, to organise, almost single-handedly, the death of 300,000 of his own troops at the Battle of Passchendaele. Dixon shows that such people achieve promotion through their orthodoxy, their cultivation of superiors, and their ruthless and unfeeling behaviour towards subordinates. In intensely hierarchical structures, it seems that those who cannot think or communicate very effectively tend to get promoted *because* of these failings. Dixon also points out that the really great examples of military incompetence, the Crimea, the Boer War, the First World War, and so on, only really emerge with the first generation of children subjected to the public school environment. He asserts that separation from parents, and an attendant absence of parental warmth, with subjection to arbitrary discipline, often backed up by physical brutality, is liable to lead to the type of personality disorders that are manifest in the cold authoritarian type, unable to think beyond conventional channels, afraid of, while unthinkingly accepting, authority, zealous against the unorthodox, and so on.

I have also pointed out in Chapter 9 the positive feedback loop that exists in a hierarchic society, in which parents force their models on their children, who will tend to experience their parents as hostile and arbitrary, these children growing up to succeed in hierarchies, and treating their children in the same way. A population so nurtured will tend to have a disproportionate desire for status symbols, for rank in an organisation, and for material objects, since the child will have noted that in his world disputes are settled arbitrarily by those with the most power, and that power is associated with status and the possession of objects. Thus there is a link between the hierarchisation of society and the increasing demand for natural resources and there is also a link between the hierarchisation of society and mental illness.

Living in surroundings where important problems and questions are persistently evaded can, according to psychiatrists like R.D. Laing and Gregory Bateson, lead to mental breakdown. As Laing put it, 'Schizophrenia is just a sane reaction to an insane world.' Gregory Bateson has suggested that the lack of communication between an individual and the outside world is essential to an understanding of schizophrenia,[3] though others insist that it is all due to brain chemistry. If, for instance, we had just learnt the alphabet and were quite happy about distinguishing between A and B, something would have to give if someone appeared demanding to know what the letters AXOLOTL meant, beating us over the head to extract an answer, but at the same time denying access to extra knowledge such as a dictionary.

Someone in a severely schizophrenic state may suffer complete meta-level confusion and be unable to answer a question on the level intended. The situation can be confusing for a psychotherapist when confronted with a patient who insists on replying to a question with two conflicting answers at the same time. When asked 'Are you happy?' the person may open his mouth and say 'Yes', while scowling, and maintaining the tense body posture that says 'No'. It is for the therapist to decide which answer is 'meta' to which. The book *The Structure of Magic*[4] attempts to unravel the confused multi-meta-level communication of disturbed patients, trying to sort out which modes of communication refer to the 'surface structure', normal mannerisms for dealing with simple questions, and which refer to 'underlying structure', mannerisms connected with deeper problems of a higher logical type.

The notion of the need for ever-wider perspectives and the need to be able to shift up a meta-level to 'see over' a problem, is implicit in many Zen and Sufi teaching stories, such as those collected by Idries Shah.[5]

Confusion of meta-levels also leads to the phenomena known as logical paradoxes. To most people, for example, the statement 'no generalisation is wholly true', is a perfectly valid one. But to people who have never learnt, or who have deliberately forgotten, the tacit rules of conversation, the statement is a paradox. Philosophers might argue that the statement itself is a generalisation, so if it is true, it must not be wholly true. It then follows, they argue, that some generalisations must be wholly true, which contradicts the first assumption, but follows directly from the statement. Similar problems arise with statements like 'I am a Cretan. All Cretans are liars.' If you follow it logically through, your mind rapidly gets baffled. The problem, of course, only arises if you depart from the 'commonsense' or tacit rules of conversation. If a local inhabitant made the above statement to a visitor on holiday in Crete, most people could deduce useful information from it. An over-logical person could not. People who have problems with logical paradoxes also have problems with language in general, and are likely to be pedantic, and to complain about phrases such as, 'Hopefully, when we get there they won't have gone to bed.'

The theoretical scheme of logical levels and the hierarchic organisation of thought processes seems plausible enough. What I am suggesting is that people's personalities actually exist as a collection of small particles of personality, each with a life of its own, like in the ant-hill, and that these are hierarchically organised and related in the same way as meta-levels. Data or communication from the world will activate the appropriate groupings of particles, forming the patterns discussed in Chapter 9, and it is the recognition and manipulation of these patterns which constitutes thinking. Rational thinking requires that when an external event activates a given pattern within the brain, then lateral connections to the appropriate related patterns are made.

The hierarchic arrangement of successively more complex personality structures is demonstrated in certain bizarre and extremely rare forms of schizophrenia called 'multiple personality disorder' (MPD). In this condition, the same body may appear to be lived in by several different people at different times, and these may have different names and may even walk and sit differently. In 1910 a Pittsburgh psychiatrist by the name of Walter Prince came across a girl called Doris Fischer who exhibited at least five different personalities.[6] The break-up of her personality had been caused by the cruelty of her drunken father and witnessing the death of her mother while he was drunk. Dr Prince adopted the girl and documented the rise and fall of the many personalities in her body. They appeared to be hierarchically organised. At the bottom was a character that Dr Prince named Jane. Jane was a tape-recorder and little more. She could recite conversations right back into Doris's childhood as if she were reading a script. Next came Mary Anne. She was dull and wooden, but could maintain a dog-like friendship. Next there was Margaret, who was reasonably bright, but whose development appeared to have stopped at the age of ten. Doris herself came next, and she had almost ceased to exist when Dr Prince took the child in. Finally there was Ariel, who claimed not to be a personality at all, but a spirit sent by the girl's dead mother to sort out the mess.

The inter-relation of the alternating personalities is extraordinary. Margaret was aware of the existence of Jane, Mary Anne and Doris, and could 'switch off' Jane and Mary Anne in order to come into existence herself. She claimed that she had taught Mary Anne to speak. Margaret could read Doris's mind but had no control over Doris. Doris was not aware of the existence of any other personality, but was distressed by the way she 'blanked out'. Ariel could control all the other personalities and could 'switch off' Margaret in order to allow Doris to appear. As a result of this, Margaret deduced the existence of another personality of whom she had no direct knowledge. The various personalities would also write letters to each other. Once Doris was settled in with the Prince family, the lower personalities, Jane and Mary Anne, became younger and younger, regressing into infancy, allowing Doris to appear more and more. After two years both these personalities had 'died', Mary Anne leaving her toys to Margaret in a letter. Eventually Margaret also regressed and 'died', leaving Doris in full control. Ariel, who had no claims to the body at all, simply vanished. Dr Prince described her as the 'maturest and wisest of the quintet', and was inclined to believe that she was what she claimed to be, a visiting spirit, rather than a dissociation of personality. This case demonstrates, perhaps, that 'maturity and wisdom' are synonymous with full control over all the sub-personalities in a particular body. This effectively means having the possibility of a full flow of information between them through the medium of a personality or thought-landscape at a higher meta-level.

At the National Institute for Mental Health in Washington, tests have been carried out recently on MPD patients to check the ability of their different personalities to keep memories separate.[7] Word lists were given to each personality to learn, and afterwards tests were given to see whether the words from one personality had leaked through to the other. These tests were also given to ordinary volunteers, some of whom were asked to simulate multiple personalities and some to act normally. Strangely enough, although the MPD patients were good at keeping the word lists separate, the volunteers who were being 'normal' were better at keeping them separate than the ones who were acting at being MPDs. So perhaps multiple personality is present in all of us to some extent. Dr Putnam, who conducted the experiments, commented 'Think of dissociation as a spectrum. On the one end is daydreaming, on the other multiple personality.'

In a sense we are all schizophrenic, but some of us make a better job than others of 'keeping it together'. Arthur Koestler, in his *Act of Creation*[8], suggests that it is these fragmented chunks of personality, of logical ordering, that are at the root of humour. The story line of a joke creates a certain train of thought at a certain logical level. When the punch-line arrives, a whole new logical landscape is suddenly introduced, out of the blue. It is the clash and resolution of these two conflicting logical patterns that produces the joke itself. The need to resort to higher meta-levels of understanding to resolve the conflict is one reason that satire has always been used as a vehicle for political reform.

For narrowness of mind really does seem to affect our perception of the world. If we have never seen something before, we may actually not be able to perceive it. Credo Mutwa, in his book *My People*[9] describes some of the stories that circulated amongst the Africans who were suddenly exposed to White Europeans. The Africans were used to people having dark skin, curly hair and few clothes. When the Europeans first appeared, the Africans were at a loss to fit them into their cosmology, since the Europeans had long straight, blondish hair, wore many funny clothes and were white-skinned. Stories began to circulate that they were in fact a strange new kind of plant. Another story arose from the fact that Europeans often used to kiss in public, often as a form of greeting. The only time that the watching Africans *ever* kissed, was when making love. At the time of the appearance of the first Europeans, according to Mutwa, stories circulated that Europeans could have children simply by kissing.

It would seem that, as Arthur Koestler put it, we are both 'individuals' and 'di-viduals'. In *The Ghost in the Machine*[10] he argues that we are made up of many organisational units called 'holons', arranged in hierarchical order. Each holon is 'Janus-faced': looking both ways, organising the components of which it is made, and also being organised by a holon of a higher logical type to make up a larger sub-assembly.

We can think of an ant-hill as an entity able to recognise and interact with its surroundings. Hofstadter's ant-hill has an amiable relationship with the local ant-eater and communicates with it on one level by arranging patterns of ants and sending him the juiciest ants to eat.[1] On another level the ant-hill develops longer tunnels to keep the ant-eater at bay. In response, ant-eaters over the generations develop longer tongues.

Even nation states may be regarded as organisms, not centrally controlled just by governments, but to a very large extent by the interaction of their individuals. We may legitimately talk of countries having personalities, and viewing the world, and communicating with other countries, on levels we cannot perceive. So we may ask the question, what does it feel like to be the Soviet Union or India, or the Roman Empire?

The answer, I would suggest, is that in general you, the country or empire, would recognise very little of the rest of the world outside its role as a repository of things for you to use to maintain your hegemony. You would also recognise immediate threats to your existence, such as other threatening countries. But countries or empires are unable properly to perceive the complicated threats to their existence due to environmental and ecological factors. They can recognise and respond to more simple things such as threats from potential opponents – from other similar entities – and in the long run communication between countries tends to arms-racing and warfare. But countries are not organised so that they can recognise, and deal effectively with, the many other threats stemming from their treatment of the environment.

The reason for this inability lies in part in their nature as institutional hierarchies writ large, and the concomitant absence of internal networks with requisite variety. Specialisation breaks the country down into separate functional groupings (health service, foreign office, power supply, army, etc.) which do not communicate laterally. This means that in general countries cannot recognise the complicated and interlocked threats facing them because their institutions are only capable of looking at reality in a narrow, specialist way. But worse than that, it is the specialism and fragmentation of their world view that creates many of the threats in the first place. In effect, the essentially hierarchic organisation of countries is akin to the multiple personality disorders of schizophrenia. Elections, on one hand, and civil war on the other, can be seen as the analogue of the internal arguments and battles between parts of the schizoid personality. The fragmented nature of the agriculture, water supply, waste disposal, and energy sectors in Britain, for example, that I described earlier, is responsible in large measure for unnecessarily high energy and resource use and pollution. The fragmented nature of our institutions not only prevents them from seeing the problems and believing them to be real, but actually causes many of them. Governments being the sum total of official agencies, there is no *deus ex machina* to identify and confront these convoluted and interlocked problems. Individuals can see some of the problems some of the time but cannot possibly grasp the complexity of the whole, and nor are they able to force a government into a coherent response, because society as a whole cannot 'see' the problems. These are compounded by the features of the general and specialist media that I described in Chapter 10.

The major threats with which most modern countries are confronted are well-known – resource-shortage, energy-shortage, and pollution. But it is quite clear that most people do not appreciate the scale of the problems, nor their interlocking complexity. It is such problems on which many of the world's great civilisations have already foundered, as I have said. They usually ended up consuming or destroying those features of the natural environment on which they depended, such as soil, forest and water. G.V. Jacks and R.O. Whyte made a detailed survey of this in their book *The Rape of the Earth*, first published in 1939.[11] They argue: 'Erosion has indeed been one of the most potent factors causing the downfall of former civilisations and empires whose ruined cities now lie amid barren wastes that once were the world's more fertile lands. The deserts of North China, Persia, Mesopotamia and North Africa tell the same story of the gradual exhaustion of the soil as the increasing demands made upon it . . . exceeded its recuperative powers. Soil erosion, then as now, followed soil exhaustion . . . The gutted North-West and the Yellow River [in China] are the outstanding and eternal symbols of the mortality of civilisation . . .

'So in Mesopotamia, the River Tigris, which once irrigated and enriched the empires of Babylon and Assyria, now flows menacingly on a raised bed of eroded soil brought down from the hills when the plainsmen, seeking more water for their irrigated crops and more land to replace their exhausted soils, cut down the hill forests and were rewarded with uncontrollable floods that overwhelmed their fields and swept away their irrigation works . . .

'On the desert fringes of the Persian and Carthaginian empires, soil exhaustion, crop failures and land abandonment allowed the desert sands to encroach relentlessly.

'The might of Greece and Rome had its origin in the mastery of the art of continuous cultivation on forest land. Continuous cultivation of forest soils enabled permanent, organised communities to develop in a more favourable environment and to attain greater heights than the arid environment where civilisation could only exist by irrigation. Continuous cultivation meant continuous depletion of the soil, and always more deforestation, to secure new land . . . The decline of the Roman Empire is a story of deforestation, soil exhaustion and erosion . . . From Spain to Palestine there are no forests left on the Mediterranean littoral . . . That the Mediterranean countries have not suffered complete annihilation like the earlier empires bordering the deserts, is due to the comparative rapidity with which new soil forms from the rock beneath. But soil formation, apparently, has not kept pace with soil erosion.'

Jacks' and Whyte's description, although some years old now, remains reasonably accurate. The Romans were perhaps not quite as bad as they are made out to be in relation to soil erosion: it is now thought that vegetation in large areas of Italy and Spain was destroyed in the fifteenth century by sheep farming, leading to extensive erosion.[12]

And other causes are also present, such as sudden climatic changes. It has been argued that civilisations get used to the high output of crops during the good years, and come to depend on it. In periods of drought, not only do crops fail, but the lack of vegetable cover allows the massive and rapid development of dust-bowl conditions. Farming cultures are unable to adjust their methods to take account of poor weather conditions, and tend to stick to inappropriate practices. The Irish, for example, persisted in trying to grow potatoes for several disastrous years during the Potato Famine, when other crops might have succeeded.[13]

A centrally-controlled civilisation, consisting of cities feeding off surrounding farmland, is radically different from a dispersed culture such as the Maring, which I described earlier. With the Maring, gardening plots are abandoned as soon as they are approaching maximum output, beyond which soil breakdown would occur. So the signal to move on to fresh ground is determined by the output of the agricultural system itself. And as soon as output reaches its maximum, inter-tribal conflict ensures a war, with the losers abandoning their gardens, which are then left to regenerate. The beauty of this system is its homeostatic nature. By contrast, in civilisations where production from the farmland is controlled by demand from the cities, and there is an ethos sanctioning maximum output, there is no homeostatic control. The farmers always produce as much as possible, so that the soil is eventually exhausted.

Some civilisations have done better than others in recognising the true problems facing them. Jacks and Whyte compare China, where some of the worst soil erosion in the world has occurred, with Japan, 'where erosion does not occur to any great extent, as the Japanese have learned how to control it.'[11] Japan, of course, was a poly-centred feudal society, as opposed to a bureaucratic centralised society like China. As an information-processing system it was therefore presumably better able to respond to its environment.

The destruction of the soil, and hence agriculture, was exacerbated by a further problem encountered by, for example, Romans and Greeks: an energy crisis. The main fuel source was charcoal, derived from forest trees. The destruction of this resource was responsible, in large part, not only for the arid lands around the modern Mediterranean, but also for a lack of fuel, which was needed for industrial as well as domestic purposes. The following extract from *A Golden Thread* by Ken Butti and John Perlin describes the Greek fuel shortage.[16]

'As indigenous supplies dwindled and wood had to be imported, many city-states regulated the use of wood and charcoal. In the fourth century BC, the Athenians banned the use of olive wood for making charcoal . . . In the same century they also forbade the exportation of wood from nearby Attica. Yet Athens' own supply lines stretched all the way across Asia Minor to the shores of the Black Sea. On the island of Cos, the government taxed wood used for domestic heating and cooking . . .

'The Greeks responded to the situation by building solar-heated houses, complete with automatic control systems. They used pots of myrtle plants, whose thick leaves block the sun in summer and allow the sun's rays to penetrate when they fall in winter . . .

'Later on the Romans failed to learn from the Greeks' mistakes, and continued to ruin their environment far more efficiently and on a far wider scale than the Greeks had done . . . By the time of Christ, it was common for wealthy Romans to have central heating in their expensive villas. The hypocausts burned wood or charcoal in furnaces, and circulated the hot air through hollow bricks in the floors and walls. A hypocaust system could devour as much as 280 pounds of wood per hour.

'Indigenous wood supplies quickly disappeared from the Italian peninsula. By the first century BC, timber had to be imported from as far east as the Caucasus, more than a thousand miles away . . . Local fuel shortages and the high cost of imported wood probably influenced the Romans to adopt Greek techniques of solar architecture . . . They advanced solar technology by adapting home building design to different climates, using clear window coverings such as glass to enhance the effectiveness of solar heating and expanding solar architecture to include greenhouses and huge public bath-houses. Solar architecture became so much a part of Roman life that sun-rights guarantees were eventually enacted into Roman law.'

The relevance of the historical perspective is that our own civilisation is in danger of going the same way as previous ones, with soil erosion and energy shortage as the two horsemen of the Apocalypse. For civilisations as organisms produce ecological disaster. The most recent evidence and, since it emanates from the US government, the most disturbing, is the *Global 2000 Report to the President – Entering the Twenty-First Century*.[15] It was commissioned by President Carter, and makes grim reading.

This report attempts to project forward to the year 2000 'the probable changes in the world's population, natural resources, and environment through to the end of the century.' In the letter of transmittal to the President the authors wrote: 'Our conclusions, summarised in the pages that follow, are disturbing. They indicate the potential for global problems of alarming proportions by the year 2000. Environmental, resource, and population stresses are intensifying and will increasingly determine the quality of human life on our planet. These stresses are already severe enough to deny many millions of people basic needs for food, shelter, health, and jobs, or any hope for betterment. At the same time, the earth's carrying capacity – the ability of biological systems to provide resources for human needs – is eroding. The trends reflected in the Global 2000 Study suggest strongly a progressive degradation and impoverishment of the earth's natural resource base.'

Some of the interlinked problems foreseen in the report can be summarised:

1   For many less developed countries (LDCs) per capita food consumption will scarcely improve, or will decline.
2   Arable land will only increase by 4 per cent by 2000, so any food increase will have to come from increased use of fertilisers, pesticides, power for irrigation and cultivation, and fuel for machinery – implying higher energy use.
3   During the 1990s world oil production will approach its geological maximum. The richer industrialised countries will be able to purchase sufficient oil and other energy sources for their needs, but at high prices, creating shortages in the LDCs.
4   Needs for fuel wood will exceed supply by 25 per cent by the turn of the century, creating greater pressures on the green cover, and leading to even further soil erosion.
5   While in theory the world's finite energy supplies – oil, coal, gas, oil shale, uranium and tar sands – are sufficient to last for centuries, they are not in fact evenly distributed, and their extraction poses severe economic, political and environmental problems.
6   As increasingly dilute ores are mined for minerals, increasingly large amounts of money and energy will be required per unit of extraction. The quarter of the world population inhabiting the industrial countries will continue to consume three-quarters of the world's mineral production.
7   Regional water shortages will become more severe. In many LDCs water supplies will become increasingly erratic as a result of extensive deforestation. Development of new water resources will become more expensive virtually everywhere.
8   Significant losses of the world's forests will continue over the next 20 years, as a result of growing needs for fuel wood and forest products. By the year 2000, 40 per cent of the remaining forest cover in the LDCs will have gone.
9   There will be serious deterioration in agricultural soils worldwide, due to erosion, loss of organic material, desertification, salinisation, alkalinisation, and water-logging. Already, an area of agriculturally productive land equal in size to the American state of Maine is becoming barren wasteland each year, and the spread of desert-like conditions is likely to accelerate.

10 Atmospheric concentrations of carbon dioxide, and ozone-depleting chemicals, are expected to increase at rates that could significantly adversely alter the world's climate and upper atmosphere by 2050.

11 Acid rain from the increased combustion of fossil fuels threatens increased damage to food production and amenities by damaging soils, lakes, crops and rivers.

12 Radioactive and other hazardous materials present an ever-increasing threat to health and safety throughout the world.

The report warns that the sombre picture presented is likely to be an understatement of the problems we will face as we enter the year 2000, because in studying each sector they assumed that sufficient capital, land, water and energy would be available to meet needs, regardless of the competing needs of other sectors. It demonstrates the complexity of the problems facing us, due to the interactive nature of ecological and political processes. For instance, as minerals become more scarce, ores with lower mineral content have to be used as a basis for extraction, in turn requiring more energy for extraction, and so on. Fuel wood shortage and timber export for hard currency lead to deforestation, soil erosion and loss of food production. Downstream areas suffer flooding, since the uplands no longer absorb rainwaters, and downstream areas are in addition clogged with silt. The periodic disastrous flooding which we see on our television screens in India, for example, is a direct result of deforestation in the Himalayas, the once rich topsoil of Nepal now forming an island in the Indian Ocean off the coast of Bengal.

Most thinking people recognise that our civilisation is heading for hard times. Certainly the lives of people in the majority of LDCs have little chance of future improvement, and, despite huge aid projects, their per capita consumption is diminishing. Most people in the West console themselves that they were born in the right part of the globe, but the evidence is that the gradual economic stagnation that is overwhelming the LDCs will gradually overwhelm the West, because much of our wealth is derived from exports to LDCs. This recognition underlies the Brandt Report,[16] which has so far been effectively ignored by the West. The inescapable conclusion is that if present policies continue, the world economy will be in severe difficulties by 2000, due to the purely physical restraints imposed by the environment. Economic hard times, and competition for natural resources, inevitably make the threat of nuclear warfare more likely.

We are facing a situation in which our current mode of operation is made untenable by physical realities. Our extinction is as assured as that of the previous civilisations unless we modify that mode of operation drastically and fast.

Man has been civilised for about 0.16 per cent of his existence. For the remaining 99.84 per cent of the time he has been living in semi-nomadic groups, or small villages, ways of life bringing about none of the disastrous effects on the environment that have characterised settled civilisations.

The interactions between man and the environment in the 'pre-civilised' world can be seen as very fine-grained. There were a large number of small, local interchanges between groups of people and their surroundings, with most materials being recycled locally. Civilisations, on the other hand, are very coarse-grained. In place of many, short fine lines representing local communications, long thick ones can be imagined, branching outwards from a centre, with only very fine ones coming back to it. There are also very thick lines entering the centres, from very far away; these represent the import of materials. North Africa, for instance, was once the granary of the Roman Empire, as sub-Saharan Africa provided many of the British Empire's raw materials.

Vast imports of food, energy and materials into the industrialised countries of the West are causing immense social and economic problems in the supplying countries, in addition to ecological trouble. Michael Lotchie, for example, writing on the 'Political and Economic Origins of African Hunger' says[17]: 'Decades of over-concentration on export cultivation have left the continent's food-producing regions badly undersupplied with infrastructure, deprived of government services, desperately short of capital for development, and techno-logically pre-feudal. As a result, any attempt to improve Africa's food producing capability, will need to concern itself with a fundamental structural transformation of the rural economy.' Numerous other studies have shown that one of the main causes of starvation is that countries are geared towards the export of food and other materials, in order to pay for food which they could easily grow themselves, but instead has to be re-imported.

The existing mode of organisation within industrial society creates centralised, hierarchic organisms within countries which vie for supremacy with one another. Within each bureaucracy factions form, which try to enhance their own supremacy and power. In the wider world, collections of these bureaucracies, nations, fight one another for supremacy. If we take a biological and cybernetic view, these hierarchic structures are organisms each with their own internal language and cosmology. But none of these organisms is capable of perceiving its true problems. Most specialist agencies within and between countries are set up to do certain specific jobs – build power stations, make roads, house people, dispense pensions, set up industrial projects in the developing countries, and so on. There are no effective mechanisms for recognising 'systems-wide' problems, and then forcing reluctant governments to act.

It may be argued that within Britain, for example, parliament is, among other things, an informal network which ought to have requisite variety because of the large numbers of different opinions, experiences, professional training, and so on, represented. Unfortunately, this is not so. Most MPs are lawyers or administrators, and few, for example, have specialist technical or scientific knowledge. Furthermore, most MPs are basically interested in, and adept at, the institutionalised political games associated with trying to gain and hold political power. The political process is really no different from the internal power struggles that go on within hierarchies, writ large, and as such not about the determination of truth, but rather its distortion to suit expedient short-term ends. The adversarial debating skills, learnt largely at public school by both political parties, are deployed to the full, as each side blocks the communication of the other through trivialisation, distortion and mis-statement.

We have seen that hierarchies operate more effectively when the lateral communication within them is increased. One way to allow countries to respond more appropriately to problems is, by extension, to increase their lateral communication. The adjustments required to save our society can only be properly determined by a kind of vast interlock diagram spanning almost all institutions. It is not possible for individual groups or institutions to make decisions about these adjustments, since the problems are too complex. Only a huge interlock network, where each member understands his sphere of operation, and its interactions with adjacent ones, could carry out the necessary thinking and attain the desired result. This would be like the ant-hill, or the human brain, with patterns forming as a result of interaction between individuals. At present, each individual is blind to the overall pattern, simply reacting to his nearest neighbours. A vast interlock network, by contrast, would create a stock of tacit and formal knowledge which would inform decision-makers so that they could make appropriate decisions.

If such a network had existed in the 1970s, for instance, the situation of the peace movement having eventually to force the American government to end the war in Vietnam could have been avoided. In the opinion of Robert Giddings, head of Media Studies at Bath Technical College, who was in the United States at the time and watched the peace movement grow, it sprang from the spontaneous recognition growing from discussions between millions of ordinary Americans, that the Vietnam war could not be won, and that thousands of Americans were needlessly dying. If members of governments participated in the kind of lateral media that I have mooted, American government policy would not have been allowed to diverge so far from public opinion.

National governments are, of course, only one of the many levels of decision-making which could be affected. Any large organisation such as the CEGB, the water authorities, ministries, large companies, local councils and so on, would benefit in exactly the same way by augmenting centralised flows of information with lateral ones. The same applies to supra-national agencies confronting global issues. Just as the human body is partly under central, and partly under dispersed, control, and could not function if it were not under such a dual control system, so in the industrial West we need to develop dispersed forms of control in order to correctly guide our institutions. So far we have used and developed technology mainly to amplify central communication. Nor do central media help the situation, as they do not facilitate the formation of interlock diagrams of requisite variety within our civilisation which would enable it to recognise and deal with the fundamental problems facing it.

What we need to do is use new technology now available to develop lateral forms of communication, the type which existed in traditional societies before the imbalance of wealth led to the development of modern hierarchical structures; when each member of the community was a node in the network that passed news and social comment around, and handed down its cosmology and folklore. We need to use and invent technology that can amplify this aspect of communication.

12 *LATERAL MEDIA THROUGH TECHNOLOGY*

While the electronic revolution is still in its early days it is vital that the right choices are made. At the moment the field is wide open, and various options can be fully explored, but once technological and political decisions are made they tend to have long-term and far-reaching effects which are difficult to undo. If all the right options are not explored now, we may find that as a civilisation we get stuck with the wrong basic equipment. Our modern airliner design, for example, with its long thin fuselage and slender wings, is apparently a result of the difficulty of reversing technical decisions, since the design is basically unsuited to protecting people in a crash during take-off and landing, which is when most accidents occur. The fuselage is too fragile so that the engines tend to smash through it, and the wings are full of hazardous fuel. A much safer basic design, called the Burnelli 'lifting body' was built 50 years ago,[1] and was last delivered to the RAF in 1945. A British-built version was used as de Gaulle's personal transport plane for some years. It had a stubby, wing-shaped fuselage, less likely to break up on impact, short stubby wings and rear facing seats. Modern versions would have fuel tanks and engines able to be jettisoned. This plane could take off and land at half the speed of conventional jets. But the design was killed by Roosevelt in 1941, when he found that one of its proponents was a supporter of his Presidential opponent, Wendell Wilkie. The subsequent commitment to the airliners we are familiar with today appears to be irrevocable.

In this chapter I will make suggestions about the type of information technology we need for the future. These Information Routeing Groups (IRGs) are important not because of any particular technical details I propose, but because we must in one way or another develop technology that can correctly route information. At the moment the development of information technology is largely in the hands of the government and existing commercial companies, and it is progressing in a direction that largely perpetuates existing practices and ideas. In simply facilitating the transmission of information via existing routes, the centralisation of control organisations and governments is enhanced. Adjuncts to the consumer society are provided, such as shopping and banking by telephone.

There is no real motivation to question existing forms of central media and the organisational system they support. Any incentive to use information technology to create decentralised media to improve the functioning of our institutions and communities will have to come from beyond a narrow clique of specialists, and before it is too late.

Most official forays into the field of public information technology have been orchestrated by the telecommunications monopolies of the countries concerned, and have simply been electronic extensions of prevailing paper-based central media systems. Prestel, in Britain, for example, is essentially the conversion of newspapers and magazines, railway timetables and catalogues, into electronic form. An implicit distinction is made by such systems, known generically as Viewdata, between information-providers and information-users. The providers are large organisations which can afford the capital outlay required. Such systems, in fact, are simply a recasting of Gutenberg technology in electronic form. Historically, the economics of publishing dictate that it is only feasible to send large chunks of information such as a whole book or a whole newspaper to a lot of people. This is what gives central media their characteristic chunky, coarse-grained attributes. Viewdata is based on the same sort of economic assumptions. But the new information technology could turn traditional economics on its head. An established electronic network, connecting, say, 1,000 people, can transmit very short messages at very low cost, and to one individual almost as cheaply and easily as to a large number.

Several computer manufacturers are beginning to market electronic network systems. Probably the best developed, and certainly the best studied, is the Electronic Information Market Place, which is a sub-system of the Electronic Information Exchange System. This system was set up by Murray Turoff, of the Computerised Conferencing and Communications Centre at the New Jersey Institute of Technology. Each member has a computer terminal at home or work, connected by ordinary lines to the central computer which supports the system. Each terminal consists of a typewriter keyboard on which he sends his messages, a visual display unit (VDU), and an optional printer, on which he receives messages. The terminals can be situated anywhere in the world, and there are several British members. If the terminals are not wired into the central computer, as most are, the connection can be made via an acoustic coupler. This converts the electronic signals from a terminal into sound signals which can be fed into an ordinary telephone receiver. The advantage of the acoustic coupler is that providing the phone lines are of reasonable quality, contact with the network can be made from a public call box wherever you happen to be. Portable terminals are already small enough to fit easily into a briefcase. As jack sockets become standard on phones, the terminal will simply be plugged in.

The point of such a network would be to enable individuals to transmit useful information to others, and to groups subscribing to it. But once you have set up the hardware, joined the network, and switched on your terminal, where do you begin? How do you know who will be interested in the information you have, and how do others know that you will be interested in their information? An obvious solution would be a sort of Yellow Pages, but this is unworkable in practice, because the range of information handled by the system is too diverse. For as well as scientific, working papers and articles, general information and statistics, the system can be used to pass on jokes, hints on programming micro-computers, anecdotes, gossip and so on. Yellow Pages would be unable to cope with the fluidity of the material, or to provide mutually meaningful descriptions. Specialist jargon, for example, would be a barrier. As Murray Turoff says,[2] 'It only takes a little reflection to realise that any open marketplace for information needs a wide range or "rich" choice of communication alternatives. Only if one is focusing on very highly structured information is a concept such as the hierarchical text pages of Videotext usable for organising the marketplace. However, things such as the Yellow Pages will not work in the hierarchical classification because of the ambiguity in language and the need for cross correlations.'

The chief way that users select who to send information to, or request it from, is through an 'ad' (for advertisement). An ad is written by the 'vendor', and contains brief information about the information he has to offer. It differs from a conventional ad, in that those who have already purchased the item can attach comments or reviews to it and these cannot be altered by the placer of the ad, meaning that the number of purchasers can be displayed.

In the current design of an Electronic Information Marketplace (EIES) an ad can be used to advertise any of the following transactions:

1   Offering information for sale at a fixed price. The information may be as short as a single page, or it can be a lengthy document.
2   Placing an item up for auction. The ad will display the current highest bid, but not who made it.
3   Offering subscriptions to one of the many computer conferences or electronic newsletters.
4   Offering payment in return for filling in a survey-type document. EIES has a special sub-system which allows any member to collect survey-type data from other members who are willing.

5   Offering a questionnaire for sale. This may take the form of a self-assessment test that asks, for example, 'Are you of above-average intelligence?' The test supplies your own score, and the average one.
6   Requesting the supply of a service, such as a consultancy.
7   Requesting comment on, or editing of, an item, for a fee.

These ads can be delivered in several successive stages. If a prospective purchaser is interested after reading the simple ad, he can request a closer look, at which stage a summary, the number of sales, the expiry date, and any reviews, for example, can be viewed. If he then wishes to purchase the item he can make an appropriate payment arrangement with the vendor, cash or invoice, and take delivery via the VDU or the printer. In the future it is expected that funds will be transferred electronically via this system.

If all ads were transmitted to all members of the network there would of course be an impossibly high number of them to wade through. So the system contains several ways of getting the right ads to the right people, a significant one being the Interest List, an alphabetical list of key words and phrases held by the computer. Each key word or phrase (for example, 'Apple micro-computers', 'high-strength polymers', 'bio-technology', 'baby-sitting groups') represents a specific interest of one or more members. Any member may instruct the computer to associate him with any of the words on the list, and add new ones to it. When a person composes an ad, he simply attaches a string of key words from the list which he thinks appropriate, so it is only presented by the computer to selected people – those who have associated themselves with the keywords. When a member 'logs on' to the system, it automatically presents him with these ads, together with any other messages from friends and colleagues, as well as from other systems within EIES. If he finds an ad interesting he can call for more information, purchase an item, pass the information on to his friends, or ignore it. As a result of the Interest List, dynamic common-interest groups may form themselves. Any member can associate himself with any key word on the list, for as long as he wants. So around each there is a cluster, large or small, of members who are currently interested in a particular topic. Supplementing the Interest List is the Categories List, which is analogous to the categories in classified newspaper advertising, and which holds ads under listed categories to be browsed among by members. These sub-systems, with others, enable members to buy, sell and discuss information ranging from single pages to long documents, from scientific dissertations to jokes and recipes. An exchange may be between two individuals, or between one and the entire network.

Other services offered by EIES include a computer conference system and discussion groups. Conferences usually take the form of the attenders paying a small fee, in return for which they receive advance copies of the papers for a particular conference, which may then take place over as much as several weeks. The 'attenders' may be from all over the world, but do not have to leave their desks. They log on when it suits them, and receive, in chronological order, comments on the papers, general opinions, and so on, that have been fed in so far by the other attenders. They may then add their own comments. So the central computer stores comments as they come in, and sends them out to people as they log on.

In a similar fashion, any of the interest groups can form continuing discussion groups. Unlike conferences, there is no formal time period arranged, nor are papers circulated in advance. Discussion can be set in motion by one or more members of an interest group, and when the other members log on, they simply scan the previous day's, week's or month's input from other members, and add their own comments. It is also possible to advertise for other members to join existing discussion groups. Some are open to any network members, while others act like an exclusive club and are by invitation only. The maximum workable number of participants has been discovered to be about 50.

EIES has been in operation since 1976. Continual improvements and modifications are being made in the light of users' comments. A newcomer to computing can quickly learn the layout of the system, and how to use the various facilities. Regular users pay a monthly subscription fee of $75 (or £50) a month regardless of how many hours they use, plus an hourly charge of around $7 (or £4.50), at 1982 prices.

In general, the cost of putting a page of text onto the system is between one and 30 cents per page. Given these costs, Turoff expects sales of text at upwards of 30 cents. The system takes a commission on all sales, usually about 5-20 per cent. The economics of selling text in this way are fundamentally different from existing central media systems. For if a member has originated the text he sells, he can get back something like 80 per cent of its value, with only 20 per cent going to an intermediary. If he publishes an article through the usual commercial media, at least 80 per cent of the final value goes to the intermediary. In addition, much smaller chunks of information can be sold. It becomes economic to address information to very small groups, and even to individuals. The fact that the system that transmits the information also transmits the money to pay for it also tends to blur the traditional boundaries between the banking, publishing, printing, newspaper, broadcasting and information services.

A study of the way EIES is used has been carried out by the sociologist, Roxanne Hiltz.[3] She found that enthusiasm for it varied widely. About 40 per cent of initial users dropped out, because they did not have convenient access to a terminal, while 40 per cent made moderate use of it, and another 20 per cent became addicts. Of the latter, some went to the length of taking portable terminals to New Year's Eve parties, logging on and then using the network to tell jokes, swap stories, make New Year resolutions and comment on them – oblivious to the parties going on around them. She comments: 'The addicts set up terminals at home, and reorganised their routines so that they could be at their terminals, and logged in to EIES day and night. They reorganised their work routines, so that almost everything went through the machine. "I can't think when the computer is down," they would complain. Wives on the other hand would complain . . . "You don't talk to me now, you're always on that damn machine"' . . . and Hiltz knows of two divorces attributed to EIES.

Perhaps one of the keys to this fanatical use of the system lies in the need for social stroking which I have already described. I speculated on the changes in communication skills required by modern forms of society. I suggested that many people are starved of social stroking through social incompetence, brought about by experiences in upbringing, education and work. They are frightened of interaction, and shy and nervous in company, while at the same time craving the social stroking that accompanies it. It is easy to see how computer networks can give easy access to massive quantities of interaction and social stroking in a particularly safe form, and perhaps this is one of the reasons for its potentially addictive effects.

Much of the information transmitted by the present network is certainly of an apparently trivial nature. In their description of the Marketplace in its early days, Turoff and Chinai speculated on the likely use to which the system would be put, based on their experience with other EIES patterns of usage.[2] 'We suspect that initially users will approach the Marketplace cautiously and with the attitude of engaging in some sort of grand "monopoly game". While there will be some important early exceptions to this, the first major bulk use is likely to be a high volume of low value information related to entertainment and recreation. One can expect a large offering of things like recipes, jokes, poems, reviews of books and movies, etc. This same sort of material has been popular in a number of current public conferences that commonly represent a personification of the "electronic coffee break". As one objective of EIES is to allow the widest possible range of human communication, it is gratifying that people use this technology for recreational purposes. While this application may seem a bit frivolous on the surface, it should be realised that transactions of this type would probably make up the bulk of traffic on any system ever put into wide scale use by the public.'

The exchange of such apparently trivial information is a feature of all communities, and is indeed what creates group feeling, as well as providing important tacit information about the community's nature. Formal information within an organisation, reports, memos, letters and so on, are usually based on a good deal of unwritten tacit knowledge about its nature and power structure, but it is only private, or informally, that pieces of this vital tacit knowledge can be transmitted, often humorously. Fig 17, for example, contains a lot of tacit knowledge about the relationships within the world of local authorities. It cannot be stated explicitly and formally, but it does not go unnoticed when pinned on the wall above the photocopier. I have seen the same basic cartoon, with suitably modified captions, in an architect's office and an engineer's office.

It is the informally acquired knowledge of how things actually work within an organisation that enables people to get things done. A similar point is made in a paper by Tom Ward and Julian Newman:[5] 'From the viewpoint of management, computer conferencing, particularly in the context of the Integrated Office of the future, will have a far greater impact than conventional computer systems ever had. As Rosemary Stewart has pointed out, by far the greatest proportion of the information used by management is of an informal nature, and not readily captured in conventional Management Information Systems, and this accounts for much management disillusionment with computers (Stewart, "The Computer Promise", *New Society* 24, 1973). But the communication of informal information is readily facilitated by computer conferencing. A capability to assess both informal and formal information through a common and interactive interface, will undoubtedly be a prime desideratum in future office systems.'

Hiltz's research, mentioned earlier, also showed that although the network was originally set up for the use of scientists and research workers, other activities soon sprang up, with special conferences for children, for instance, and for single people. For systems like EIES enable people to meet other people. Having met each other on the network, users often travelled great distances to see each other face to face. This is in contrast to telephone technology, for example, which only enables you, as a rule, to contact people you already know, or know of.

Another important effect of EIES, and similar systems, is its

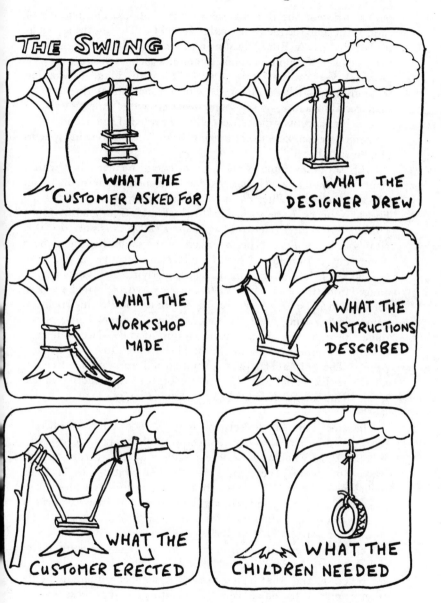

Fig 17 The swing

powerful decentralising influence on organisations. This effect is of course crucial to the theme of this book, and I will be returning to it in the last chapter. As Rory Johnston, reporting on Hiltz's study, wrote in the *Guardian*,[3] 'Communications techniques such as this can act as a powerful decentralising force. One US company found its working relationships had been changed, with a concomitant threat to its managerial structure, by the spontaneous growth of a message system that senior executives did not even know existed. Little wonder that US computer companies are hurrying to develop conferencing systems of their own to sell.'

EIES is one example of the type of lateral media, albeit with a central computer, which have so far been used in the main by an educated, scientific élite. But a completely different type exists – the Enfield Network. It was started in 1979 by Francis Sealey, a BBC Open University producer. Network, as its users call it, was started with a clear aim in mind: to bring members of the somewhat anonymous community of Enfield in North London closer together, in a spirit of mutual self-help and enjoyment. The underlying philosophy can be gauged from the *Handbook* for 1980: 'For the past decades we have been surrounded by state bureaucracies, corporate profiteering, political game playing, and failed revolutions. These are now being placed under increasing strain, and in the future, it is the development of community initiatives that will be vital in our efforts to survive as a free people. The only alternatives to mutual aid are a savage free-for-all where life could well be "nasty, brutish, and short", or extreme dictatorships dedicated to the domination of the many by the few.'

The chief function of Network is to provide a means whereby services can be offered by one member to another. The idea is to place in touch those who have a service, a skill, or a facility, with someone who wants them. There are currently 300 subject/interest areas, including cookery, DIY, dance, brick-laying, music, social sciences, plumbing, languages, and printing. Languages, for instance, consist of 23 sub-groups, including those for Armenian, Sinhalese, Swedish and Swahili (see Appendix II, p. 233).

On joining Network, each member fills in a questionnaire, giving details, as much or as little as he wishes, of the kind of thing he is interested in, and what he has to offer. A member wishing to use the service contacts the office, where a voluntary worker checks through the card index, and gives details of anyone fitting the description. The member then contacts the names he has been given, and arranges the transaction. The arrangements arrived at are entirely up to the individuals concerned: it can be done as a swap, for cash, or for free.

Another service that arises out of the system is the creation of interest groups such as sports groups, a baby-sitting circle, a camera group, a philosophy group, a publishing co-op, and so on. There is also advice available in areas such as accountancy, consumer affairs, job training, for parents, youth, and so on.

Francis Sealey reckons that the drop-out rate is about 20 per cent, but more new people join each year than those who drop out, so the membership is continually expanding, and is now well over 1,000. All members pay an annual fee of £2.25. There are about 30–50 referrals a week, on average, and 10 group meetings. The venture has recently received an MSC grant, which will enable three full-time and eight part-time workers to be employed.

Network provides another example of existing lateral media. The simple exchange of DIY knowledge or language skills is not the end of the matter, of course. By the time people have spent time together exchanging a skill, they will have got to know one another, and if they get on, they may engage in other mutual activities. An article in *Time Out* quoted Fred Melvin, aged 74, who has lived in the area since 1938.[5] 'Network gives people that initial *excuse* they need to get started with one another. They might want the badminton or to join one of the food co-ops. Or they might want the children's workshop or the under-5s information service or the baby-sitting circle. Or someone else might want to do a Network skill-swap – you know, I'll teach you bricklaying if you teach me accounting or the piano. But whatever it is people actually want, the best part of it is they get to meet and help each other, to know each other, and it goes on from there.

'With my father being in the army, we moved around a lot when I was young, but I've never seen a community like this one. It's all classes, races and ages, and it *works*. Prejudice only comes out of fear, isolation, and niggling on about people when you don't really know them. But Network sort of brings out the humanity. We have discussion groups on public issues, we went to the big CND rally in Hyde Park, we're involved with things like the Peace Movement. Anything which gets people to understand each other better. And when they do, it's not just pleasant. What with the way the world's going, I think there's an urgency about all this now.'

The *Time Out* journalist also observed, 'Any sociologist in search of a thesis should take a stopwatch and a clickometer and go hang about in Palmer's Green High Street for a week. He will discover an extraordinarily high incidence both of greeting behaviour and verbal exchange between passers-by. The proportion of people prepared to cross a busy road for a chat would be worth a graph in itself. The sense of community there is very infectious.'

The effects of Network are in contrast to central media in the form of local newspapers, for example, which on the whole have a negative effect on interaction, for reasons I described in Chapter 10. Such media are also intimately connected with stimulating the consumption of goods and services, by the creation of spurious meta-worlds, placing an ever-increasing strain on the environment, and diverting people from the real concerns of their lives, and from the people around them, raising the level of fear and prejudice against outsiders.

If EIES promotes co-ordinated action at an intellectual level among élite groups. Network co-ordinates more closely the operation of a community. EIES is a high-tech system, using a sophisticated central computer, and local as well as international telephone lines. The Enfield Network is relatively low-tech, a central card index and the telephone being the basis of the system. But both are a reversal of the general trend in society since the Industrial Revolution towards the breakdown of communities, brought about by the suppression of public festivals which were the public celebration of a joint cosmology; the use of powerful central media; the development of specialist groups with specialist technical languages and world views; specialist education leading to professional hierarchies; featureless housing estates, and so on.

The system I am proposing, which I call Information Routeing Groups, falls somewhere between the two approaches. As a preliminary, it must be appreciated that it is estimated that within the next two decades almost every middle-class home in the industrial West can be expected to have its own micro-computer.[2] These will be very different from the micros of today, which use difficult and rather inefficient programming languages, such as BASIC. Those of the future will be much easier to use ('user-friendly' in the jargon), being able to communicate with the user, in ways that are more 'natural' than at present, and guiding him in the use of the machine. Indeed, if plans to produce a so-called 'fifth-generation' computer are successful, it may even be possible to address the computer by voice, and for it to talk back in a fairly relaxed conversational style, instead of using the stereotyped styles today's computers require.

The big question is, however, what will we do with such sophisticated equipment in our homes? Beside providing ever-improved video games, doing our accounts, controlling heating systems and burglar alarms, acting as diaries, providing remote banking and shopping, and so on, what do we want such systems to do? Current computer technology seems capable only of making battery hens of us, with all our physical and communicational needs piped anonymously to our houses, and with only rare glimpses of other human beings.

One of the themes running through this book has been that man is essentially a communal animal, but that the effect of civilisations, and in particular of modern civilisation, has been to destroy much of our opportunity for the expression of this need. I have argued that central media and educational systems, and indeed our modern attitudes towards language and communication deny this basic fact. I contend that information technology has reached a point where it could be used in a way that is congruent with man's need to be part of a community, creating in the short term a society where people were happier and more fulfilled, but also indefinitely sustainable. At the moment our society is clearly not very successful in these terms, nor likely to be long sustained.

The question remains, of course, whether those who presently control technology in this country would actually allow developments to take place which would make such a society possible. For the state has always been frightened of unofficial communication. I have already referred to the restriction on the Xerox machine in the Soviet Union; there the use of the telephone is also restricted. The bureaucracy prefers to use more cumbersome means, such as writing and visiting, if possible, since these can be monitored more easily by the state apparatus. Here, in our British bastion of democracy, it is worth noting that the state has also always maintained efficient means of inspecting the mail of likely troublemakers. And as soon as radio's potential for unofficial communication was realised, the government controlled its use, and for many years only the highly-centralised, anodyne world of BBC radio was on offer. It was only with the greatest reluctance that local radio was allowed on the scene, and ham radio was allowed by the state only because it was seen as a harmless hobby for government radio operators, who had to pass stiff tests to qualify for a licence. Even so, and just in case, all users are effectively forbidden to discuss political matters. The same fear of unofficial communication caused the Home Office for years to block the use of CB radio.

Undoubtedly, then, attempts to create an electronic society, with fair access for all to the system, will come up against stiff political opposition from those groups who feel threatened by it. Powerful vested interests would much prefer us to sit at home and watch *Coronation Street*, or tele-vote in response to spurious political questions concerning, say, politicians' hairstyles, after the manner of the *Eurovision Song Contest*, rather than discuss real issues. Questions such as the following could prove embarrassing: 'Were you asked if you minded your local shops closing down and being replaced by anonymous hypermarkets?' 'Why did it take a public campaign to remove lead, one of the most potent neuro-toxins ever made, from petrol?' 'How did asbestos companies get away with poisoning their workers for so long, when the facts about its carcinogenic properties were known before the First World War?' 'Why is it that when the railway-bashing season arrives no one mentions that the annual subsidy for British Rail is less than the subsidy to motorists, via company-car tax relief?' 'Why do politicians complain about the subsidy for public transport without mentioning that Whitehall subsidises the private motorist by giving grants for the construction of multi-storey car-parks?' With good lateral communication, enabling issues to be discussed in fine-grained detail, matters such as these would be illuminated, which would of course inconvenience many vested interests. There would certainly be a great deal of opposition to unrestricted lateral communication, which may well become a major political issue. The description of Information Routeing Groups that follows assumes that the political will to create a better and more viable society by such means exists.

An Information Routeing Group is a group of between 20 and 50 people who all have micro-computers and who share a common interest. This interest could be virtually anything, a profession, employment in the same company, a hobby, tropical-fish keeping, the history of the Manchu, jokes, a fan club or a campaign. It might be geographically local, or scattered worldwide. Each IRG could be started by an individual or group who recognise some mutual benefit in forming it. Enough people (up to 50) sharing the interest are invited to join, by a mixture of personal request, personal recommendation (friends of friends, acquaintances of colleagues, and so on) and, possibly, advertising. It is similar to the way the interlock networks described in Chapter 6 could be formed, or indeed the way people already get together to form a baby-sitting circle, or a darts team.

An IRG would be 'joined' by filling in a record such as the one described in Chapter 6 which asks various questions. The exact format of this could be decided by the originators of the IRG, and then adjusted in the light of experience. The process of designing and filling could easily be done using a computer and programme available on a standard audio-cassette or disc. The members would then fill it in using the keyboard to answer each question as it came up on the screen.

With fifth-generation computers possibly in the 1990s, it should be possible for the computer to vocalise the question and for the member to talk back; the computer, say, asking the member's particular interest in tropical fish, and the member answering fish for use in irrigation schemes to control bilharzia. The same programme which enabled a record to be designed and filled in, could also produce an index of all entries. So if the record contained six headings, the programme would produce six separate indices, one for each heading.

Each member, on receipt of the programme disc, would feed it into his micro at his convenience, answer the questions, and make any suggestions he had for amendments to the profile. Later that night, using cheap-rate telephone time, the originator's computer (we could call him the 'network manager') will ring each of the new members' computers in turn. This is called 'polling', and can be an entirely automatic operation. The manager's computer then adds this record to the existing ones, indexes them all again, and sends an updated list of all profiles to date, plus the new index, back to the new member over the phone. Apart from actually turning the machine on, and answering the questions, no further human intervention is required. The manager's micro will automatically poll each member each night, so that within a short space of time all 50 members will have an up-to-date set of all the other members' profiles, plus the index. The real cost of using the telephone network in this way is very low, in that the type of transaction described can be carried out in a matter of seconds. This is not necessarily reflected in telephone tariffs at present, for they were not designed with such data calls in mind.

We can then distinguish three possible types of interaction between our notional 50 members:

1 Messages between specific individuals – 'Gossip section'

This is the electronic-coffee-break type of fare – jokes, gossip, snippets of news and interesting facts. It would take place between people who knew one another, and enjoyed interacting. The beauty of the network in this respect is that if you were to come across something, or think of something, that you know a friend would find interesting, you would simply type or speak it into the machine, or, in the case of written articles or extracts, feed them into a scanner, and these messages would be collected on the regular evening poll and delivered to your friends or contacts that day, at very low cost. If a message was urgent, the machine could be instructed to send it directly. This message-sending facility avoids the problem of forgetting to pass on interesting or urgent messages, or even forgetting to act on them, as a record would exist.

Another advantage of actually sending the message through the system would be that all such messages, sent or received, would be stored and retrievable by key words. So if a member wanted to write an article on any topic, all the messages ever sent or received could be instantly reviewed, for the computer would be able to search for items containing particular key words.

Since most members of the group would know initially only a small number of the people in the group, say five, this mechanism of exchanging personal messages would allow interesting and relevant messages to diffuse gradually through it. This is the analogue of the sort of exchange that takes place in a research group or an office, for example, in the casual capricious meetings in the corridor, or as a result of dropping into someone's office for a chat. The important feature emerging from the system is that each exchange is tailored to the recipient, either by style or content, and this explicit recognition of the person's individuality by the group makes him feel part of it. This is unlike the present central media, where every recipient gets the same message, an intrinsically alienating procedure.

2 Conference-level material

When the member logs on, and has reviewed his personal messages, he might call for the conference material. This body of material would have started right back when the IRG began, and would be presented to the member on the screen in the form of a page, like the transcript of a conference now. Normally he would only be presented with the last page, but it would be an easy matter to wind back through preceding pages to see what had been said in the past. Or he could do key word searches on the entire accumulated conference material to see what had been said on a particular subject. He might add a comment of his own to the conference data, should he have something to contribute. As with an ordinary conference at present, protocols could be developed to control the proceedings, such as a rotating chairmanship, and rules of debate. On EIES, some people have been ejected from conferences for swearing. These protocols can be developed by and for each group, in the same way that CB enthusiasts have developed their own protocols and jargon. The conference type of message is distinguished by the fact that all members of the IRG can have access to a message sent by one member. If, of course, a member should not be interested in the thread of the debate, he would simply ignore it. But the conference would normally stick to the shared interests of a group, whether or not it did being entirely up to the members.

3 Selective messages

This type of message, which might be an ad as on EIES, or a one-line comment, or a printed extract, is one to which a member attaches a string of key words corresponding to the type of person he thinks it will interest. His computer would then send it to all those in the IRG with the relevant key words somewhere in their profile. From the recipients' point of view this would mean that every other member in the IRG is a potential source of information of the type he has specifically mentioned on his profile. But his listed interests might also implicitly attract information he had not listed. In a civil engineering IRG, for example, one member might have come across the bilharzia problem. He could send a brief message to all civil engineers who have mentioned 'irrigation' or 'Third World' on their records, pointing out the problem and where to go for further information. By means such as this the relevance paradox is attacked.

These three types of interaction I have outlined could of course be added to. They will all, in any case, to a large extent interact. When a member logs on, he could call for whichever mode he wanted – personal messages, conference, or selective, and review them separately. But a personal message might well become the basis for a comment on the conference mode, which might jog members' memories into initiating selective messages, which might in turn trigger personal messages, and so on. Ads received by key words could be passed on to friends as personal messages.

In addition to the exchange of simple messages, the basic IRG configuration could be used for the exchange of services such as those described in connection with EIES and Network – advice, consultancy, physical help, tuition in some skill, surveys, questionnaires and self-assessment tests, soliciting comments on written work, and so on. The basis of these exchanges would be the particular protocols developed by each independent IRG. Within a particular system, for example, services might be exchanged on the basis of tokens. Each member would start off with the same number of electronic tokens, and each hour of assistance to a member of the same IRG would be worth one token. When the member ran out of tokens he would have to earn some more. This would work like a baby-sitting network, where each couple is given a set of tokens which are exchanged on the basis of one per hour.

In time one would expect that an IRG would gradually become more of an entity, with a large body of tacit, informal knowledge concerning the abilities of the group as a whole, and the strengths and weaknesses of individual members. So it would develop into a rich and well-integrated information-exchange group – a sort of co-operative brain, where a single stimulus might initiate patterns spanning the whole group.

A typical middle-class professional might be in four or five IRGs, these roughly corresponding to his local community, leisure, hobby, cultural, political and professional interests. Or he might simply be in several work-oriented IRGs – production, quality control and planning, for instance. He might, for example, be a civil engineer specialising in irrigation, with a leisure-time interest in tropical fish. In the tropical fish IRG that he belonged to, there could well be biologists and doctors who would be aware of, say, the bilharzia problem. It might come up on the conference one day that there is a type of fish that eats snails, one of the bilharzia parasite's intermediate hosts, and that it might be useful in controlling the disease and providing food at the same time. Our civil engineer might enquire, in the conference or in a personal message, what the bilharzia problem is, and be told, thereby transferring important information from a leisure IRG to a professional one. Once the engineer had grasped such a problem he could raise it in his engineering IRG conference, and so on. In the same way, if I can anachronistically bring forward the IRG idea by 20 years, a member of a NASA IRG might in his leisure time be a member of an IRG studying English history. He might notice in the NASA IRG that the space-suit team is having trouble with the articulation mechanisms. He may have just studied his history IRG, and noticed that someone said that Henry VIII had particularly fine armour that solved the same problem, and thus be able to make the appropriate suggestion to the space-suit team.

This sort of cross-fertilising conversation already goes on, of course, but apparently not nearly enough. When people meet and discuss things in organisations, they generally do so in pairs or small groups, and it is unlikely that each person is aware of all the problems and all the odd unexpected skills of all the other people in the organisation. So highly relevant matters might tend not to get raised. An IRG system would make it much clearer what problems are being encountered elsewhere, so that those who wanted could get involved. I claim that a world-wide network of IRGs, all interlocked by the simple fact that each member would be in several different ones, would vastly improve the transmission of both formal, and more importantly, informal information. The way that an item of information – a simple fact, an idea, a view – could diffuse rapidly through an entire network of random interlocking IRGs is in fact the same as the way in which diseases, gossip, fairy stories, jokes and tales spread – like wildfire.

An interesting experiment has been carried out in the United States which sheds some light on the question of how many IRGs a particular item, say, a request for a consultancy service, or an ad for an article, or a report, might have to penetrate, before all likely recipients, worldwide, have received it.[6] The experimenters selected several hundred people as volunteers, through newspaper advertisements. These people were given a folder, and asked to send it on to someone they knew personally (defined as knowing his first name), with a request that he do the same, with the ultimate aim of the folder reaching a chosen target – a stockbroker on the other side of the United States. The object of the experiment was to find out the average number of intermediaries between the randomly-selected sources and the targets. Over a third of several hundred folders got through, and the average number of intermediaries was about six. A similar result was achieved using a non-random group of originators (stockbrokers). So if an author were to write an ad for a research document he has written, and send it (selectively or indiscriminately) to his IRG contacts, he might send it to a total of 250 people. His computer would automatically select people by scanning their profiles for key words. Some will ignore it, others may re-inject it into their own IRGs. As the ad entered each new IRG the number of times it was multiplied would depend on whether it was relevant. The method of routeing through key words means that it is more likely to gravitate rapidly towards those IRGs where people are most interested in it. Once in a vein of IRGs where people are likely to be interested in it, it would be multiplied many times, each time it moved. I would guess that most people likely to want an ad are about six to ten IRGs away from the original source.

There is another reason why IRGs are likely to be better at selectively disseminating information than conventional systems. As the ad passes through each IRG it can have its original key words altered to suit the local information and professional territory through which it is passing. This is important, because when people are asked to give key words for a topic, they can usually think of only five or six. These words will also be the ones used in their private technical languages, reflecting the way they perceive the world – one of the main obstacles to universal classification systems. But with the IRG system key words could be added to as an ad entered new territory. An ad concerning the use of the snail darter fish as part of a biological control system, for example, might start off with the key words THIRD WORLD PROFESSIONALS, AGRICULTURALISTS, BIOL-OGISTS, EPIDEMIOLOGISTS, PHYSICIANS, but pick up on the

way ECOLOGICAL STUDIES, INTEGRATED PROJECT DE-
VELOPMENT, WATER INDUSTRY JOURNALISTS, PARA-
SITOLOGY, VECTOR CONTROL, and so on.

The fact that people would bother to engage in such activity would
stem from the operation of the basic IRG as I have outlined it. As long
as the incentive of mutual self-interest causes people to co-operate in
one IRG, then, since they would be in overlapping ones, this kind of ad
enhancement is bound to occur. In the same way that Network seems
to build a sense of identification with the local group, and that EIES
apparently fulfils a basic need in people besides that of mere technical
information gathering, I see no reason why the informational assets
and social rewards should not compensate for the comparatively mild
effort required in being in an IRG. In the United States there are
already many information networks similar to EIES and IRGs, and
these exist simply because people enjoy them. Free computer bulletin
boards are also springing up all over the country. They are rather like
electronic notice boards on which ads and messages can be placed to be
reviewed by others, and there is apparently ample motivation to use
them.

In this brief outline of the IRG concept I have not attempted to deal
in great detail with any of the technical problems. My intention is
rather to indicate the usefulness of the concept. Nevertheless, it is
possible to organise IRGs in the way I have described using existing
telephone technology and today's computers, developments in technology merely making it easier and cheaper. One interesting step,
particularly for developing countries, is the use of short-wave radio,
which can transmit messages over long distances if conditions are right
at very low power and cost, compared with the telephone. Co-
operative members of IRGs with short-wave radios could bounce radio
messages from computer to computer. This would mean that regular
information exchange over long distances would be extremely cheap.
For the actual cost to an intermediate 'relay' of picking up and re-
transmitting such a message would be comparatively small – and he
would probably be on the air anyway, waiting to pick up messages for
himself.

Other problems that people raise in connection with computer
networks are of a social kind, such as a concern about security of
information, information overload, being asked for too much information, junk mailings, and so on. Again, I have not gone into these
questions in detail because solutions to these problems are largely
technical, and this is not meant to be a technical manual. Suffice it to
say here that there are many techniques available for dealing with such

problems. Crypto-systems are available, in principle, for instance, to make all messages and data indecipherable except to key-holders. It is also possible to devise automatic techniques to weed out uninteresting information or material from known 'electronic bores' or time-wasters. Ultimately, of course, users are free to give only as much information as they wish. In the existing networks such problems have either not yet materialised, or have not proved insuperable.

It is true that many of the potential services that a widespread IRG system could give are already offered by existing computer networks. But these networks so far appear to me in the main to be élitist and disintegrative, in that they are segregated into specialists and enthusiasts of a certain area, with no overlap or interaction between them. Each therefore merely develops its own special cosmology. Since I have been arguing throughout this book for a more integrated approach to social and professional life, proposals to extend existing networks seem to me to merely perpetuate the divisions which in the long run will doom our civilisation.

The basic IRG proposal that I have made in the latter part of this chapter, overlapping 50-person groups, using micro-computers and the public telephone or radio network, is perfectly possible with today's technology. It is, however, still a relatively expensive system. A 'network manager's' equipment would cost about £4,500, and the average member's about £2,500. In addition, a fair degree of computing skill would be required. So initially IRGs would be restricted to the well-off and well-educated members of society. In three to five years, however, it is estimated that the price of the basic equipment, including standard software packages, will have fallen sufficiently to make most of the equipment available to most people in the West.

The basic IRG concept can of course be made available at very low cost to groups of people: societies, clubs, voluntary and environmental groups. In this situation the expense of disc storage and telephone communications is not really necessary. The cheapest micro-computer, currently selling at under £50, can be used to produce a paper version of an IRG, providing a copy for every member. The computer and television screens could be available for up-dating and message-exchanging at meetings. Virtually no computer skills would be required, except for elementary knowledge on the part of the person setting up the system. In groups of people such as these, an IRG could be very helpful in stimulating informal exchange, and making the skills and attributes of group members visible to one another. Appendix I shows an extract from a local IRG. It demonstrates the astonishing range of talents and contacts available even in quite a small group. As equipment costs fall, and computer literacy rises, these simple IRGs, infrequently up-dated and without conferencing and electronic mail facilities, could be gradually converted to the IRG format I described earlier.

In France, for example, the government has a considerable commitment to the 'information society'. Part of its plans include a free Prestel-type terminal in every telephone subscriber's home, by 1992. In computing-power terms, this terminal would have roughly that required by an IRG terminal. The French reckon that it can be done for about £52. The system will have full electronic mail facilities, the message being typed into the terminal, with the phone number, and the system delivering it to the nominated terminal. Other items in the package will include a cheap facsimile machine, which will enable one user to feed a document or drawing into it, and a Xerox-like reproduction to be sent to a nominated address; this will also double as a cheap photocopier for the user. A cheap telewriter will also be available, a tablet on which you will be able to write or draw with an electronic pen. The drawing will be transmitted through the network to another user's identical screen. Two users will be able to write or draw or erase simultaneously. So two surgeons could discuss a particular operation over the phone, with the aid of the same sketch, visible to them both. The French government plans illustrate how ubiquitous sophisticated pieces of electronic equipment are likely to become in quite a short space of time. And there are no technical or economic reasons why IRGs should not become equally ubiquitous.

The aim of these systems is not to create a society where people spend all their time huddled over computers, tapping away. This would, to my mind, be a dreary addition to the current trend towards more and more non-participatory activities such as watching television and video. I would anticipate that people would use their IRG computer in time otherwise spent reading the newspaper, say, or watching television. The evidence indicates that the interaction with other people that it would involve would lead, naturally, to increased communal activity.

APPENDIX I

Extracts from the index of profiles of a small community-based IRG.

GROUP PROFILE SHEETS,
INDEXED UNDER SUB-HEADINGS

Work
Expert
Activities
Interests
Contacts
Local Skills offered
Local Skills needed

Activities

Interests

Contacts

Local Skills Offered

Wildlife Management 037
Xeroxing, possibly some
  cheap 038
Yoga 004

Local Skills Needed

Accommodation in Bath,
  after dances 006
Accountancy 009
Aikido Teacher 026
Bicycle Maintenance 001
Brain Surgery 003
Builder 012
Car Maintenance 021
Carpenter 035
Carpentry, help and tuition 005
Cat Minding 021
Darning 002
Dark Room (use of) 039
Electrical, bits and pieces 005
Electrical, gadgets fixed 001
Electrician 035
Empty Cellar, or similar for
  wood workshop 013
Food Co-op, space for 036
French Tutor 030
Garden Labour 012
General House Maintenance 048
German Conversation 002
Guitar Tuition 028
High Ceiling Painter 038
Info on Homeopathy and
  Herbs 019
Info on Philosophies/Religion 019

Information on Organic
  Gardening 019
Info on Tailoring/Soft
  Furnishing 019
Insurance 009
Invoicing 009
Layout and Paste-up Artist 035
Learning Bridge 029
Learning How to Write 002
Mini Maintenance 013
Models for drawing 005
Moped maintenance and
  repair 005
Nature Cure Advice 018
Organic Gardening 006
Photo Printer 039
Plasterer 035
Pottery Facilities 038
Recycled Bags/Containers 036
Rotovator 013
Secretarial 009
Sewing Altering 003
Shiatsu Tuition 026
Skilled Woodworker (turner) 022
Tax Problems 009
Tent to buy, needed 035
Tool Loan 009
Typing 004
Use of Power Jig Saw 034
Veganism, advice 006
Wholefood, evening meals
  and lunches (pay) 002
Wholefood recipes 016
Window Cleaning 048

APPENDIX II

COMMUNITY NETWORK

Network is a democratically run community organisation in this area. It sets about finding out what people in our neighbourhood need, and then, through community co-operation, establishing the means to satisfy these needs.

Network education

There are now over 1,000 members in Network offering each other nearly 400 different skills and subjects – from macramé to playing the flute, and from German to bee-keeping. This exchange of learning forms the basis for a series of short courses, seminars and conferences that Network organises several times each year.

Network groups

Members also tell us what group activities they are interested in and we then try to get that activity off the ground. This way, Network has seen the growth of several groups – a Children's Workshop, a Children's Book-group, Yoga, Bridge, Badminton, Singing, Theatre visits and several others.

Network co-ops

With the aid of the Network information base, Network has seen the growth of several co-operatives. About 9 food co-ops have sprung up offering food at discounted prices. There is a crafts co-op that sells crafts at exhibitions, fairs and through the Community Shop. There is a publishing group, providing Network literature and a Community Shop that is run on a co-operative basis.

Network services

Network also provides a pool of volunteers and organisers to offer services to each other and to the general community. There is an English Language Service offering English conversation to those whose first language is not English, an under-5s information service, a 'phone-in advice service, and a baby-sitting service. Other services are being planned for the future.

Network entertainment

The entertainment side of Network is also growing. Network now holds regular dances and other forms of popular entertainment. It also has cultural evenings as well as regular coffee evenings for members. We try to provide every opportunity whereby members can meet each other on a social basis.

NETWORK

NETWORK is a community project based mainly in the London Boroughs of Enfield, Barnet and Haringey. It is a democratically run community organisation. It sets about finding out what people in our neighbourhood need and then, through community co-operation, establishes the means to satisfy those needs.

EDUCATION COUNCIL
SHORT COURSES
FEBRUARY–MARCH 1983

Gardening for beginners
This will be a short 3-4 week course concentrating on basic skills – type of tools needed, planning and buying seeds, preparing the soil, seed sowing, planting and care, laying a lawn, etc.

Bookkeeping for beginners
This 3-week course will consider how to use a cash book and ledger, reconcile a bank account and how to control collection and payment of cash. Depending on what students want, it may also cover preparing profit and loss accounts, cash flow statements and using a petty cash system.

Meditation
Network has received many enquiries about doing a meditation and relaxation course. We have now contacted the Buddhist Centre and they seem willing to put on a course for us in this area.

Nutrition
For those interested, we plan to organise a course on nutrition – what is the body and how does it function, food and its value, protein, fats and carbohydrate, vitamins and why we need them.

Contempo – Jazz dance
Learn the fundamental rudiments of dance movement; savour the sizzling sounds and relax (sort of) to the rhythms of a contempo-jazz dance class. Class structure includes:
a. standing warm-up
b. floor work
c. dance routines

Ex-dancercise teacher – I am also available for private or semi-private coaching at £2.50 per hour.

Machine knitting
This group has a tutor for beginners and advanced knitters. Please bring your own machines.

Tap dancing
This is a class for adults. You need no experience or previous training – the class is for beginners. Keep fit with music. All you need is a sense of rhythm and a love of dancing.

Yoga
This is a new class so it should be a particularly good time to join. It will be a class with a relaxed and relaxing approach to yoga for mental and physical health.

NOTE: The teacher is willing to teach two or three people in her home, in the daytime, at a time to be arranged with those concerned.

National country dancing
English, Scottish. European etc. –

good fun, good exercise (mental and physical), nice music!!!

A 6-week course, part of a continuing weekly group successfully started before Christmas. Experts, beginners, young and not-so-young are all welcome. Will possibly include an introduction to group singing of international songs.

Indian cooking

This will be a 6-week course on Indian home-made cooking. The course will teach you how to cook and prepare Indian breakfasts, lunches, dinners and snacks. It will show you both vegetarian and non-vegetarian menus. There is only a limited number of places available on this course, so please book early.

Keep fit for the over 60's

The course will consist of exercises and dancing plus a talk and discussion on dieting. It will be a 6-week course.

Buying a house

Network Education is planning a course particularly for first-time buyers on 'Buying a House'. This course will be 3 weeks and will describe the role of the estate agent, the building society and the solicitor in the transactions. This course will be in March and a separate leaflet will be issued. If you are interested, then please contact us and let us know.

Literature group

We meet once a month on a Monday at each other's houses. The group selects a novel or a short story or a poem and the group discusses it. This is a very informal evening to heighten your enjoyment and share your enthusiasm for literature.

Introduction to micro computers

This is a course for complete beginners. If you want to know about micro-computers, their uses and how to operate them, then this is the course for you. There will be machines available and this will give each student a chance to use a small computer.

Trace your family tree

A 4-session course in tracing your 'Family Tree', designed specifically for those who are totally inexperienced and in need of practical assistance to get themselves started. The form of instruction will be very informal and structured to the personal needs of the individual. If you are interested, then please contact us with name and telephone number and we will let you know the date and venue.

Bridge group

Network has a bridge group which meets regularly to play bridge. You do not have to be an expert to join.

In the examination I have made in this book of the communication routes underlying organisations at different levels of society, I have frequently chosen specifically British examples. My observations apply, however, to all industrialised societies, East and West, to a greater or lesser extent. To summarise, the problem is that we have centralised, hierarchic, bureaucratic institutions, which operate in isolation from one another, producing non-integrated solutions to problems. These solutions frequently attack only the symptoms of a problem rather than the root cause, and ultimately create further ones, either for the hierarchy itself or for adjacent ones. This lack of integration of policy-making, in part due to the coarse-grained structure of the institutions, is compounded by an educational system which breeds specialisation from an early age. This is further compounded by specialist central media, which enhance the growth of private meta-worlds with their own languages, opaque to outsiders, professional and non-professional alike. Coupled with this institutional and professional control system split into essentially non-interactive parts, is a child-rearing one which is inherently divisive in that it trains people to be individualistic and essentially non-communicative. Institutional hierarchies, then, tend to promote those with the least ability to communicate effectively. As a result, most of them are internally split by wrangling, empire building, back-stabbing and squabbling over policy, which further diminishes their ability to produce effective action. Central media portray these internal battles as aberrations when they surface in public, but they are in fact quite routine. Institutions in general only function because of systematic rule-breaking, and deception of superiors by subordinates. The larger the institution the worse are these internal features, due to the greater scope for misunderstanding, failure of lateral communication, and the increased attraction of the larger, more hierarchic institutions for authoritarian-type personalities.

For the population at large, small communities have been broken up by a combination of the demolition of areas where they used to flourish, and their relocation in anonymous housing with little scope for interaction; the construction of homes in which it is impossible to conduct family life in the manner in which it has been carried on for millions of years, based on a variant of the extended family; and the pressure of central media systems on the traditional role of community networks. The breakdown of the extended family has also been hastened by the fact that many modern children resent and are resented by their parents, are ashamed of or embarrassed by them, and the lack of mutual understanding. This is largely due to inappropriate styles of communication, which are the result of a faulty authoritarian model derived from the prevailing style of education and employment. That, in its turn, was caused by the need to create large institutional hierarchies as a prelude to, and necessary component of, large-scale, centralised, industrial production. This breakdown in traditional communication, along with the quasi-religious festivals that used to celebrate the purpose and origins of the community, has led to feelings of alienation and frustration which are compensated for by an ever-increasing stream of goods and services, at ever-increasing cost to the environment. Whereas in traditional communities people celebrated membership of them, and sought status as measured by their norms, they now celebrate their status, measured against the spurious, arbitrary standards provided by central media.

In suggesting how Information Routeing Groups could bring about an improvement in this situation, the scenarios chosen for specific applications of the use of IRGs are intended to exemplify how they could address these problems. When I refer here to IRGs, I do not necessarily mean to confine myself to the system outlined in the last chapter. It may be that for various considerations a system in which groups are differently composed, or larger, or have slightly different ways of operating, with any combination of the features of EIES, IRGs or Network, would be more appropriate. I use the term rather to refer to the general concept of lateral media.

1 Parent groups

Anyone who has looked after a young pre-school child for any length of time knows the difficulties this presents. Most small children need almost constant attention, but the countervailing pressures on the parent of housework, cooking, shopping and work lead to a good deal of irritable confrontation and emotional upset. Most parents put much of their energy into organising freedom for themselves from their children, and yet still spend most of their time in their exclusive company. The parent, as a result, usually suffers to some degree from feelings of isolation, frustration, resentment, and depression. The child is a victim of the intensity of this relationship. In traditional societies the mother does not have the exclusive burden of young children.

Grandparents, aunts and uncles, brothers and sisters, older children, and other families, all of whom share the load of child-care, are always near at hand. Colin Turnbull, writing in *The Forest People*, of the Bambuti pygmies of the Ituri Forest, says, 'It is no accident that you call everyone who is of the same age group as your parents either "father" or "mother"; those still older you call "grandparent"; those of the same age as yourself you refer to by a term which could be translated as either "brother" or "sister", and anyone younger is "child".'[1] Each child in a traditional community can learn important behaviour from slightly older children through play, conversation, songs and games. The parents can get on with their own activities in congenial company, while keeping a watchful eye on the children. Such a social structure must be a healthier environment for parent and child than the virtual prison of many modern homes, both middle and working-class ones. The rich, of course, can afford nannies, and have always done so.

Although labour-saving devices have made much of the work of parenting physically easier, they have at the same time alienated mothers from the community. For millions of years men and women spent their time in essentially communal activities. Intrinsic to these was membership of a group and the associated lateral media providing tacit information on life, children and the universe, as well as essential social stroking. The modern mother is surrounded by central media, in the form of women's magazines, women's programmes on the radio and child-care books, which reinforce her sense of loneliness, isolation and failure.

In response to this predicament, pre-school playgroups have evolved. In addition, mother and toddler groups have sprung up, which are run on a shoe-string by dedicated volunteers, often in church halls, and sometimes with barely adequate toys and facilities. Their popularity shows how much they are needed. For they offer a chance to meet other mothers or fathers, and give a break from the children's need for constant attention. According to Penelope Leach,[2] mother and toddler groups are for parents, with the child benefiting from what his parent receives there. Belonging to such a group, with its network of relationships, replaces some of the aspects of community that have greatly diminished in modern society. At the very least, the chat and gossip found there can make the parent's life more enjoyable. It also provides an arena in which the mother can assess her achievement in comparison with real people, rather than the exemplary family in the soap powder advertisement, or the arbitrary standards provided by child-care books. But there are other, more significant benefits to be derived from participating in this apparently simple system. In the group to which our child goes, the group leader was one day rung by one of the fathers in despair. The father explained that his wife was on the verge of a breakdown, due to the strain of both his children having whooping cough, with ensuing sleepless nights. The group leader was able to ring a few of the people in our group, and arrange for them to help out with cooking, cleaning and looking after the children for a few weeks, until the crisis was over. In this particular case the only alternative would have been for the desperate father to have rung the social services and asked for a home help. To get one of these requires a note from the doctor, a visit from the social services, an implicit means test, and - if all goes well - the arrival of a complete stranger. The process can take about three weeks before any help at all is forthcoming. And at the end of the crisis the 'help' disappears again. With the informal system, however, the possibilities of lasting friendship and mutual future help exist.

The comparative cost to the state of the two methods of finding help are very telling. The cost to the state of obtaining it through the mother and toddler group was zero. The cost of the husband approaching social services can be estimated on the following basis: in Britain there are approximately 57,000 social workers, attending to 914,000 clients.[3] The figures available suggest that social workers spend about 28 per cent[3] of their time in personal contact with clients, and the rest on travelling, writing reports, appearing in court, and so on. So we can calculate that in one year they spend something like 26,254,000 hours per year with clients. Now in 1980-1, the social services budget for all categories of support, including fieldwork, residential care, support services, and training and research was £1,844 million.[3] So the average cost per hour of a social worker's contact time with a client would seem to be £70 per hour. In fact the true figure is even higher than this, since the figures do not include the capital cost of residential care, which might have been involved in the example if informal help had not been immediately available. To look at the social services figures another way, the average annual cost of a client is about £2,000. A cynic might suggest it could be cost-efficient to pay clients £1,500 a year to stay away from the social services.

Examples showing how informal networks save the state a vast amount of money, and at the same time contribute to the quality of people's lives, can be endlessly multiplied. But the real point is that an institutional hierarchy cannot in principle cope properly with such problems, whereas a network can. The reason is, quite simply, the law of requisite variety. The sheer volume and variety of predicaments that people can get into in a modern society defeats the capacity of any hierarchy to respond speedily and appropriately. Only a network can respond with the necessary speed and flexibility.

To illustrate the flexibility of a network compared to a hierarchy, consider what happened when a baby-sitting circle was formed in our neighbourhood recently. The practical problem was that we needed to supply each couple with 30 tokens for use as a means of exchange, and that these should be cheap to produce and not easily counterfeited. One member, who is a wood-turner by trade, offered to make some wooden rings. A few days later, walking into town, I bumped into one of the members, who told me she had seen the wood-turner's wife and heard that he was having trouble making the tokens without the wood splitting, but that he was now trying with some different wood. Later on I passed a tool shop and enquired about the cost of 300 washers and a metal stamp, meaning to ring the wood-turner that evening, to see how he had got on. As it turned out, I in fact met him on my way home, and he told me that what we wanted could not be done with wood. So we agreed to buy the washers. As I was going home and he was going into town, he bought them and dropped them off to me on his way home. I then stamped them, and gave them to the other members, or their friends, as and when we met. The whole cost of the operation was very low in time, money and memos. A centralised bureaucratic solution to our requirements would have required the setting up of committees, the commissioning of reports on various options, studies, reports, more committees, tenders for the supply of stamped washers, and so on.

But the expensive and ineffective bureaucratic way of dealing with things is exactly how our social services, for example, try to cope with social problems. The call on them is becoming greater each year because society generates problems at a far higher rate than a hierarchy can generate solutions.

How might the networks I am proposing as a solution, be set up? Taking mother and toddler groups as an example, the existing voluntarily-established groups clearly contribute to the well-being of the participants, and no doubt absorb some problems that might end up on the social services' budget. But there is no doubt that the effectiveness of these groups could be increased even further. However good the leadership is, it is still difficult for newcomers to overcome initial barriers and feel sufficiently part of the network to ask and be asked for help. What is needed was put into words by the 74-year-old mentioned in the previous chapter in connection with Network: 'that initial excuse they need to get started with one another.'

I would envisage the group leader of a mother and toddler group asking each mother as she joined to fill in a profile. The format and content of this would evolve in response to suggestions by users, in the light of experience. A micro-computer would be available for the group at each meeting, since in the short term it is unlikely that there would be enough home users (although judging by the rate of penetration into homes of colour television, stereo, video recorders, and so on, that time will not be far away). The group leader would ask an existing member familiar with the system to help the newcomer fill in the profile. It could look like the example set out below.

Profile for Mother and Toddler Group

NAME	Jaqui
ADDRESS	36 Acacia Avenue
TELEPHONE NO	324790
CHILDREN (names and ages)	Kate, $2\frac{1}{4}$
TRANSPORT (lifts you need or can offer)	Can give lifts to group for 1 mother and child
BABY-SITTING (Do you want to join the circle?)	Yes
SKILLS OFFERED (by yourself or by your contacts)	Have trained as a jeweller and can undertake the occasional commission or repair for cash or exchange. Husband has a small metalwork lathe and will do odd piece of turning if not too busy.
SKILLS WANTED	Would like advice on setting up an aquarium. Also would like tuition in French before holiday in September.
CONTACTS	Have friend who can get lots of waste paper from office for drawing on. Know a good cheap plumber. Husband is computer programmer and will help people with home computer problems.
OTHER IRGS (you are a member of)	Local craft-workers; whole food co-op.

The tea urn stews the tea and
                                              makes it rather bitter.
                                              Why don't we organise outings
                                              in the summer to a zoo or to the
                                              beach?

The advantage of the computer system is that mothers can change
their profile each week, if and when their interests change or an
emergency arises. Access to messages and conference material would
probably best be achieved on paper. Each week or month every
member would then receive a listing of personal messages and a record
of the conference material, and the terminal could also be used at
meetings to look at profiles through the indices. Once a month, say, an
edition of the indexed profiles could be made available for perusal at
home. Each profile could have a recent photograph to help connect
names with faces. What would emerge in time from an exchange of
profiles is an excuse for mutual co-operation, with small groups of
people who wish to work together developing. No compulsion would
exist to fill in a profile, of course, since part of the attraction of such
associations is the freedom to come and go without commitment. But
the group in general would become more dynamic if everyone did,
allowing mutual trust to develop which in turn could support a greater
volume of practical and emotional help.

There is no reason why an initially mother and toddler IRG should
not be extended to include others who could offer directly-related
mutual benefits. Old people, for example, are often lonely and
deprived of a function in the community, and mothers are often
desperately short of child-minding help. If interested older people
filled in the same profiles, it would provide an excuse for the two groups
to make contact. People could be sized up in informal situations before
things developed, and useful exchanges arranged as a result – baby-
sitting for shopping trips, and so on. This would address the ludicrous
situation that sometimes occurs, of frantic mothers and bored, lonely
old folk using the same village hall on alternative days.

In my experience, many people are afraid that such a network might
generate an uncontrollable number of requests, and that they would
be forced to get involved with people they did not like. In practice such
fears are unfounded. If an individual does not want to lend something,
or help a particular person, there is no compulsion to do so, and the
usual excuses will suffice: 'I'm too busy', 'It's broken', and the like.
Network certainly reports no problems of this nature. It is also possible
to stipulate on each profile exactly the terms under which any

transaction will be carried out, in order to avoid resentment over, for example, whether or not money for petrol during lifts is expected.

In my own area various local bodies are getting together to try and organise courses on parenthood. Parenting skills belong to the realm of tacit knowledge. What is needed to enhance them is a Network-style discussion involving both parents and children, from which can emerge a shared body of tacit knowledge. Such a network could very easily be a related off-shoot of a pre-school playgroup or mother and toddler one. In conference mode, a discussion on parenting would take place. Theories could be aired, problems presented, and possible solutions discussed. Such a continuous conference among a small group of people would be of far more value in the long run, in my view, than any number of books on child-rearing, which always seem to offer conflicting, coarse-grained advice, based on authors' opinions and prejudices. A group of 50 or so people in dialogue would be much more representative of reality, and each person would personally know the one who was making any statement, and so could better judge its value.

There are also plans in my area to set up a directory of all the supportive agencies and resources available to families. I would suggest that this is the wrong approach to use. Directories, for a start, are out-of date almost as soon as they are printed; secondly, people are often either alienated by the impersonality, or simply forget to use them. I would suggest that a better approach would be to create one or more networks containing members of all the different local family support bodies. The profile would include entries such as those below:

Profile for Family Support Bodies

ORGANISATION	Samaritans
CONTACTS	Women's Aid; a marriage guidance counsellor; several local co-counsellors; MIND: housing co-op; community policeman
INFORMATION AVAILABLE	Used to work in social services and can advise on family entitlements to benefits
	etc.

Members of such a network would inevitably belong to other networks, depending on their varying interests. Access to their profiles in each network would reveal, say, special knowledge of family support resources, allowing the person to become a gatekeeper to that resource. A system of interlocking networks like this would allow the relevant information to percolate through the population much more effectively than a directory.

It is my contention that some official funding of IRGs by the existing social services would be money well spent. What presently exists is not a conspicuously successful system, in the eyes of consumers, providers or observers. So there should, in theory, be no great objection to putting some funds into experimenting with the network approach I have outlined. I believe that many people, particularly the elderly, the lonely and the poor, resort to the social services simply because they do not have friends and relatives available to help out in difficult periods.

IRGs organised in a similar way to Network could be offered a subsidy according to the amount of socially-useful work they carried out. If it costs the country £70 per hour of client contact time to attend to someone's need in a bureaucratic fashion, why not pay the organisers of IRGs with any social work component £7 an hour for any direct work they undertake: the provision of home helps, temporary foster care, help for single mothers or counselling? One way of administering such a scheme could be along the same lines in which British Gas entrusts sub-contracted gangs of labourers with the repair of potentially highly-dangerous gas mains. The gas boards tell the contractor where a leak is, and the gang organise the whole job themselves, the board simply paying their bill based on time and materials. Checks are made, of course, by board inspectors. Similarly, networks could submit a monthly bill to the social services department showing what they had done, with whom and for how long; this could be vetted by an impartial third party, employed to check up on the quality and quantity of the work.

An example of this approach already exists – the Maygrove Project is run in conjunction with Camden Council and Paddington churches in London, and there are also other similar fostering arrangements elsewhere. The Council pays a man an annual fee a year to be a father to three teenage boys who would otherwise be in a boys' home. What he does with the money is up to him, as long as it results in the boys being acceptably looked after. It has been found that the cost of looking after the boys in this way is far less than the equivalent cost of caring for them in an institution at about £450 per week each, and all the available evidence suggests that it is far more beneficial to the boys.

So it can be seen that although the geographic and employment patterns of modern living have to a large extent destroyed opportunities to form informal networks, electronic lateral media can stimulate their regeneration. An IRG can be used to generate the traditional form of face-to-face community connected with some shared activity, or informal activity can actually take place via a terminal. Both forms of network are valuable sources both of tacit knowledge and of emotional and practical help.

2 University course preparation

The material for the following account was provided by a course team chairman at the Open University.[4] 'During the first eight years of its existence, the Open University Technology Faculty produced over 20 undergraduate courses. Unlike those at conventional universities, Open University students study from their homes, wherever they happen to live in Britain. Their contact with the university staff is through specially-produced correspondence material, experimental apparatus which they use at home, through television, radio, and, for some courses, a one-week residential summer school. Thus, production of an Open University course is a complex operation, involving a team of academics, editors and designers, technicians, BBC producers, administrators and secretaries. The complete production cycle takes $2\frac{1}{2}$ to 3 years.

Each of the 20 or so 'course teams' developed its own particular style of working, with ideas passing from one course team to another, principally when there was an overlap of membership. Some teams found more efficient ways of operating than others, but there were also occasional disasters, with a team unable to produce material within its deadline.

In 1979, the members of the Technology Faculty Board decided to assemble their collective experience to determine the best working methods that had been developed and to help themselves avoid further disasters. They set up a working group which had several meetings, interviewed people, read documents, and finally produced a report with a series of recommendations. This was accepted by the faculty board. Matters ended there. Very little change resulted, even though many of the ideas in the report were very valuable, and these ideas were implemented mainly by subsequent course teams containing members of the working group who later complained that their work appeared to have been largely wasted.'

This demonstrates yet again how deeply-ingrained are formal – and frequently inappropriate – solutions to organisational problems. The problem in the faculty in fact concerns the transmission of tacit knowledge. In the same way that reading physics books cannot help someone to ride a bicycle, that teaching five-year-olds the rules of grammar does not help them to speak, you cannot help people function better as a course team by appointing committees to extract the relevant knowledge with a view to writing it down in a form that will enable other people to benefit from it. It is rather like trying to organise a course for people who do not know how to behave at parties, and hiring sociologists to produce reports on successful party behaviour, including diagrams of people standing around in groups, tables of the average group size and sex-composition, and charts showing the frequency of circulation from group to group.

The real problem at the Open University was lack of dialogue between members of the faculty and the absence of a well-used network of contacts among members. In Chapter 5 I showed how important personal networks are in transmitting tacit knowledge through dialogue. The appropriate solution in this case would be to create the conditions under which informal networks could flourish. The clue to the problem lies in sentences: 'with ideas passing from one course team to another, principally when there was an overlap of membership' and 'these ideas were implemented mainly by subsequent course teams containing members of the working group.' What is needed is an increase in such overlap, and an increase in the amount of informal contact that occurs between people in the faculty. IRGs should be an effective way of achieving this. One or more could be set up in the Technology Faculty, based on a profile including items such as those below:

Profile for Technology Faculty

NAME	G. Learner
ADDRESS (home)	72 Acacia Avenue, Bletchley
(internal)	Wimpey 3a
TELEPHONE NUMBER (home)	75362
(internal)	6451
POSITION IN ORGANISATION	Team Chairman in Technology, Human Ecology and Energy Conservation Courses

COURSE UNITS WORKING ON	Home Computers, PSTI05; Advanced Structural Mechanics, XZA109; Sociology Foundation Course, RFT104
COURSE UNITS WORKED ON	Energy in the Home, PRF105; Introduction to Geology XLR-236
COURSE PREPARATION SPECIAL INTERESTS	Communication and special group techniques; folk music; theatrical techniques in improving group behaviour
TECHNIQUES AVAILABLE (developed by you, or familiar to you)	Various group-function enhancing techniques
TECHNIQUES WANTED	Use of theatrical/revue techniques
OTHER INTERESTS (leisure and general	Classical piano; local choral society
OTHER ACTIVITIES IN OU	Member of Senate, Member of Co-ops Research Unit
OTHER IRGs	Psychology and practice of successful child-rearing; holistic medical network; alternatives to prison; computer graphics

Computers are in plentiful supply at the Open University, and at quite low cost everyone in the faculty could have regular access to a terminal. The object would be to use the profile to stimulate lateral communication between members, which is exactly what computer conferencing in small groups can achieve. In fact non-course-related IRGs would also promote the same thing, whether it be through pot-holing, drama or baby-sitting. The example given is representative of a type of problem that exists throughout the university, and indeed any large organisation.

In addition to setting up IRGs at the Open University, to continue with this example, steps could also be taken to improve the general social climate. Until the BBC production department moved to the campus there was nowhere to get a good meal and relax in a convivial atmosphere, despite the fact that 2,000 academics and administrators worked there. There is now a good restaurant, but it closes at 6.30 p.m., so there is really nowhere to meet in the evenings. The pages of *Who's Who* reveal that the people who own and run the country all belong to several clubs, thereby gaining access to a vast lateral media spanning the upper echelons of industry and government. Every evening over dinner or drinks tacit knowledge is exchanged by the captains of industry and the mandarins of Whitehall.

There is no reason why any clause of a work contract should not include mandatory paid attendance at group activities such as an annual week spent mountain-climbing or on a canal barge, with more frequent weekends spent in similar pursuits. What is actually done on these occasions is irrelevant, so long as everyone can physically participate. Such activities generate shared experience which is the basis of communication. The Energy Research Group at the Open University, a body of 20 or so people just as prone to internal wranglings as any organisational hierarchy, went one weekend to Wales. The first day we spent visiting the nuclear power station at Trawsfynydd, followed by a lively party in the evening. The next day we visited the Centre for Alternative Technology at Machynlleth. The effect on group morale was quite noticeable, and for many months afterwards an enhanced air of co-operation and goodwill pervaded the group. This impromptu outing should be seen in contrast with a residential get-together I attended when I first joined the group. This consisted of a formal meeting at a vacant university hall of residence. People read papers addressing topics such as 'Where is the Energy Research Group going?' 'Problems facing Energy Research' and so on. The result was that doom and gloom pervaded the group for months afterwards, with an ensuing negative effect on its operation. It may seem to some people that public money is thus being spent on enabling employees to have fun, but this should be seen as a cost-effective way of improving the effectiveness of an organisation, in the same way that it is accepted that people work better in attractively-decorated offices.

IRGs can also be used to augment the formal functions of universities, the production of courses, documents, reference books, and so on, depending on the efficient circulation of information. For IRGs can circulate information very much more cheaply and rapidly than existing systems, and if necessary more widely. With current paper systems a memo or a report tends only to be distributed to people on the circulation list, since it is relatively expensive and time-consuming to photocopy and deliver or post such items. Once a memo or report is on a computer system, however, it can easily be sent on to others who might be interested or find it useful, by simple instructions to a computer.

3 Individual advantage

IRGs could be used as an information access system, rather like present libraries or computer data bases. Professionals working in any field – researchers, engineers, social workers, writers, historians, and so on – all accumulate information as a result of their jobs, their personal experience, their contacts with other people and those with central media. A social worker, for example, in time accumulates collections of cuttings from professional journals, newspapers and other sources, on matters of particular interest to him or her, just as energy researchers collect newspapers, reports and cuttings connected with that. At the present time, classification and filing systems have major drawbacks, in that it is often hard to decide which category a particular item belongs to, so it is frequently difficult to retrieve it in a hurry. An article in my files on, for example, quality circles, could be filed in my system under 'language' or 'Industrial Relations'. When I want the cutting, I have to remember where I decided to put it. A micro-computer would of course help here. As each item came in, it could be given several key words. In my example I could list language, quality circles, industrial relations, Wedgwood, Marks and Spencer, potteries and Japan. I would then tell the computer which category I had decided to put it in. If years later I wanted to retrieve the item, but couldn't remember which category it was in, I would simply type in or perhaps speak, using as many possible key words as I could remember. The computer would then print up on the VDU all the items on file containing these key words, with the string of key words that each item was originally given, the date of acquisition and the source. It is then a far easier matter to locate the desired article.

An extension of such a filing system is to put the entire document on computer file. This could be done by feeding it through a scanner, which would read and convert it to a form suitable for computer storage. Although scanners are at the moment expensive, the price will inevitably fall. We can expect to see them in our high streets in the updated equivalent of the photocopy shop, where documents will be read for a small fee onto a disc or cassette. This would entirely eliminate the need to think up a list of key words for each item, since when doing a search a computer could look through the entire data base in a relatively short time. When the searcher wanted to retrieve a document he would merely have to recall a few words occurring in the text. There is additional value in placing documents in categories, so that they can be browsed among. The computer could place a copy in each nominated category.

Numerous centralised computer data bases have sprung up over the years, some specialist and some general, and containing vast amounts of information on many different topics. Some are very specific, and contain large numbers of scientific papers on a certain speciality. AQUALINE, for example, produced by the Water Research Centre, contained in 1980 21,000 abstracts 'selected since 1974 from the world's literature on the basis of their relevance to water and waste engineers and scientists, and anyone concerned with environmental water pollution.'[5] Similar systems exist for other specialities. Such systems are usually now searched with the assistance of an experienced operator, such as a librarian at a remote terminal.

The limitation of such undoubtedly valuable systems is that they contain only formal knowledge. As I have been at pains to point out, not everything that is useful can be written down. Nor can such systems ensure that you are asking the right questions. I have already illustrated this problem in connection with bilharzia. Such large centralised data bases have to be organised on the basis of a universally applicable cosmology, which then tends to perpetuate existing practices and divisions, often arbitrary and unproductive ones.

Take, for example, someone who is looking for information on ways of increasing the efficiency of power stations. Conventional systems might simply refer him to the technology available for increasing the efficiency of steam turbine ones. But there are several kinds of non-steam plant available which offer much higher efficiencies. The relevance of these, however, can only be seen in connection with the new technique of homeostatic control, so they would tend to be missed by the searcher, or rejected. Similarly, the conceptual leap of combined heat and power, which effectively trebles energy efficiency, requires a completely new paradigm to be adopted by the searcher.

Part of the reason for the blockages that tend to exist in the transmission of information on significant new developments is that the situation is frequently one of non-specialists trying to get into a specialist area, a situation rather like trying to cook a meal in a friend's kitchen – everything is there but you don't know how it is organised. Journalists and civil servants do not often use data bases and other similar information sources to form their opinions, but go to existing specialists and experts who can act as guides. A journalist's natural inclination may well be to go to the CEGB on energy-related issues, where he is very likely, for reasons I outlined in Chapter 7, to receive only conventional wisdom from the organisational hierarchy.

With the role that I envisage could be played by IRGs, however, the situation would be very different. A journalist, civil servant, or any other information seeker would find it far easier to discover a group of experts whom he could consult. For he would belong to several IRGs covering his areas of interest, and he could monitor these for interesting items on the conference or through personal messages. If he wanted more information on a subject, or news of a new one, he would use the key words search facility, or the index, to look through his IRGs to find someone to consult. If there was no one suitable, he would then scan the other IRGs of the people closest to his purpose, and these could give him access to several hundred new people. This process could be continued indefinitely until he found a suitable person or people. If necessary he could, with their permission, extract items from their files. In time, people would build up not just lists of names and addresses, as they do now, but lists together with IRG records. Profiles, in fact, could probably be coded onto plastic, rather like telephone credit cards, and exchanged like visiting cards. So although a person might only actively participate in four or five IRGs, he could, if he wished, gradually accumulate hundreds of useful contacts. In effect he would have access to a highly-efficient, interactive data base. And through contact with these people he would have access to their models of the world, their tacit knowledge and, if they were willing, to their files.

This provides a new way of looking at information-gathering and dissemination. Instead of seeing it as being stored and described in a universal language, obtainable through a universal indexing system, we can think of it as being accessed through *people who know its context*, and can make sure that the enquirer understands this and its relative significance. Thus the person investigating higher efficiency power stations could be re-educated, if necessary, by his information source as to the benefits of homeostatic control and C.H.P.

When using an IRG to obtain information, the searcher is not just dealing with a list of anonymous people, but with a group of 50 or so who all know one another. So if a searcher enters an IRG through a certain member, that member can use his knowledge of the strengths and weaknesses of others to point the newcomer towards someone who can help, and can also provide reservations: 'He has a bee in his bonnet about windmills, but he knows what he's talking about', for instance.

In the same way that centralised data bases already charge for their use, there is no reason why IRG users should not charge one another for their services. There is then an added incentive for accuracy in filing, and keeping key words up-dated. After an initial contact has been made, the information-seeker would be free to use the contact's personal data base. This would make the idiosyncratically-filed information of various 'experts' available to others, as well as their informal knowledge.

Various controls would of course have to be built into such a system. The full IRG facilities of message-leaving and conferencing would only be routinely available to bone fide members of that particular IRG. Visitors, as it were, or 'friends', who had been given details of it, would only be allowed access to its facilities if they did not abuse them, by, for example, swamping the IRG with junk mailings, or passing the details on to third parties who abused the privilege. It is in fact relatively easy to eliminate unwanted visitors by using a password system. Messages would not just enter an IRG, but would come from another terminal, which would have to identify itself; if that terminal had been misbehaving, then it could be blacklisted. This is simply the same as exchanging business cards. People only do it with those they trust, and the recipient does not abuse it, since he knows that to do so would rebound on him. In the same way, most people in the business and academic worlds already know the value of keeping confidences, and the rules. If a confidence is broken, then to some extent credibility is lost with the person to whom it is revealed, and certainly with the person who originally placed the trust.

A professional could, then, use his IRG computer to file and retrieve information of particular use to him, whether it is derived from conventional central media sources, or through the IRG system itself. Interlocking membership of different IRGs, and the passing around of records between acquaintances could open these private data bases for inspection by others, if desired, and this could be a source of income. The benefits of providing information are, in any case, usually mutual.

An additional benefit of such a computer network approach would probably be a reduction in the size of members' telephone and postage bills, not to mention travelling expenses. In general, it is already quicker and cheaper to send messages electronically than through the post, and computer conferences save an enormous amount of time and travel for people who would otherwise have to travel to a central point to meet. Under the right conditions, which include access to a terminal, adequate training, and adequate encouragement from a 'network manager', there is little doubt that most people could make extensive use of such systems, and find them an extremely pleasant, useful and rewarding experience.

The outline of the IRG system I have sketched here – each individual being in four or five groups of 50 people, and each provided with a profile of the interests of the others – implies that each member has consciously to make a decision to pass on interesting items to other people in his five IRGs. He also has to make a decision to receive or read items sent to him. There is no reason, however, why software couldn't be developed which would automatically take over these key functions.

The IRG user would allocate priority points to the items on his profiles, so that the software could rank each day's input and print out in newspaper format a given, specified amount of information each day. Similarly, the software could allocate a fixed amount to other IRG users, again on a priority system, set by the recipients.

Each day, entirely automatically, a user would get an interesting set of information from known sources, tailored to his exact demands.

14   *IRGs AND THE FUTURE*

In this final chapter I would like to speculate briefly on the long-term effects of the widespread introduction of Information Routeing Groups. I am not, of course, suggesting that they will usher in a promised land of problem-free perfection, but a revision of attitudes to organisations, communication, child-rearing, and so on, is clearly necessary. I believe these changes in attitude would be made very much more easily through the introduction of IRGs.

The way in which information is handled by the existing informational framework of hierarchic organisations and central media can be demonstrated by its treatment of certain recent medical advances based on folk remedies. Researchers at Birmingham's Dudley Road Hospital have 'discovered' a new treatment for diabetics.[1] They apparently noted that certain long-term immigrant sufferers from diabetes were free of the normal debilitating symptoms, such as poor eyesight, associated with the disease. Their investigations revealed that the patients from Asia and the West Indies used certain plants to combat their condition. The researchers were confident about the potential of their discovery because they knew that these treatments had been used for centuries without apparent harmful side-effects.

It is surely rather arrogant and blinkered to refer to a 'discovery' in such a situation, rather like India being discovered by the British, as if it had not really existed before then. Secondly, having 'discovered' these remarkable plants, did the research team immediately make available the names of the plants, suppliers, the methods and quantities for their use, and so on? Certainly not. 'We are preparing extracts from the plants to find the active ingredient,' said one of the doctors involved. 'Then we will tinker with its chemistry to improve its performance before passing on our discovery to a pharmaceutical company which can begin manufacturing suitable treatments.'[1] And in the process, an existing cheap and effective remedy will be transformed into an expensive pill which may, as a result of this Western reductionist approach, have harmful and unforeseen side-effects.

The vested interests of the researchers, the pharmaceutical companies and the central media are all too obvious. The drug companies play a major role in the allocation of research funds and the provision of grants. And there is no money to be made from patenting plants unless they have been through the expensive process of testing for side-effects and can be sold as 'drugs'. The 'active' ingredient must be extracted, synthesised, named 'Tripoundshillings and penceoxyoate', patented, and sold for profit. And medical correspondents, reporting this, have to adopt a suitably respectful stance towards the medical profession if they are to be fed any juicy medical news stories in the future.

So in this case the information processing systems – the central media and the hierarchic institutions, the medical profession, the drug companies and university researchers – do not operate to produce what one might expect to be their aims, a well-informed public and cheap and effective medical treatment. The reasons for this have formed a major part of this book. It is my claim that IRGs would function quite differently, and that their widespread existence, spanning the immigrant and indigenous communities, would greatly help this particular situation. The fact that certain plants are very effective remedies is precisely the kind of information snippet that would be circulated very fast through IRGs, rapidly reaching all diabetics if they had expressed an interest, in their profiles. The widespread dispersal of this knowledge would presumably create a demand for the plant, which could then be bought cheaply from stores in much the same way as herbs now are for cooking.

Let me emphasise that I am not objecting to the current medical profession, its doctors, researchers, drug companies, as a whole. What I am saying is that in certain well-defined areas it can be seen that current arrangements do not promote the health and well-being of the nation at the lowest cost. In fact they *cause* ill-health and high cost. Certain of their activities could more appropriately be carried out by the individuals themselves if they were better informed by a network of IRGs, not only at lower cost but to far greater effect.

The treatment of diabetics is far from being an isolated case. Dr Court, a reader in Pharmacognosy at Bradford University has said that 'it is fair to state that a large proportion of drugs in current use are either naturally-occurring or derived from plants.'[2] Interviewed on the radio programme *Medicine Now*, he said of herbal remedies that 'my experience of them is that they are probably slower-acting, but for many conditions they are just as effective.'

An article appearing in 1978 in the *Sunday Express* described the remarkable success achieved by Mrs Jenkins from Cardiff in using sandwiches made from feverfew, a common weed, to treat her crippling bouts of migraine and her severe rheumatism.[3] The article reported that fourteen other people in Cardiff had followed her example and had been similarly freed from pain. Nearly five years later another article on the subject appeared in the *Sunday Times*, under the heading 'Herbal Remedies on Trial'.[4] It reports that 'thousands of sufferers of migraine find relief by using a herbal remedy dating at least from Shakespeare's time', and that the plant is finally undergoing clinical trials, after a deluge of enquiries from members of the public. The results have been so promising that the doctor carrying out the trial, and two plant chemists, have 'filed an application to patent the substances isolated from feverfew, with an eye on the potential market among Britain's 10,000,000 migraine sufferers.' However, 'From a commercial point of view the active substances may be very difficult to synthesise in the laboratory and this has so far put the drug companies off,' Dr Johnson is quoted as saying.

I have chosen medical examples of inadequate information flows, but the phenomenon can be found in almost any information system that is dominated by powerful hierarchies and central media. I have given many other examples in the course of this book, where sophisticated organisations such as the CEGB inevitably and systematically fail to carry out their apparent aims. The medical hierarchy does not make people healthy; the CEGB does not produce cheap and non-polluting power; food aid schemes result in more hunger. And so on, and on.

Throughout this book I have argued that hierarchic, centralised systems will *inevitably* get it wrong. Within hierarchies, the lack of variety the higher one goes; the information overload due to bureaucratic in-fighting; and the personality damage inflicted by a status-oriented child-rearing and educational ethos, produce an information-processing system which will inevitably produce wrong, or irrelevant outputs. Operating in parallel with these institutional hierarchies, we have central media which at the mass level suffer grossly from low variety models, and at the specialist level, are couched in terms of tacit meanings which make them opaque to outsiders. So at a mass level all issues are seen and treated as fragmentary, and unrelated to one another, whereas they may well be interrelated. Specialist central media accelerate the growth of private jargon and hence world views, which at the same time as obscuring issues to outsiders confer on the initiates a spurious air of omniscience. So specialist groups see themselves and their specialist concerns as unrelated to other parts of the real world.

Only well-informed networks of individuals outside the official systems can force existing hierarchies to act sensibly. For years, for example, members of private networks interested in health have been aware of the evidence that poor diet is responsible for the majority of degenerative diseases that afflict Western man and fill our hospitals. There is a wealth of firm evidence, for example, to show that the widespread eating of refined carbohydrate (in, say, white flour) is responsible for, or aggravates all kinds of conditions such as diabetes, diverticular disease, inflamed colon, heart disease, varicose veins, and so on. Detailed evidence, much of it dating from the 1930s and 1940s, for connections between a low-fibre diet and degenerative diseases is given in Dr Andrew Stanway's book *Taking the Rough with the Smooth*,[5] but until the last ten years or so standard medical treatment for the disease caused by its absence was to put the patients on a diet of puréed foods entirely devoid of fibre. Only in the last few years has the medical profession agreed that fibre in the diet might be a good thing. It is on the face of it a staggering paradox that the very professional group which is supposed to make people healthy, actually opposes or ignores the truth of the matter.

It is again and again apparent that it is these private networks of people who as a whole can see the validity of arguments, that force any issue. Unofficial networks, operating outside and transcending conventional bureaucratic boundaries, are those that can force appropriate action. The myth is that what is called 'democracy', the 'free press' and conventional institutions operate effectively. This myth only survives within the confines of the conventional paradigms offered by the central media and conventional institutions. Standing back from these conventional views, a different perspective is revealed. The CEGB wastes energy and money; the NHS makes people ill; governments are leading us to the brink of nuclear or ecological disaster. Private networks have forced the medical establishment to recognise that white bread is making us ill. Private networks also forced the government to agree to reduce the lead content of petrol. In West Germany, the environmental party, the Greens, has forced a reduction in pollution from many existing power stations.

Going down a meta-level, I have given examples of private networks within central governments and institutional hierarchies concerned with compensating for their inevitable errors. I am arguing that, in the same way that within organisations lateral media can compensate for failures, lateral media at a higher meta-level can compensate for larger failures within countries and civilisations. So what is initially needed is the widespread introduction of the means for useful lateral communication between individuals, spanning normal boundaries of society, profession and geography.

In the introduction to this book I described the idea of cargo cults. The history of these cults is really that of people trying to accommodate new and strange events into an existing cosmology that cannot cope with it. In the case of what Peter Worsley has called 'millenarian cults', these strange new events were the coming of oppressive colonialists, richly endowed with superior material goods. Worsley relates how the lateral spread of millenarian ideas gradually united entire regions into stable political groupings, in which the people, rather than seeing themselves as members of small isolated villages, usually hostile to one another, came to see themselves as part of a wider grouping, behaving more as a cohesive organism, able to resist the exploitation of the colonialists. It is clear that these ideas about the world, no matter how bizarre they may seem, spread from person to person in a lateral and (from the centralist point of view) disorganised manner, but that in time they united people and gave them a new and coherent world view.

It is possible to see what is happening today in the industrialised countries in these terms. Many people recognise that existing world views are leading us to disaster. If current trends are continued, then in the next 50 years or so we will probably have a massive nuclear war ending in the ecological destruction of the planet. If we, by some chance, avoid a nuclear war, then the destruction of the ecosystems, upon which all life depends, by poisoning, by pollution, by the destruction of the soil structure, and a general shortage of raw materials, will not only make life much tougher for everyone, but also increase the pressure for war.

Conventional institutions and conventional media, lead people to see problems in such a way that they can only produce more 'solutions' of the kind that actually exacerbate the problem: more police for more crime, more spending on arms for more insecurity. In the Third World, economies have generally declined, or remained static. At the same time, their arms expenditure has increased exponentially. So the amount of money available to the people declines. We see that the price for central control in this case is starvation.

But the major aim of any government, considered as an organism, is its own preservation and growth, rather than the protection of its people, a government only protecting and succouring its people if that ensures its own survival. In Western democracies, an organism tends to develop which consists of the most powerful people in the country. It is not a conspiracy, but a simple outcome of numerous dialogues occurring between members of the existing establishment. The main tacit rule has become 'keep things as they are', 'maintain stability', 'don't rock the boat', 'we know what's good for you', and so on.

The people who control the output of central media, the censor in totalitarian countries, and the owners, editors, and advertisers in capitalist ones, ensure that perspectives and world views they espouse suit the continued existence of the central organism. And quite apart from this tacit conspiracy, the central media cannot, by their very nature, give information in such a way that people reach a true view of what is happening. If there are too few houses, then we must build subsidised council houses; if rents are too high, then we must control rents; if transport is difficult, then we must build more roads for cars; if there is a Third World food shortage, then we must have a Green Revolution or more dams. Central media present the issue in a simplified way, and professional hierarchies carve off the problem from the rest of reality, and try to establish an exclusive right and capability to solve it. Take heroin addiction: every week in the press we hear stories of massive heroin hauls, each one bigger than the last, together with the periodic smashing of drug smuggling rings. The implicit suggestion is that the problem is being solved, but the inescapable fact is that heroin addiction is on the increase. And a solution is implied by the way the problem is presented in the media – international gangs of master criminals trap gullible youngsters into using the drug, so the criminals must be caught, the fines and punishments of offenders increased, and more police and customs officers provided. But the more success the authorities have in controlling the drug, the more valuable it becomes, which draws more efficient and ruthless criminals into selling it, making profits proportionately greater. Despite (or because of) increasingly strenuous efforts by the authorities in Britain and the United States, the scale of drug abuse has increased enormously. A holistic solution, as Julian Huxley pointed out many years ago, would recognise that people use the drug because they lead miserable lives, mainly due to severe emotional damage as children; this indicates an entirely different course of action.

Existing information-processing systems, then, guarantee that the problems facing us will get worse. In the terms I introduced earlier in the book, there is a series of positive feedback relationships going on. The solutions proposed to particular problems either make them immediately worse, fail to solve them, or make someone else's problem worse. There have, of course, been many previous critiques of organisations and the media, but these generally take the form of pointing out their failings, and then saying that in effect they must do better in future. I am saying something different: that the whole approach is doomed to failure. Central media, and hierarchic institutions will always in the long run fail to work. In the language of cybernetics, they will always have models and solutions without requisite variety. Only networks operating largely outside official organisations and central media can generate and force appropriate solutions on such systems. Central systems should not be done away with entirely, but lateral systems and lateral media should augment them, forcing appropriate action.

There are already many precedents for such international networks based largely on lateral communications. These have produced profound changes in our thinking about the world, and forced action on many governments. The many environmental groups which appeared in the 1970s have spearheaded the defence of the natural world in the face of 'rational' opposition from varied vested interest groups and central media. The latter were quick to portray these groups as long-haired, brown rice-eating, sandal-wearing, bearded eccentrics, irrespective of the content of their arguments. My central claim is that it is the membership of informal networks by ordinary people, based on the lateral communication systems of the telephone, cheap transport, and the Xerox, which enabled these groups to spring up in the first place, and which has had a powerful cosmology-changing effect.

If we make lateral communication easier, and at the same time more structured, in the form of self-generating, self-assembling networks on the IRG model, then they will also have a powerful controlling effect. Government and international agencies will become more intelligent. And we will have created a homeostatic control system with requisite variety, similar to that which operates in the human brain.

REFERENCES

INTRODUCTION

1. PETER WORSLEY, *The Trumpet Shall Sound: A Study of Cargo Cults in Melanesia,* MacGibbon and Kee, 1957.
2. IAN CLEMENTS, 'Technological Irrelevance of Post O-Level Maths', *Educa,* 11 March 1981, Guildford Educational Services.
3. 'Unintentional Duplication of Research', *New Scientist* 377, 6 February 1964; John Martyn, ASLIB Research Department, personal communication.
4. IVAN ILLICH, *Limits to Medicine: Medical Nemesis, the exploration of Health,* Marion Boyars, 1976.
5. BERT LODGE, 'Cold Water on Survival Theories', *Times Educational Supplement,* 23 July 1982.
6. Bogota strike information: the National Morticians' Association, in the *National Catholic Reporter* (USA), 12 November 1976; Israeli strike information: the Jerusalem Burial Society, in *Jewish Press,* 29 June 1973.
7. Table 6, *Digest of Energy Statistics 1980,* Department of Energy, 1981.

CHAPTER 1: Skimmerton Rides, May Day and the Traditional Sense of Community
1. BOB BUSHAWAY, *By Rite: Custom, Ceremony and Community 1700–1880,* Junction Books, 1982, pp. 111–17; R. W. Malcolmson, *Popular Recreations in English Society, 1700–1850,* CUP, 1973, pp. 62–4.
2. ANTONIO GRAMSCI, *Selections from Political Writings,* Quintin Hoare and Geoffrey Noel Smith (eds.), Lawrence and Wishart, 1971, p. 323.
3. G. O. SAYLES, *The Mediaeval Foundations of England,* Methuen, 1950, p. 69.
4. SIMON ROBERTS, *Order and Dispute: An Introduction to Legal Anthropology,* Penguin, 1970, Chapter 7.
5. E. EVANS-PRITCHARD, *The Nuer,* OUP, 1940, p. 181.
6. M. FORTES and E. EVANS-PRITCHARD (eds.), *African Political Systems,* OUP, 1961, p. 2, p. 34.
7. JOHN FLETCHER, 'Verbal Violence', from *More Words,* BBC Radio, 1977.

8. VICTOR TURNER, *The Ritual Process: Structure and Anti-Structure*, Routledge and Kegan Paul, p. 97.
9. ROBERT WERNICK *et al*, *The Family*, Time-Life International, 1976, p. 35.
10. N. J. O'CONNOR, *Godes Peace and the Queenes*, OUP, 1934.
11. DOROTHY DAVIS, *A History of Shopping*, Routledge and Kegan Paul, 1966.

CHAPTER 2: Natural Lateral Control Systems
1. See for example, Stafford Beer, *Designing Freedom*, John Wiley, 1974, p. 22.
2. See Stafford Beer, 'Death is Equifinal: Eighth Annual Ludwig von Bertalanffy Memorial Lecture, *Behavioural Science* 26, 1981, p. 186.
3. D. A. COLINVAUX, *Introduction to Ecology*, John Wiley, 1972, p. 407, 473.
4. MARTIN HARRIS, *Cows, Pigs, Wars and Witches – The Riddles of Culture*, Hutchinson, 1975.
5. CLIVE COOKSON, 'Using Micros to Smooth out the Highs and Lows', *The Times*, 4 June 1982.

CHAPTER 3: Language and Communication
1. Quoted in Ivan Illich, 'Vernacular Values', First Schumacher Lecture, 1978, printed in *Resurgence* 72, February 1979.
2. ANTONIO GRAMSCI, *Selections from Political Writings*, Quintin Hoare and Geoffrey Noel Smith (eds.), Lawrence and Wishart, 1971.
3. THOMAS HARDY, *Tess of the d'Urbervilles*, Macmillan, 1926, pp. 24-5.
4. JEAN AITCHISON, *Language Change: Progress or Decay?* Fontana, 1981, p. 24.
5. IAN G. HEGGIE, *New Civil Engineer*, 22 July 1982.
6. DEIRDRE WILSON and NEIL SMITH, 'Understanding Language', *New Society*, 24 July 1980.
7. K. D. BANDHAM, *The Guardian*, 18 January 1978.
8. Interview with Maureen Cleeve, *The Observer*, 4 July 1982.
9. *Sunday Times*, 25 July 1982.
10. *Observer Review*, 26 January 1980.

CHAPTER 4: Television and its Long-term Effects
1. ANN M. CLARKE and A.D.B. CLARKE, *Early Experience, Myth and Evidence*, Open Books, 1976, p. 29.

2. ROBERT WERNICK, *et al*, *The Family*, Time-Life International, 1976.
3. R. GULLIFORD, *Backwardness and Educational Failure*, NFER-Nelson Publishing Co, 1969.
4. JAMES BRITTON, *Language and Learning*, Pelican Books, 1972, pp. 87–8, 94–5.
5. L.S. VYGOTSKY, *Thought and Language*, MIT Press, 1962.
6. IVAN ILLICH, 'Vernacular Values', First Schumacher Lecture, 1978, printed in *Resurgence* 72, February 1979.
7. MARIE WINN, *The Plug-in Drug*, Viking, 1977, pp. 105, 107, 98.
8. PHILIP SHORT, *From Our Own Correspondent*, BBC Radio 2, October 1983.
9. DENIS HERBSTEIN, 'A Four-year-old Cry for Help', *Sunday Times*, 27 January 1980.
10. HERBERT FILL, *The Mental Breakdown of a Nation*, New Viewpoints, 1973.
11. 'Children See Too Much Television', *Daily Telegraph*, 6 September 1979.
12. JEREMY CAMPBELL, *The New Standard*, 24 June 1980.
13. MARTIN LARGE, *Who's Bringing Them Up?* self-published, 1980, available from 1 Berkley Villas, Lowers Street, Stroud, Gloucestershire.
14. DAVID LEWIS, *The Secret Language of Your Child*, Souvenir Press, 1978.
15. *Crosstalk*, National Centre for International Language Training, 1979.
16. EDWARD NORBECK, 'Man at Play', *Natural History*, December 1971.
17. DONALD GOULD, *The Guardian*, 22 January 1980.
18. Quoted in *Long Island Press*, August 1972.

CHAPTER 5: Tacit Knowledge and Lateral Media

1. H.M. COLLINS, *The TEA Set: Tacit Knowledge and Scientific Networks*, School of Humanities and Social Sciences, University of Bath, reprinted in B. Barnes and D. Edge (eds.), *Science in Context: Readings in the Sociology of Science*, Open University Press, 1982.
2. ROBERT WERNICK, *et al*, *The Family*, Time-Life International, 1976, p. 40.
3. JAMES COLEMAN, ELIHU KATZ, HERMAN MENZEL, 'The Diffusion of an Innovation amongst Physicians', *Sociometry* 20, 1957, pp. 253–70.
4. T.J. ALLEN, 'Organisational Aspects of Information Flow in Technology', *ASLIB Proceedings* 20, 11 November 1968, MIT.

CHAPTER 6: Interlock Research

1. *Energy from Biomass by Anaerobic Digestion*, Watt Committee on Energy Report 5, 1979.
2. *Communication and Integration within the Agriculture, Water, Waste and Energy Sectors*, Open University Energy Research Group, 1980.
3. JOHN MADELEY, 'How the village of Xinbu learned to love the biogas unit', *The Guardian*, 5 August 1982.
4. 'An Indian Village Agricultural Ecosystem: Case Study of Ungra Village', *Biomass* 1, V, 1981, pp. 77–88.
5. G.M. FOSTER, *Traditional Societies and Technological Change*, 2nd ed, Harper and Row, London, 1973, pp. 80-1; Jas Gill, 'Fuelwood and Stoves in Zimbabwe: a System in Change', Second EC Conference on Energy from *Biomass*, West Berlin, 20-3 September 1982.

CHAPTER 7: Hierarchies and their Problems

1. *Institute of Public Health Engineers' Journal*, Spring 1982.
2. HAROLD JACKSON, *The Guardian*, 2 January 1982.
3. See, for example, Norman F. Dixon, *On the Psychology of Military Incompetence*, Jonathan Cape, 1979, pp. 164–8.
4. GERALD LEACH and SIMON PELLEW, *Energy Conservation in Housing*, International Institute for Environment and Development, November 1982.
5. 'Blocked energy report vies with Lawson', *The Guardian*, 14 March 1983.
6. *The Observer*, 2 January 1983.
7. *US Intelligence and the Soviet Strategic Threat*, Macmillan, 1977.
8. *Sunday Times*, 20 January 1983.
9. 'Lysenko and Darwinism', *New Scientist*, 29 April 1982, p. 298.
10. *The Guardian*, 8 September 1980.
11. *Sunday Times*, 24 October 1983.
12. *Integrating the Individual and the Organization*, John Wiley, 1964.
13. JOHN HUXLEY, 'Electrical Silence alarms Whitehall', *Sunday Times*, 19 September 1982.
14. MARSHALL C. YOUITIS, GEORGE T. JACOBI and GORDON D. GOLDSTEIN, (eds.), *Information Input Overload: Symposium on Self-organising Systems*, Spartan Books, 1962.
15. 'Heart Disease: Action Now Proof Later', *New Scientist*, 28 April 1983.
16. H.G. MATHER *et al.*, 'Myocardial Infarction – a Comparison between Home and Hospital Care for Patients', *BMJ*, 17 April 1976.

17. MARJORIE TEW, 'Is Home a Safer Place?', *Health and Social Services Journal*, 12 September 1980.
18. DAVID STEWART, 'The Five Standards for Safe Childbearing', NAPSAC International, Marble Hill, Missouri, 1981.
19. CHRIS ARGYRIS, *Increasing Leadership Effectiveness*, John Wiley, 1976.
20. HUGO YOUNG, *Sunday Times*, 24 October 1982.

CHAPTER 8: Alternatives to Hierarchies
1. DONALD A. SCHON, *Beyond the Stable State: Public and Private Learning in a Changing Society*, Temple Smith, London, 1971.
2. *The Guardian*, 11 January 1983.
3. *Sunday Times*, 17 January 1983.
4. *Daily Telegraph*, 8 January 1983.
5. ROBERT JUNGK, *Brighter than a Thousand Suns*, Penguin, 1982.
6. *Sunday Times*, 17 October, 1982.
7. 13 January 1983.
8. BRYAN SILCOCK, 'Developing Creativity', *International Herald Tribune*, 6 January 1983.
9. In JOHN F.C. TURNER and ROBERT FICHTER (eds.), *Freedom to Build*, Macmillan, New York, 1972.
10. NICK WATES, 'Freedom to Build – Dweller Control of the Building Process', *Architects Journal*, September 1982, pp. 57-8.

CHAPTER 9: Communication, Language and Behaviour
1. KARL PRIBRAM, 'Holographic Memory', *Psychology Today*, February 1979.
2. THOMAS GORDON, *Parent Effectiveness Training*, New American Library, 1975.
3. DEIRDRE WILSON and NEIL SMITH, 'Understanding Language', *New Society*, 24 July 1980.
4. NEIL LYNDEN, 'Legacy of Hate', *Sunday Times Magazine*, 5 September 1982.
5. JOHN ARDAGH, *France in the 1980s*, Pelican, 1982, p. 368.
6. SUSAN LASDUN, *The Victorians at Home*, Weidenfeld and Nicolson, 1981, p. 44.
7. E.P. THOMPSON, 'Time, Work, Discipline and Industrial Capitalism', *Past and Present* 38, pp. 84-5.
8. JOHN FLETCHER, 'Verbal Violence', from *More Words*, BBC Radio, 1977.
9. JEAN AITCHISON, *Language Change: Progress or Decay?* Fontana, 1981.

10. NORMAN F. DIXON, 'Some thoughts on the nature and causes of industrial incompetence', *Personnel Management*, December 1982.
11. L. IREMONGER, *The Fiery Chariot: a study of British Prime Ministers and the search for love*, Secker and Warburg, 1970.
12. *Sunday Times*, May 1983.
13. *Sunday Times*, 19 December 1982.
14. JOHN B. CARROLL (ed.), *Language, Thought and Reality: Selected Writings of Benjamin Lee Whorf*, MIT Press, 1976.

CHAPTER 10: Central Media and the Corruption of Information
1. Clarendon Press, 1959 and 1969.
2. 'The Urchins' Opera', *News of the World*, 16 February 1982.
3. HERBERT FILL, *The Mental Breakdown of a Nation*, New Viewpoints, 1973.
4. ERIC BERNE, *Games People Play*, André Deutsch, 1966.
5. JOHN EZARD, *The Guardian*, 11 May 1978.
6. RENATE MRESCHAR, 'Fairy Tales', *German Tribune*, 13 July 1980.
7. POLLY TOYNBEE, *The Guardian*, 26 March 1982.
8. J. WISEMAN, July 1980.
9. DAVID ANDREWS, 'The Importance of Knowing the Right People', *The Guardian*, 20 March 1980.
10. ERIC LIGGETT, *The Guardian*, 20 March 1980.
11. FEONA HAMILTON, *The Guardian*, 17 April 1980.
12. I.P. HAIGH, *New Civil Engineer*, 27 January 1983.

CHAPTER 11: Problems of Centralised Societies
1. DOUGLAS HOFSTADTER, *Godel, Escher, Bach: an Eternal Golden Braid*, Penguin, 1980.
2. NORMAN F. DIXON, *On the Psychology of Military Incompetence*, Jonathan Cape, 1976.
3. GREGORY BATESON, *Steps to an Ecology of Mind*, Ballantine, 1972.
4. JOHN GRINDER and RICHARD BANDLER, *The Structure of Magic*, Science and Behaviour Books, California, 1975.
5. IDRIES SHAH, 'On the Nature of Human Consciousness', in *The Teaching Story - Observations on the Folklore of our Modern Thought*, Robert Ornstein (ed), Freeman, 1973.
6. COLIN WILSON, *Mysteries*, Hodder and Stoughton, 1978.
7. *New Scientist*, 5 May 1983.
8. ARTHUR KOESTLER, *The Act of Creation*, Hutchinson, 1969.
9. CREDO MUTWA, *My People*, Blond and Biggs, 1968.
10. ARTHUR KOESTLER, *The Ghost in the Machine*, Hutchinson, 1967.
11. Faber and Faber, 1939.

12. FRIEDRICH M. HEICHELHEIM, *Man's Role in Changing the Face of the Earth - the Effects of Classical Antiquity on the Land*, 1939, p. 179.
13. M.L. PARRY, *Climatic Change, Agriculture and Settlement*, Dawson-Archon Books, 1978, pp. 64, 69, 72.
14. KEN BUTTI and JOHN PERLIN, *A Golden Thread, 2500 Years of Solar Architecture and Technology*, Marion Boyars, 1980.
15. GERALD O'BARNEY, Study Director, Council on Environmental Quality and the Department of State, Government Printing Office, Washington, 1980.
16. *North South: A Programme for Survival*, Report of the Independent Commission on International Development Issues, Willy Brandt, Chairman, Pan Books, 1980.
17. MICHAEL LOTCHIE, *Journal of Modern African Studies* 13, 4, 1975.

CHAPTER 12: Lateral Media through Technology

1. 'Flying in a wing and with a prayer', *Sunday Times*, 30 January 1983.
2. MURRAY TUROFF and SANJIT CHINAI, *An Electronic Information Marketplace*, Computerised Conferencing Center, New Jersey Institute of Technology, 1982, pp. 7, 10.
3. Reported by Rory Johnston, *The Guardian*, 26 March 1982.
4. TOM B. WARD and JULIAN NEWMAN, 'Computer Conferencing and Post-Industrial Regional Policy', *Working Research Paper Series* V, 8, School of Business Management, Ulster Polytechnic, 1981.
5. From unedited version of article, 'Help Thy Neighbour', *Time Out*, 20 January 1983.
6. J. TRAVERS and S. MILLIGAN, 'An Experimental Study of the Small World Problem', *Sociometry* 32, 1969, pp. 425–43.

CHAPTER 13: Information Routeing Groups

1. COLIN TURNBULL, *The Forest People*, Picador, 1979, p. 117.
2. PENELOPE LEACH, Vice-President, Pre-School Playgroups Association, in an address to PPA, Bristol, 1983.
3. D. HICKS and R. CARTER, *The Organisation and Management of Social Work*, DHSS, 1981, Chapter 12; table 1302, p. 280; table 1202, p. 261.
4. DR GARY ALEXANDER, Lecturer, Technology Faculty, Open University.
5. AQUALINE, Water Research Centre, Medmenham Laboratory, Henley Road, Medmenham, Marlow, Bucks., and Stevenage Laboratory, Elder Way, Stevenage, Herts.

CHAPTER 14: IRGs and the Future
1. ROBIN MCKIE, 'Folk Remedies Work', *The Observer*, 21 November 1982.
2. *Medicine Now*, BBC Radio, 6 November 1982.
3. ROBERT CHAPMAN, 'Garden Weed Sandwiches End a Woman's Migraine', *Sunday Express*, 21 May 1978.
4. JULIAN CHAMET, 'Herbal Remedies on Trial', *Sunday Times*, 13 February 1983.
5. ANDREW STANWAY, *Taking the Rough with the Smooth*, Souvenir Press, 1976.

INDEX

Active listening 149-53
Ardagh, J. 154
AQUALINE 250
Argyris, C. 120, 124-5
Ashby's Law (Law of Requisite Variety) 34-5, 46-7, 50, 60, 100, 110, 183, 239
Aswan High Dam 104-5
Authoritarianism 116-17, 158-9, 185-6, 237 *see also* Central government control, Hierarchies
Barriadas (Peruvian housing) 140
Bateson, G. 186
Berne, E. 168
de Bono, E. 14
Books 176-9 *see also* Central media, Libraries
Bread and blood riots (as informal control mechanism) 29-30, 136
Butti, K. 193-4

Cargo cults 1, 17-18
Central Electricity Generating Board (CEGB) 44-50, 64, 118, 120-1, 139-40, 199, 251, 256-7
Central government control 54-5, 116-17, 193, 198-9 *see also* Hierarchies
Central media 17-19, 164-82, 199, 210-11, 214, 236-7, 259 *see also* Books, Newspapers, Radios
Centralised societies 183-99 *see also* Hierarchies
Chieftain (role of) 23-5
Child-rearing practices 148-55, 178, 185

Chomsky, N. 59-60, 152
Church (as a hierarchical institution) 108
Church orchestras (as informal control mechanism) 28-9, 35
Civilisation, problems of 190-9
Coarse grained policies 119, 127, 173-5, 178, 197, 236
Collins, H.M. 77, 83-4
Common sense 22, 54, 63
Communication systems 52-65, 98, 211, 236-7
  problems of 114-15, 149-53, 158-60, 185, 198
  see also Grapevines, Old-boy networks, Informal (communication) networks, Central media, Lateral media, Hierarchies
Community
  breakdown of 210
  lack of 168-9
  self-control *see* control mechanisms
  sense of 20-33
Computer conferencing systems 206-8, 242
Computers (as a means of communication) 201-2, 206, 210-12, 218, 242, 247
Control mechanisms (community self-) *see* Informal control mechanisms
Control systems *see* Central government control, Dispersed control systems